MIRACLES OF THE SAINTS

by Rodney Charles

Miracles of the Saints

Rodney Charles

© Rodney Charles

Published by 1stWorld Publishing
P.O. Box 2211, Fairfield, IA 52556
tel: 641-209-5000 • fax: 866-440 5234
web: www.1stworldpublishing.com

First Edition

LCCN: 2008929206
SoftCover ISBN: 978-1-4218-9884-1
HardCover ISBN: 978-1-4218-9883-4
eBook ISBN: 978-1-4218-9885-8

All rights reserved. No part of this book may be reproduced or utilized in any form or by any means, electronic or mechanical, including photocopying or recording, or by any information storage and retrieval system, without permission in writing from the author.

This material has been written and published solely for educational purposes. The author and the publisher shall have neither liability or responsibility to any person or entity with respect to any loss, damage or injury caused or alleged to be caused directly or indirectly by the information contained in this book.

For

Mother Teresa

Acknowledgment

I offer thanks to the hundreds of authors, biographers, historians and legend-tellers from whose works I have borrowed heavily to compile this collection of miracles.

Contents

Preface 9

January. 11
February. 59
March 95
April 133
May. 177
June. 219
July 257
August. 295
September 337
October. 383
November 427
December 471

About the Author 526

Preface

Are miracles real? Yes, of course. But in this century of scientific inquiry, they have lost some of their appeal. Science is based on repeatable, predicable observations of the world, whether galactic or subatomic, and the study of miracles has not yet conformed to these rules. However, as scientists investigate deeper into nature, their findings uncover truths about the unseen world. What was once considered a miracle is not miraculous at all. Miracles are simply laws of nature, not yet fully discovered, that apply when the human spirit, or consciousness, interacts with the spirit, or consciousness, of its creator or creative force.

It would be ridiculous to think that the stories in this collection are entirely fictitious. Perhaps many are merely legends, and no doubt others are embellished products of over-zealous, religious devotees. But the majority of entries in this volume are genuine and include appropriate references so you may undertake your own research and draw your own conclusions.

For those who have a subjective understanding of miracles, remember that someone who is blessed with miracles, visions, psychic abilities, or healing powers is not necessarily a saint. Sainthood is more than the demonstration of extraordinary powers.

We may think that our species has not progressed quickly on this planet, but four hundred years ago only a handful of people believed the earth was round. As we evolve, our latent potential for miracles will manifest more fully—until every day a miracle will happen for all of us.

Rodney Charles

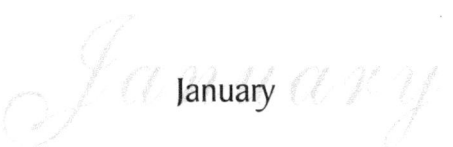

January

1 Princess of Hungary
2 Grateful Mother
3 Genevieve and the King
4 Weeping Madonna
5 Ever Mindful
6 Most Ignorant
7 Gifts of the Senses
8 Legend of Hamme
9 Where There's a Will
10 The Almighty: An Equal
11 Simplicity Desired
12 Fragrances of Heaven
13 Determination Rewarded
14 Lord of Battles
15 Surprise Visit
16 A Saintly Sum
17 The Eyes of a Child
18 No Bread in the House
19 Suspended in Prayer
20 Miraculous Administration
21 Patroness of Purity
22 Nest of Fish
23 The Raft
24 Sweet Speech
25 The Organizer
26 Old Friend
27 Bubbling Spring
28 Self-made Man
29 Ina Poonbato
30 The Dove's Veil
31 Formula for a Miracle

Princess of Hungary

Margaret was no ordinary princess. As a child she was surprisingly affectionate and possessed a warm and quiet manner which made her irresistibly charming. Her royal father, the great King Bala IV of Hungary, knew, by divine inspiration, even before her birth, that his child would be gifted with miracles. Accordingly, he educated her under the guidance of nuns in a new private island monastery built in her honor.

During these years, she outstripped even the most advanced in devotion and took great delight in serving everyone as though she were his or her personal valet. She never spoke of or made references to her royal family and never revealed the many miracles which occurred to her daily.

In time, however, her visions, prophecies and heavenly communications extended beyond her ability to conceal them. Her secret was first discovered one New Year's morning, when the sisters observed her lifted in an ecstasy and floating in the air twenty inches from the ground. Again and again this miracle occurred and soon became a routine delight. One could particularly look forward to her levitations on days of celebration, especially All Saints' Day.

Though qualified, Princess Margaret never entered the world of royal tradition and politics. Instead, she preferred a simple life of fasting and meditation and remained unnoticed in the world until she gave up her pure soul to God at age twenty-eight.

She is honored in all the churches of Hungary by virtue of a decree by Pope Pius II.

Margaret of Hungary died on January 18, 1271, and was canonized in 1943. The private island monastery where Margaret spent her life is located on the Danube River near Budapest, capital of Hungary.

Grateful Mother

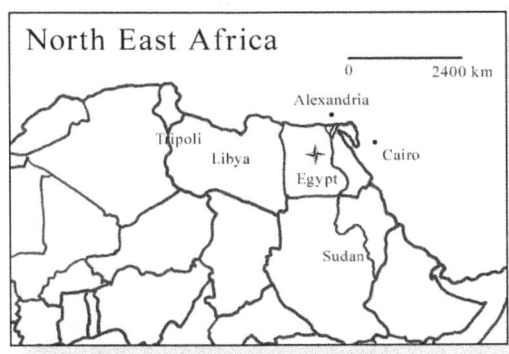

An unusual event occurred in the forest home of Macarius of Alexandria at the end of the fourth century. A hyena unexpectedly appeared at his doorstep carrying her infant cub which she laid at his feet. Macarius, astonished at this act, examined the pup and found it to be blind. He touched its eyes with his finger and immediately the helpless creature regained its sight.

The following day the grateful mother hyena appeared at the hermit's cell again, but this time she brought a sheepskin with her, as if to offer her thanks. Macarius, being thus honored, wore the sheepskin ever after until the day of his death when he gave it to Malania, his disciple.

Having gained a level of proficiency in miracles, while studying under masters renowned for their sanctity in Upper Egypt, Macarius retired to a cave in the desert near the borders of Libya, Egypt and the Sudan. In ancient art, Saint Macarius of Alexandria is portrayed with a hyena and her cub as his companions. The acts of his life are documented in the Acta Sanctorum, January 2.

Genevieve and the King

Genevieve was no stranger to the royal court. She was loved by King Childeric, King of the Franks, who was incapable of denying her the smallest request. However, in the course of his royal duties, he was obligated by law to condemn to death a number of captives taken in war. He knew well that Genevieve would protest and accordingly commanded that the city gates be bolted and locked lest she intercede for the prisoners' liberation.

As expected, when the news reached Genevieve's ear, she hurried to Paris intent on stopping the executions. She found the gates were indeed shut tight, but with a touch of her hand they were instantly unlocked and flew open of their own accord. She proceeded at once to the king and fell to her knees refusing to rise until the prisoners were set free. Thus, the captives were released and the murderous deeds averted.

According to Manager Guerin, Chamberlain to Pope Leo XIIL there is a lamp in Saint Denis' Church before the shrine of Genevieve. The oil in this lamp is always consumed, but never diminished in quantity. This is still more noteworthy, since the priests continuously distribute the oil for remedial purposes.

The "Patroness of Paris," Genevieve lived from A.D. 420-500. She is celebrated on January 3rd. The accounts of her life are recorded in Lives of the Saints, by Baring-Gould.

Weeping Madonna

Following eight years of investigations and consultations with the Holy See, messages and supernatural phenomena connected with a statue of the Madonna, in Akita, Japan, were approved for public recognition. Testimonies from more than five hundred witnesses, of various occupations and faiths (many of them Buddhist), stated that they had seen the statue weep and shed blood. The miraculous statue, which stands three feet tall, is carved from a single block of wood taken from a Katsura tree.

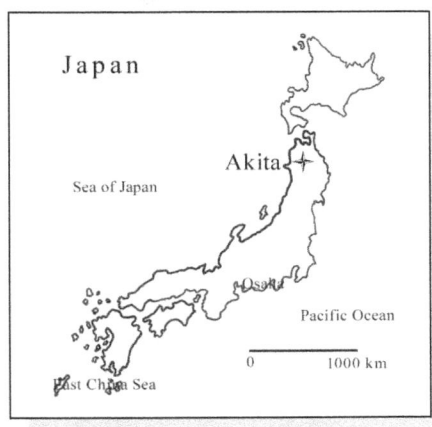

These events were first recorded by Agnes Katsuko Sasagawa on June 12, 1973, when she witnessed mysterious beams of light suddenly emanating from the tabernacle in Akita. For two days this phenomenon recurred and then stopped. During the weeks that followed the statue began to bleed. At this time, a voice from the Madonna spoke to Agnes, commending her for her purity, and warning of calamities that would befall the world should it fail to seek a path of peace and recognize the gifts of its creator. "Prayer is necessary," the Madonna said. "Already souls who wish to pray are on the way to being gathered together. Without attaching too much attention to the form, be faithful and fervent in prayer to console the Master."

Two years later on January 4, 1975, the statue of the Madonna began to weep tears. It wept one hundred and one times over an eighty-month period, and is documented with testimonies and photographs. Tens of thousands of pilgrims and curiosity seekers have found their way to the village of Akita, and in 1984 the supernatural phenomena was officially recognized by Bishop Ito and the messages were deemed *credible*.

Ever Mindful

When Antony, the revered desert father and founder of monasticism, turned ninety, he journeyed to visit Paul, the remote hermit of Lower Thebaid, who had reached the age of one hundred and thirteen years. While they conversed a raven settled on a nearby bough. Then alighting on the ground, it offered a loaf of bread at the hermit's feet. "Ah," said Paul, "the Almighty is ever mindful and loving. For sixty years this bird has come every day with a gift of half a loaf of bread, but now that you have come, he has doubled the allowance."

Paul the hermit lived until A.D. 342. At age ninety-five, he retired to a cave in the deserts of Egypt said to be the retreat of money-coiners in the days of Cleopatra, Queen of Egypt. The accounts of his life are documented in the original Greek manuscripts edited by Saint Jerome. He is celebrated on January 5th.

Most Ignorant

"I am only a man, just like you." How many times did Alfred Bessette repeat these words? Probably thousands. For most of his adult life he was talked about in terms of miracles, to the extent that the Canadian press dubbed him "Miracle Worker of Montreal."

He particularly did not like the titles he was given and worked hard to convince others that the miracles they attributed to him were really the product of their own faith, not his. Yet, he said many times to the people who journeyed to his side seeking a cure, "I'll pray for you," and time after time, cures took place. To the sick, he often recommended wearing a medal of Saint Joseph or rubbing with oil from the lamps that stood at Saint Joseph's statue. "Such things are acts of love and faith, of confidence and humility," he would say.

Brother Andre was an inspiration to those who felt they were slow learners or lacked proper education. He himself, having been orphaned at an early age, was entirely illiterate at the age of twelve, and throughout his life he read only with difficulty. "It is not necessary to have been well educated, to have spent many years in college, to love the good God. It is sufficient to want to do so generously."

As a young man, this miracle worker worked at a number of unskilled jobs in Canada and for a time journeyed to the United States where he heard the opportunities were better. However, no job ever fully satisfied his heart. In 1870 at age twenty-five, he discovered where he belonged and joined the Congregation of the Holy Cross.

For forty years afterwards he joyfully washed floors, windows and lamps, carried firewood, served as a doorkeeper, a porter and a messenger and performed any task that was needed.

As a child, Brother Andre once had a dream of a beautiful church. Through his efforts the church of his dream is now a reality. The magnificent Oratory of St. Joseph is an enormous shrine which took fifty years to complete and stands as the highest point in the city of Montreal-over five hundred feet above street level. When the press asked him what talents he had to undertake so ambitious a project, he replied, "Personally, I am nothing. God chose the most ignorant one. If there was anyone more ignorant than I am, the good God would have chosen him."

Brother Andre died on January 6, 1937 at the age of ninety-two, having won the hearts of French and English speaking Canadians alike. Newspapers reported that over one million people climbed the slopes to St. Joseph's Oratory, in the rain, sleet and snow to pay their final respects to Canada's most ignorant servant of God.

Alfred Bessette was born August 9 1845, in a small town thirty-two miles southeast of Montreal. Today his tomb is still a popular sight of pilgrimage, due to reports of miraculous cures. Brother Andre was Beatified by Pope John Paul II on May 23, 1982.

Gift of the Senses

As a mere child Saint Frodibert cured his mother's blindness. At a moment when his youthful heart overflowed with love and pity, he kissed her darkened eyes and gently touched them with his fingers. Instantly her sight was restored and was keener than ever.

In another instance, while being interviewed by Abbot Theudecarius the child was spontaneously caught up into the divine regions of the third heaven. Unexpectedly he was transfixed by celestial sounds and heard a heavenly choir singing, "Holy, Holy, Holy, Holy Almighty. Thou art all that has been, all that is now and all that will ever be." Ravished by the unspeakable beauty of this melody, Frodibert prayed that the abbot might be permitted to share his divine ravishment. His prayer was answered, for the abbot was suddenly transfixed and caught up in the same miraculous vision. It is through his testimony that this miracle became known.

The accounts of his life are recorded in the Life of Saint Frodibert, by Lupellus.

Legend of Hamme

Saint Gudula was respectfully buried on January 8, A.D. 712. When her body was brought to the churchyard of Hamme for burial, a tree standing just beyond the cemetery suddenly burst into full flower. Remarkable? Maybe. But even more remarkable is that the event took place in midwinter!

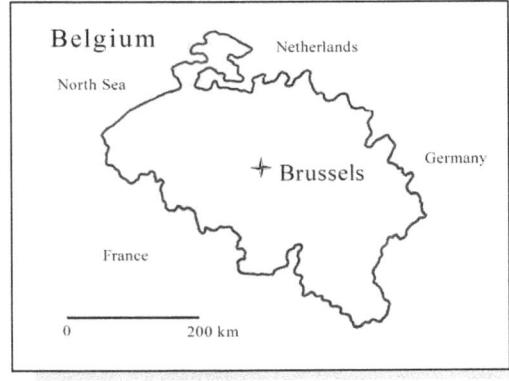

The body of the saint was subsequently moved from Hamme to Saint Saviour's Moosel. The following morning, the same tree which had first blossomed in Hamme, miraculously appeared, maturely rooted and fully flowered, directly opposite the church door of Saint Saviour's Moosel.

Many miracles have been credited to Gudula. The accounts of her life are documented in Life of Saint Gudula, *by Nicholas of Durham. She died on January 8, A.D. 712. Her relics lie in Saint Gudula's Church in Brussels, Belgium.*

Where There's a Will

Fillan was an Irishman, well educated, endowed with an incurable love for writing, and blessed with miracles. As a student, his passion for penmanship consumed him, often drawing him well into the depths of the night.

In later life, he elected to enter the monastery of Wexford where he was informed by his superiors that the use of candles was not permitted after certain evening hours. He assured them he would respect the monastery rules to the letter.

Determined to continue his writing, he unbridled himself of this restriction by way of a miracle. When the curfew hour approached he simply held up his left hand, which shone like a candle, and illuminated sufficient area to continue his writing. Hence, Fillan wrote with his right hand, by the light given from his left.

Fillan lived during the eighth century. He is celebrated on January 9th. The accounts of his life are recorded in Lives of the Saints *by Baring-Gould.*

The Almighty: An Equal Opportunity Employer

The first layman ever to be elected pope was in the right place at the right time.

It happened that Fabian, a Roman soldier, was in the right place on a certain occasion in January, A.D. 236. He inadvertently entered a church in Rome at the precise moment the synod had gathered for the election of a new pope to succeed Anteros. No candidate had been nominated, and the electors were in doubt about whom to choose. Then the miracle occurred.

From the louvre of the catacomb a brilliant, heavenly dove appeared. Fluttering for a moment, it made its way to the passage from which Fabian had entered and as if to indicate God's choice for pope, it settled upon the head of the soldier. The electors were more than a little surprised. This phenomenon was not uncommon in the history of the church, but God's choice for pope had never before been a soldier. Could this sign be right?

After days of debate and much investigation it was unanimously agreed that Fabian's qualifications were exceptional. He was the first layman ever to be elected pope and his rulership justified the choice. In the words of his contemporaries, "No man more worthy ever ruled the church."

Fabian was elected pope on January 10, A.D. 236. He reigned until the day of his death, January 20, A.D. 250.

Simplicity Desired

Theodosius was a hermit, or at least he wanted to be. At an early age he retired to a cave, not far from Bethlehem, where he resolved to live a simple life free of worldly complications. Seldom, however, does original greatness go unnoticed, and in time his natural sanctity became recognized.

Many young men continually sought his mastership and stubbornly demanded to be accepted as disciples. In time he agreed, surrendered his simple life, and rejected no one.

It became necessary to construct a monastery, but before doing so, he instructed his students to fill a censer with charcoal and incense and pray that God would ignite it when they found the perfect spot.

Bursting with enthusiasm the new monks journeyed from the highlands near Bethlehem to the shores of the Dead Sea, but there was no sign, not even a smoldering. Perhaps there was no land fit for a monastery in this area, they thought. Though reluctant, the monks returned to their master and it was then that God intervened. As they approached the cavern hut of their own Theodosius, the charcoal suddenly burst into flame and clouds of sweet incense filled the air.

It was here! This was the perfect spot! No other place was more sanctified than the home of their own master. So here it was that the monastery was constructed; on the very spot that Theodosius had chosen for a simple life.

In time the monastery grew beyond itself and may be better described as a city of saints in the midst of a desert. It contained four churches, three hospitals, several public buildings and accommodations for hundreds of pilgrims.

Such was the life of this hermit who lived for a hundred and five years to rule in his own kingdom. He died in A.D. 529 and was buried in the "Cave of the Magi," named for the three wise men who are said to have lodged there.

Fragrances of Heaven

Saint Benedicta was an observer of heaven, and the paragraph which follows is paraphrased from her personal observations. Her writings particularly discriminate the differences, in fragrance, of the occupants of heaven:

"There are many odors in the regions of heaven and all of them are divine. Among them the fragrances of the angelic hierarchy are most noticeable and they are as different and numerous as the perfumes of flowers. Each angel exhales a fragrance of divine sweetness which is distinctly his or hers alone, but none of them is so ravishing and potent in sweetness as that of the queen of men and angels, Mary.

Still, there is one perfume which surpasses in an infinite degree any of the odors I have yet to perceive. It is the sweet perfume which exhales from the Baby Jesus, child of Mary."

Benedicta was herself distinguished for her divine fragrance. During her ecstasies she would often exude a natural perfume whose potency would render witnesses utterly intoxicated. Moreover, these divine bouquets were perceived from remarkable distances.

Her biographers tell us that her breath was like the sweetest roses. Her clothes and everything she touched were all sweet with an ever-fresh perfume emanating from her body; a perfume which suffused on all those around her a vision of the kingdom of heaven.

Determination Rewarded

Veronica was not the type to follow the styles and fashions of the day. Even as a child this was true. With her confidence, determination and strength of character, she was able to gain the sympathies of heaven, a merit which led her contemporaries to title her "The Visionary of Milan."

As a child she desired only one thing: to be ordained a nun. More than just the romantic fantasies of childhood, her ambitions were genuine and uncompromising. She would delight at the very thought of becoming a sister, but her natural enthusiasm was not enough. She was disqualified, time and time again, because she was wholly uneducated, unable even to read.

To overcome her academic ignorance she studied many long hours each night, going over her alphabet and spelling. She found it very difficult and her progress was slow. She prayed for a tutor, or someone to help.

One night during her studies, someone did come to help. It was Mary, the Queen of Heaven. She was clothed in a garment of dazzling blue, as soft and brilliant as the summer sky.

"My child," said the celestial queen, "trouble yourself not with scholarship. The knowledge one amasses in one's mind will never equal the purity one amasses in one's heart. For you, I have three words of wisdom. Faith, hope and charity. The greatest of these is charity. Ponder them in your heart."

Saying this, the celestial damsel vanished, leaving Veronica in an ecstasy of joy. This was the first of many visions for Veronica. Shortly afterward her ambition was realized; she was accepted as a sister in the convent of Saint Martha.

Veronica lived during the fifteenth century. Her relics are preserved in the convent of Saint Martha in Milan, Italy. The accounts of her life are recorded in the Acta Sanctorum, January 13.

Lord of Battles

At the turn of the sixth century, a war began. In the year A.D. 513, Clovis elected to march against the oppressive and barbaric forces of Alaric the Arian, King of the Goths. What moves the heavens to enter into the affairs of man is known to God alone, but on the battlefield that morning, the heavens intervened.

A heavenly light was seen proceeding from a church not far from the battlefield of Poitiers. As the light advanced, it was clearly defined as the image of Saint Hilary, the bishop who had served in the church 146 years earlier. A voice burst forth from the light and cried aloud, "Up Clovis, and delay not, for as captain of the Lord's hosts I have come to you. Today the Lord of Battles will deliver the foe into thy hands."

Clovis advanced against the Arian Goths fully assured of victory, and before the third hour he had routed the foe and won a victory in a battle second-to-none in this world.

Recorded in the Historia Francorum, Book II Saint Hilary is celebrated on January 14th.

Surprise Visit

Above all, Saint Bont was a man of profound sensitivity. His shy disposition and natural introversion kept him far from the arenas of ceremonial or public display. He preferred a monk's life and chose to sit in silent prayer throughout his evening hours.

One evening, while deep in meditation in Saint Michel's Church, his privacy was disturbed by unexpected guests. He was aroused from his empty silence when Mary, Queen of Virgins, accompanied by a small gathering of saints and angels, appeared before him.

The heavenly visitants paid little notice to Bont and busied themselves arranging the articles for the celebration of mass. When the articles were all collected and put in their proper places, one of the celestials inquired of the Virgin, "Who will officiate the mass?" "Bont," she replied, "who is already in the church."

These words pierced Bont like an arrow. He was filled with an unexpected fear, and, almost unconsciously, pressed himself against one of the church pillars, expecting to remain hidden. It was a futile attempt, however, for the moment he touched the pillar of stone, it instantly became soft, and an impression of his body remained imprinted there.

A moment later angels gathered around him, and taking him by the hand they escorted him to the Virgin Queen who asked in gracious tones, "Will you officiate the mass?"

Unable to speak, but filled with confidence, he ascended to the altar to officiate. As he did so, he was assisted by heavenly saints and angels who took part in the chanting of the service. By the conclusion of the mass, his soul was elevated to ecstasy.

With a smile of loving approval, the Virgin Queen approached him carrying a heavenly chasuble in her hands.

"Keep this garment as a pledge of my favor," she said softly. Then handing him the delicate cloth, she and her retinue disappeared.

This chasuble, a fine delicate material, remained in the cathedral at Clermont, France until 1793, eleven hundred years after it had been given to Bont. This account is recorded in the Acta Sanctorum, January 15.

A Saintly Sum

In the biographical records of Saint Gonsalo of Amarante there is a story of how he erected a bridge over the Tamega River.

Gonsalo applied to a neighboring count for the funds to purchase the materials and pay the laborers for the construction of the bridge. The nobleman, thinking Gonsalo to be little more than a religious mendicant, contrived to get rid of him. He scribbled a couple of lines on a scrap of paper and commanded Gonsalo,

"Take it to my wife, the countess!"

Gonsalo did so and when the countess opened the letter she read it aloud.

"The poor fool, the bearer of this letter wants to build a bridge. Let him have in cash the weight of this slip of paper."

"So be it!" cried Gonsalo, "I accept!"

Fully intending to pay Gonsalo a veritable nothing, the countess placed the slip of paper on a scale. Contrary to her intentions, she discovered that its weight measured an enormous sum of money. She tried to adjust the scale, but the measure remained the same. Repeatedly she made corrections, but the balance continually registered a remarkable sum.

Finally, in frustration and sincere humility, she begged the pardon of the saint. Convinced that Gonsalo was indeed divinely blessed, she handed him his allotted sum and offered her additional assistance should his project require it.

Gonsalo lived until 1259. He is respectfully celebrated on January 16th. The accounts of his life are recorded in the Life of Saint Gonsalo, by Didacus de Rosario. Gonsalo's bridge is located in Amarante, a small, picturesque wine-producing town in the Porto District of northern Portugal.

The Eyes of a Child

Our Lady Of Hope appeared only to children. A vision occurred on the evening of January 17, 1871 when a farmer, Caesar Barbadette, and his two sons, Eugene, age twelve, and Joseph, age ten, were busy at work in their barn. Tired and a little bored from his daily chores, young Eugene wandered to the barn door for fresh air and a look at the weather. Gazing into the evening sky he was immediately transfixed by a vision five feet above the roof of their barn. It was a heavenly lady, more beautiful than Eugene had ever imagined, even in a dream.

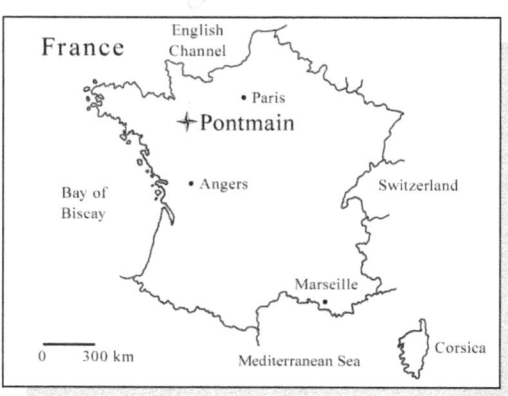

She was dressed in a gown of deep royal blue studded with gold stars. The sleeves were fully extended to her hands. Her feet were adorned with blue slippers tied with a gold ribbon in the shape of a rosette. Her hair was completely covered with a veil, and on her head was a gold crown with a single peak in the center. More importantly, she was smiling, directly at Eugene.

At the same time, Jeanette Detais, a neighbor who was helping the Barbadette family, also stepped outside the barn. Eugene, unable to speak and showing considerable concern, pointed to the sky to direct her attention to the apparition. But Jeanette saw nothing. She called for Caesar and Joseph, but when they came the mystery only deepened. Young Joseph saw the vision just as his brother did; their father saw nothing. In the moments that followed the two boys were so irresistibly absorbed by the vision, they were utterly oblivious to the presence of others.

Caesar and Jeanette tried in various ways to break their spell, but were unsuccessful. Sensing the religious nature of his sons' entrancement, Caesar summoned the nuns from the village school, but they too saw nothing and were equally perplexed. Minutes later, two girls from the same school joined the gathering, Frances Richer, age eleven and Jeanne Marie Lebosse, age nine. Both were immediately entranced, just as the brothers had been.

As the evening grew later, many members of the township, old and young, gathered at the Barbadette's farm, but the vision was seen only by the children. Even a two-year old baby held by its mother stretched out its arm and showed by unmistakable signs that he, too, was enraptured by the vision.

Father Guerin, the town priest, was summoned by one of the nuns, and when he arrived he led the assembled crowd in songs and recitation of the Rosary. All the while the children remained entranced a period of three hours.

Unaware of the crowd around them, the children watched as the vision evolved. First, a heavenly oval sphere appeared. It was a brilliant blue and encircled the Lady as though she were a picture being framed. Within the heavenly frame four candle stands appeared. Each candle stand contained unlit candles which, in the passage of a moment, was lighted by stars proceeding from the Lady's blue gown.

The stars then multiplied and a small red cross, like a badge, appeared at her breast. As the gathering recited the Rosary, stars collected, two-by-two, below the Lady's feet. Finally, a white banner, about a yard wide and forming a perfect rectangle, appeared beneath the stars. Within it a message was engraved: "But pray, my children, God will soon grant your request. My son allows himself to be moved by compassion." When the vision concluded a thin white veil covered the figure of the Virgin, first at her feet, then rising slowly to the crown above her head. Giving her last smile to the children, she withdrew from their sight.

This apparition has since been sanctioned by the highest ecclesiastical authority and is venerated under the title of Our Lady of Hope of Pontmain.

No Bread in the House

The sun had set and the cool night air sent a chill into the darkness when Theodosius and several of his disciples arrived at the home of Marcian, a local monk. Marcian graciously invited them in and offered the full extent of his hospitality. He had little to offer in the way of good food, but brought to the (table a small plate of lentils which was all he possessed. He bowed humbly to Theodosius and apologized for having no bread in the house. Theodosius, however, observed a small crumb on the monk's habit and remarked, "How say you brother there is no bread in the house?" Then lifting the crumb, he handed it to him.

Somewhat perplexed, Marcian took the crumb and carried it to the pantry, but before he had reached there the crumb miraculously enlarged to a full loaf of bread. Startled, Marcian hurried back to the table and set the miraculous loaf before his guests who ate it heartily until their hunger was satisfied. The remaining loaf was taken to the pantry for storage, but by morning it had multiplied to such a degree the entire pantry was filled to overflowing, and the door had been forced open by the abundance of bread that spilled through.

Saint Theodosius the Cenobriarch lived for 106 years until A.D. 529. He is remembered for the many miracles in which he multiplied bread through his prayers.

Suspended in Prayer

"With his face aglow like heavenly fire," Francis Xavier was often lifted into the air while absorbed in prayer. In a manner similar to Margaret of Hungary, Francis of Assisi and Theresa of Avila, "he frequently hovered miraculously above the ground where he remained suspended, sometimes for hours, before returning to the earth."

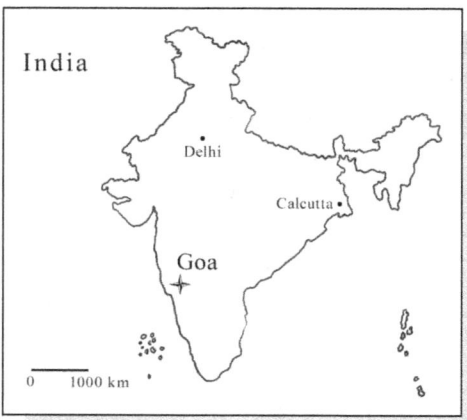

Francis was born of royalty in the castle of Xavier. Educated at the University of Paris, he chose a vocation of mission work, journeying to India, Ceylon, Malacca, the Molucca Islands, the Malay Peninsula and Japan, spreading a message of peace and understanding.

He brought reforms to numerous relaxed Catholic colonies notorious for their cruelty, open concubinage and neglect of the poor. He taught by example, living among the poor, often sleeping on the ground in huts and eating only rice and water. Yet all the while his miracle of levitation continued. At times, when his body was buoyant with ecstasy, Francis, unable to contain himself, would cry aloud, "Satis est Domine! Satis est!" ("Enough, Lord! It is enough!")

After his death in 1551, his body was returned to India where it remains incorrupt and enshrined in the cathedral bearing his name.

This account is given in Cardinal de Monte's speech before Pope Gregory XV, at the canonization of Francis Xavier, January 19, 1622.

Miraculous Administration

No matter how turbulent his life became, Euthymius always had a ready smile and a calmness which was relaxing and inspiring. He was a man of exquisite sensitivity who was loved with equal enthusiasm by both his disciples and those outside the abbey. He was gifted with miracles, but firmly maintained that he possessed no such administration. However, stories from the abbey tell otherwise.

On one occasion a riotous band of Armenians gathered at the monastery gate. Utterly destitute for lack of food they begged Euthymius to feed them. There was too little food in the monastery to last the resident monks even a single day, to say nothing of an additional four hundred mouths, but to the monks' surprise, Euthymius ordered food to be set before the travelers.

In strict obedience, the monks hurried to search the storeroom. Where there had been little more than a few loaves of bread, some oil and wine; now the storeroom was filled to the ceiling with food. So much food, in fact, that the pantry seemed in danger of collapse. Food and wine were distributed to each of the four hundred travelers whose genuine appreciation could best be measured by the extent of their hearty appetites.

Euthymius the Great lived until A.D. 473. He was born in Melitene, Armenia, but lived most of his life in a cave near Jericho. Here, due to the many miracles he performed, a large following of Arabs were initiated as his disciples.

Patroness of Purity

The following account may be the most romantic tragedy recorded in the history of documented miracles.

Procopius was young and ambitious and was as feared as his father, the Governor of Rome. Like many noblemen of the city, he was stung with excitement by the beauty and riches of a tender young girl named Agnes. The daughter of one of the first families of the city, Agnes was barely thirteen, yet possessed a beauty which seemed more than mortal. She was blessed with an astonishing intuition and an attractiveness which made her the object of admiration throughout Rome.

Procopius vowed he would possess her and pressed his suit of marriage, but Agnes refused, replying that she had consecrated her virginity "to a heavenly husband, not seen by mortal eyes."

The rejection caused Procopius to fall ill. The governor sent for Agnes and told her she had the choice of two proposals—either marry his son or lose her life.

With outward self-confidence Agnes replied she would do neither. This impudent declaration so incensed the governor that in a fit of rage he declared her to be a public strumpet and commanded that she be led naked through the streets of Rome and deposited in a brothel "with liberty to all persons to abuse her person at pleasure."

It was a futile sentence, however, for Agnes was blessed with miracles. When the soldiers arrived to tear away her garments, "her hair was caused to grow to such length and thickness that it covered her whole body like a cape." This spectacle terrified the guards, and believing Agnes to be a witch, they dispatched her to a whorehouse and abandoned her. When she entered the brothel an angel appeared and clothed her in a seamless white robe "more radiant than any earthly material." Making no attempt to escape she remained in the brothel unafraid.

Many young libertines ran to the house "but were seized with such awe at the sight of the saint, they durst not approach her-only one accepted." Lovesick, Procopius approached. Filled with anger and lust he seized her and "was that very instant, by a flash of lightning from heaven, struck blind and fell trembling to the ground."

When the news reached the governor, he rushed to the brothel with his attendants. Seeing for himself the state of his son, he implored the young saint to restore him. Agnes agreed.

She ordered the attendants to withdraw from the room and closed her eyes in silent prayer. Procopius arose, "restored to his sight and health." With tears the commander embraced his son, but his hatred for Agnes deepened. He continued his persecutions with greater vigor, and in time young Agnes surrendered her life to martyrdom.

Saint Agnes lived during the fourth century. She is celebrated on January 21st. The accounts of her life were recorded by Saint Ambrose, Saint Jerome, Prudentius and many others. She is the Patron Saint of bodily purity. This testimony was taken from De Virginibus, by Ambrose.

Nest of Fish

Since the days of childhood Saint Dominic was a charmer. His natural intensity was a magnet that made others want to listen to the thoughts he had to share. He could mesmerize a crowd with a straightforward discussion of the most delicate and personal nature, but he was no fanatic.

As a young man he chose a religious life and with his irrepressible charm, piety and natural leadership, he was soon elected as abbot of the monastery of Sora.

On one occasion, the monastery was sent a donation of fresh fish by a local nobleman. Dominic was pleased to hear of it and came himself to the monastery gate to receive it. However, the attendant hired for the task of delivering the gift separated a part of it for himself and hid it under a tree along the road. Dominic received the gift on behalf of the monastery and remarked to the man, "Don't forget the fish under the linden tree, good man. Good-day."

The attendant was startled and returning along the road he asked himself how the abbot could have known about the missing fish. When he reached the tree where his stolen treasure was buried, he discovered that his deceit had gained him nothing at all. Where the fish had once been buried, now remained only a nest of serpents.

Saint Dominic was born in Sora, Italy and lived from A.D. 946 to 1031. He is celebrated on January 22nd. The accounts of his life are recorded in the Acta Sanctorum.

The Raft

At times the miracles of Raymund of Penafort seem utterly astonishing, both in quality and quantity. Lists of supernatural phenomena accredited to him fill sixteen pages of the ecclesiastical records. He was a man of remarkable self-confidence, and at

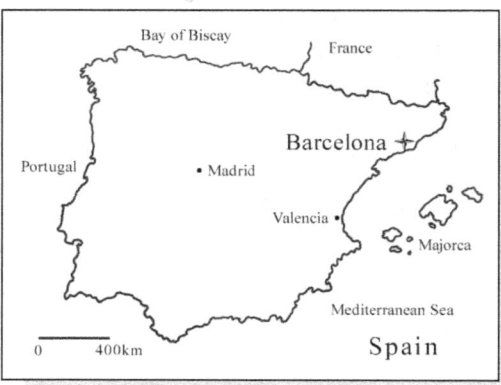

times it seemed that nothing could stand in his way. Although descended from the counts of Barcelona, he contained no grain of arrogance or false superiority and never flaunted his extensive educational accomplishments. He seemed to be loved by everyone, from the pope, who took him as his personal confessor, to his lowest countryman whose receptions often made one think the safety of the kingdom depended on his presence.

The most famous of Raymund's miracles is said to have taken place when he accompanied King James to the island of Majorca. Even though the king was married, he openly indulged in sexual dalliances with other women. Raymund warned him that he would no longer abide in the court, a witness to such open violations of the law. Despite Raymund's entreaties and the king's promise to mend his ways, the dalliances continued.

Raymund requested the king's permission to return to Barcelona, but the king refused him and gave strict orders to all shippers, under penalty of death, not to convey Raymund off the island. Full of confidence, Raymund responded, "An earthly king withholds the means of flight, but the King of Heaven will supply them." He then walked to the sea and in plain sight, spread his cloak over the waters and climbed aboard as though it had been a raft. Holding up one corner of the cloak for a sail, he reached the harbor of Barcelona in six hours, a distance of one hundred and sixty miles. Numerous witnesses received him when he landed, and and on reaching the shore he drew up from the waters his cloak, which was "not in the slightest way damp," put it on, and stole through the crowd to his monastery.

A tower was later built at the sight where Raymund landed, so a memory of this miracle might be retained for posterity.

Raymund was born at Penafort, in Catalonia, in 1175. He died on January 6th, one hundred years later, and was honored at his funeral by numerous miracles, witnessed by thousands, including two kings and all the princes and princesses of their royal families. He was canonized in 1601, his celebration being set for January 23rd. This account is recorded in the bull of his canonization.

Sweet Speech

Francis of Sales was both reserved and dynamic, cool on the surface, but a flame inside. He was educated in Paris, but later transferred to Padua to study law. There he rose to be a master of diplomacy and was renowned as a brilliant orator who spoke spontaneously from intuition.

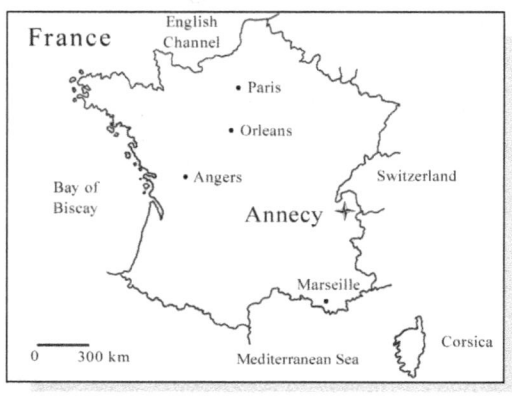

His talents won him the appointment of Counselor of the Parliament of Chambery, but he firmly refused. He believed his talent would be properly exploited only as a priest.

As a speaker representing the opinions of God, he was nothing less than astonishing. He spoke with such wisdom and sweet eloquence that even the heavens approved. He was in great demand for public assemblies because it was there that one could expect the miraculous.

On one occasion he spoke in the church of St. Dominic to a gathering of Senators who had come to confirm the reports of his apparent holiness. It was a grey, dark day, thick with clouds, but the moment Francis spoke, magnificent rays of light, clearly not of this earth, emanated from the church crucifix and showered his whole person with light. He appeared to be on fire, his face shining "as bright as the sun." The assembly was wonderstruck, but Francis ignored the sight and behaved as if nothing had happened.

When the spectacle subsided, the atmosphere was charged with energetic mumblings which filtered through the church. Again Francis ignored the excitement. He directed their attention back to his discourse with a gentle reprimand and spoke with such power, simplicity, eloquence and humility, that he himself seemed more miraculous than the miracle.

When questioned on the remarkable nature of his lecture, he replied, "More flies are attracted to a spoonful of honey, than a barrel of vinegar."

Francis of Sales {Patron Saint of writers} was canonized in 1665. Born in Savoy, France at the Chateau de Sales, Francis lived from 1567 to 1622. His incorrupt body and relics are preserved at a shrine in Annery, France.

The Organizer

If it wasn't perfect, then Saul wasn't happy. He was a man of precision and intelligence with an inclination for organization and structure. He was a Roman citizen and a Jew educated in Jerusalem under the tutelage of Gamaliel, a most illustrious rabbi. Saul declared himself an enemy of the Christian movement and organized rallies condemning their leader, Jesus, whom he believed was a threat to the teachings of the ancient Hebrew prophets. To ensure the survival of Israel, Saul zealously took part in persecuting the Christians and participated in the stoning death of Saint Steven.

At age thirty-five, while he traveled the road to Damascus, a miracle occurred.

"I set out with the intention of bringing the prisoners I would arrest back to Jerusalem for punishment. As I was traveling along, approaching Damascus, around noon a great light from the sky suddenly flashed all about me. I fell to the ground and heard a voice say to me, 'Saul, Saul, why do you persecute me?' I answered, 'Who are you sir?' He said to me, 'I am Jesus the Nazarene whom you are persecuting.' My companions saw the light but did not hear the voice speaking to me. 'What is it I must do, sir?' I asked and the Lord replied, 'Get up and go into Damascus. There you will be told about everything you are destined to do.' But since I could not see, I had to be taken by the hand and led to Damascus by my companions."

Profoundly influenced by this miracle, Saul assumed a new name, Paul. Following his destiny he became the champion of the cause which he had tried to overthrow. He structured an organization which still stands today and his writings are the most prolific and influential among the apostles of Christ.

The Conversion of Paul (the apostle).

Old Friend

Androclus was a Roman slave who was condemned to death and sentenced to encounter a lion in the amphitheater. However, when the hungry lion was released, rather than devour his captive prey, he lay down at Androclus' feet and licked them. Androclus was summoned before the Consul and the following tale was narrated:

"I was compelled by cruel treatment to run away from your service while in Africa. One day I took refuge in a cave from the heat of the sun. While I was in the cave a lion entered, limping and in great pain. Seeing me, he held out his paw, from which I extracted a large thorn. Soon the beast was able to use his paw again. We lived together for some time in the cave, the lion catering for both of us. At length, I left the cave, was apprehended, brought to Rome and condemned to be torn to pieces. The lion was my old friend and he recognized me instantly."

On hearing this tale, the Consul pardoned the slave and gave him the lion as an award.

This account is recorded in Noctes Attica, Volume XV, by Aulus Gellius.

Bubbling Spring

Julian was a thinking man who made others think in new ways. He was born in Rome, and as a youth his natural sense of leadership kept him busy with one crusade for justice after another. In manhood his sense of Justice did not leave him, and when he chose a religious career he brought with him a fresh new expression of social morality.

His many natural qualifications made him the obvious choice for the appointment of first Bishop of Mans, and it was there that his true talents emerged.

In ecclesiastical art Julian is represented in pontifical robes, planting his staff while a maiden fills her pitcher with water at his feet. These works of art were inspired by the miracle he produced while reigning as the religious leader of Mans.

During a time of siege the inhabitants of Mans, exhausted for need of water, applied to Julian for help. Their circumstances were exceptionally grave, and their need was immediate. Resolved to help, Julian planted his pastoral staff in an open plain, and in the sight of every citizen of Mans, a sumptuous, bubbling spring was produced.

His biographers write: "This is the more remarkable in that the spot elected by the bishop is wholly destitute of natural springs." Saint Julian's Spring still flows.

This story is given in the History of the Church of Mans. Julian is celebrated on January 27th.

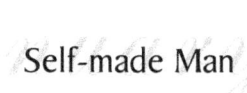

Self-made Man

James was a man of noble character with strength and substance. He loved hard work, outdoor living and well-cooked food. He was often impatient and difficult to get to know, but he set high ideals for himself and was determined to move forward tirelessly.

He was always involved with one cause or another and wasn't afraid to tell others what was on his mind. He was a self-made man with an indomitable spirit and he liked to live life by his own set of rules. No one knew this better than his own disciples who told this story.

The monks of Saint James were busily engaged in the task of erecting a new church. They were felling trees in a nearby forest when a rampant bear attacked and killed one of the oxen employed in drawing the timber. Fleeing in fear of their lives, they hastened to James and informed him that their progress had been impeded by a bloodthirsty bear. With a look of stern reproval in his eyes, the saint rose to his feet, marched directly to the ravaging beast and declared, "I, James, command thee, thou cruel beast, to bow thy neck to the yoke in place of the ox which thou hast slain."

The bear was harnessed and the work continued until completion.

Saint James lived during the fifth century. The foregoing account is given in the Life of Saint James of Tarentaise by Pope Calixtus II.

Ina Poonbato

The remote regions of the Zambales mountains in the Philippines were once the tribal lands of the aboriginal hunters, the Negritos. Djadig, their leader, was a special man revered for his unmatched skills in hunting with bow and arrow. No one in all the tribes could run as fast as he, and it was known that even without arrows Djadig could capture the fleetest deer. Among the Negrito people he was the acknowledged leader of leaders.

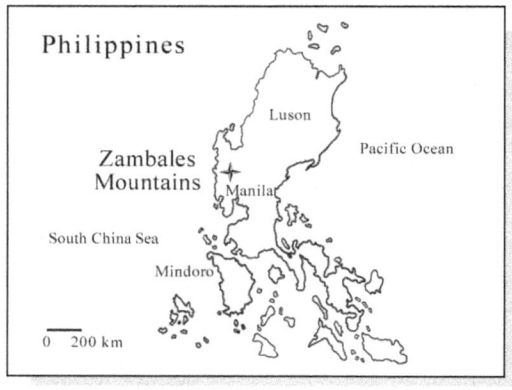

It was during a hunting expedition with his three sons that he first experienced a miracle. The hunting party had stopped to rest at the bank of the Pastac River when an ethereal voice filled the air, commanding, "Get up, Djadig. Look for me. Come and take me home with you."

The voice had come from the top of a towering rock where Djadig alone saw a beautiful lady shining like the sun and dressed in shimmering gold. Her hair was like the sunlight, her eyes dark and filled with compassion. He was drawn to the spot instinctively, like metal to a magnet, all the time his eyes entranced by the vision. As he drew closer the vision dematerialized and the beautiful Lady remained only an image carved on shining gold wood.

"Take me home with you," the ethereal voice commanded again, and Djadig instinctively obeyed.

When he reached home, his wife was unwilling to believe his mysterious tale. Angry that he had neglected his duties as a hunter, she seized the wooden image and cast it indignantly into their fire pit. Flames shot up instantly, burning the walls and ceiling, and before help could arrive, Djadig's hut was reduced to ashes. "Wait! Look!" exclaimed the children, who were poking the glowing embers with a bamboo pole, "The shining image is not burned." It was true. The image was intact and still shining like gold. With due honors, the Negritos reverently enshrined the image on the selfsame rock where Djadig had discovered it.

Many years later the first Europeans landed on Philippine soil. As they colonized the islands, the culture which preceded them was vanquished. Christianity was introduced to the new civilization, and when an image of the Virgin Mary was presented to the Negrito people, they were delighted to see that it was a replica of their own patroness, "Ina Poonbato."

When the shining image discovered by Djadig was revealed to the Spanish missionaries, they were forced to believe that their own Reverend Mother had preceded them. The Negritos explained that "Ina Poonbato" was the source of many miracles to them. She was their patroness and the bringer of rains, filling the mountains with deer and an abundance of food.

Ina Poonbato has long been recognized in the Philippines for the many miracles accredited to her, but only as recently as 1985 was she carried to Rome and officially sanctioned by His Holiness, Pope John Paul II.

The Dove's Veil

Aldegundis was the daughter of Prince Walbert of Hainaut. She was an enterprising child who was capable, competent, and competitive. She had a courageous determination to succeed and measured her worth by her own self integrity. As a child she believed that she would one day be a master of miracles, which at times seemed almost believable to her family and friends.

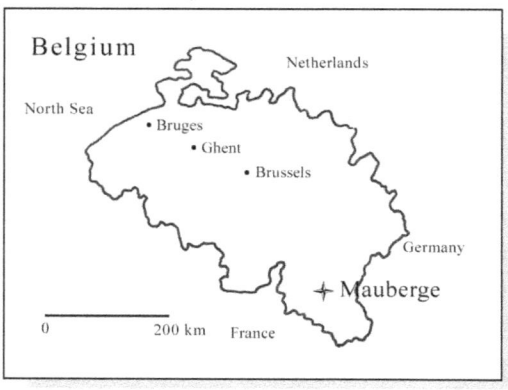

According to royal custom, when she reached her early teenage years her marriage was arranged to a suitable neighboring prince. Prince Eudo was selected for the honor, and being charmed by the sweet countenance of the girl, he pressed his suit of marriage.

Aldegundis was much too free-spirited to blindly participate in the politics of family marriages, and determined to resolve the matter, fled to a nearby monastery for protection.

She explained her dilemma to the monks and after due consideration the reverend fathers advised her to receive initiation into the abbey at once. She readily consented, believing her actions to be in league with God's will.

The ceremony proceeded, but at the moment the sacred veil was to be presented to her, by some mistake, there was none at hand. It was a fatal mishap and would have obliged Aldegundis to defer the service. Further, it would give time and reason for her espoused Prince Eudo to intervene. It was then that the miracle occurred.

In the midst of this perplexity, an effulgent dove appeared from above the altar. In its beak was a veil as white and resplendent as itself. It circled Aldegundis several times, then dropped the veil which wafted downward and rested on her head.

The assembly was ravished by the spectacle and Aldegundis was elevated with joy.

Aldegundis lived from A. D. 630 to 689. She lived most of her life at the Monastery of Mauberge located in Southern Belgium, and built on the site of one of Caesar's ancient camps. She is celebrated on January 30th. Acta Sanctorum.

Formula for a Miracle

The Second Book of Hermes-Commands

Command 9: Again he said unto me; remove from thee all doubting; and question nothing at all, when thou asketh anything of the Lord; saying within thyself: how shall I be able to ask anything of the Lord and receive it, seeing I have so greatly sinned against him?

2. Do not think thus, but turn unto the Lord with all thy heart, and ask of him without doubting, and thou shalt know the mercy of the Lord; that he will not forsake thee but will fulfill the request of thy soul.

3. For God is not like man, mindful of the injuries he had received; but he forgets the injuries and has compassion upon his creatures.

4. Wherefore, purity thy heart from all the vices of this present world; and observe the commands I have before delivered unto thee from God; and thou shalt receive whatsoever good things thou shalt ask, and nothing shall be wanting unto thee of all thy petitions; if thou shalt ask of the Lord without doubting.

The foregoing narrative is taken from the manuscripts edited from the Bible by its compilers, the Council of Nice. In the early days of the church, the book from which this excerpt is taken was read aloud publicly, along with the other works of the New Testament.

February

1 The Milkmaid's Blessing
2 Emperor's Nominee
3 A New Generation
4 All's Well
5 Cloud Canopy
6 Unburned Flower
7 God's Favor
8 Fires of Freedom
9 Seven Tiny Stars
10 Heavenly Nectar
11 Notre Dame de Lourdes
12 Legend of Marina
13 Alphabet Lesson
14 Valentine's Day
15 Innkeeper's Miracle
16 Royal Escort
17 Holy Cow
18 Flaming Swords
19 Fresh Food
20 Bishop of Choice
21 Farmer's Rule
22 Two Lovers of Clermont
23 Herbs and Roots
24 Bread Shovel
25 Physician's Dream
26 Heavenly Dew
27 Native Revival
28 Antoinette of Florence

The Milkmaid's Blessing

Bridget of Kildare, affectionately named "Mary of the Gael," is known throughout Ireland for her many miracles. She was a spiritually gifted young girl who possessed a quiet, unimposing dignity, and her genuine modesty revealed no hint of her God-given talents. As a child she was raised on a farm, but before her twentieth birthday her reputation had reached all parts of Ireland.

She was once visited by several religious dignitaries wishing to see if the many tales about the child were true. She graciously received her guests but being of humble means, had nothing to offer them for refreshment. Excusing herself, she set to work milking a cow which had already been milked twice that same day. For Bridget, however, the milk was inexhaustible. The cow that had previously been milked dry now issued sufficient milk to fill three large pails, enough for all her guests.

Saint Bridget is celebrated as Patron Saint of Ireland. Cowkeepers throughout Europe honor her with pilgrimages to Hanay in Belgium to ensure that their cows will be ample producers of milk.

She lived from A.D. 453-523 and is celebrated on February 1st.

Emperor's Nominee

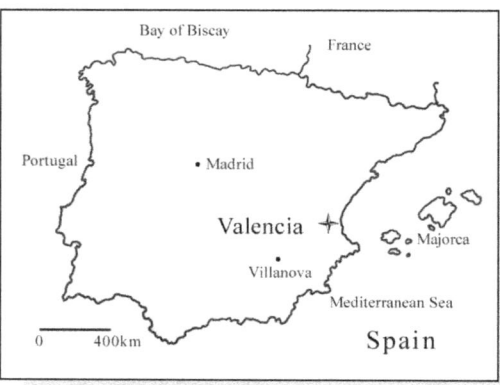

Thomas of Villanova was nominated by Emperor Charles V to the archbishopric of Granada. It was an appointment which Thomas readily declined, but as providence would have it, through certain clerical errors, his name appeared before the emperor again. This time the emperor commanded that Thomas accept the post. This Thomas did, but he was greatly distressed at his new found authority. Power and false appearances surrounded him like prison walls. So great was his distaste for this appointment that on February 2, 1555, in the middle of his sermon, he cried out, "My Father, My Father, can I be saved and yet hold this powerful position?" His answer came promptly. In the presence of the assembly, the crucifix came to life and consoled him with the words: "Thomas, afflict not yourself, but be patient. On the day of My mother's nativity you shall receive the recompense of all your troubles."

Proof of the revelation remains in the mouth of the crucifix, which before was closed, now was opened. Still more surprising is that it showed a set of teeth made of copper and styled to such exquisite perfection that no art or human instrument known could possibly have fashioned them.

Thomas of Villanova lived from 1488-1555. He was canonized in 1658. His written works have so influenced the literature of Spain, and the world, that several universities in the United States, Australia and Cuba have been named in his honor. His relics are preserved in Valencia, according to his wishes. The accounts of his life are recorded in the Acta Sanctorum, Volume V.

A New Generation

Patricia Talbott was sixteen years old and desperately had her heart set on becoming a fashion model for the clothiers of cultural Ecuador. She had never imagined she would be the recipient of divine apparitions, but on an unexpected moment in 1988, at 4:30 a.m., she was awakened from a dream to find her room filled with celestial light. The source of the light, the Virgin Mary, said, "Do not be afraid. I am your mother from heaven. Fold your hands over your chest and pray for peace in the world, for it is now that it needs it most."

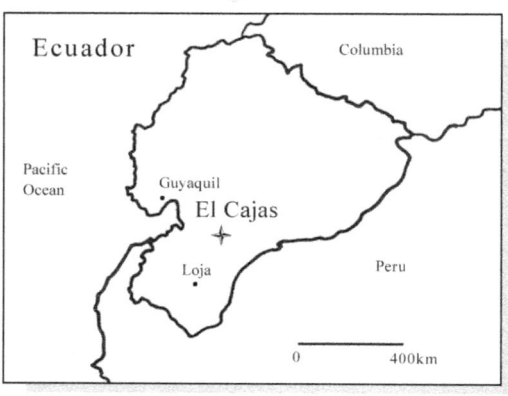

Many further apparitions have occurred since then and Patricia was encouraged to pray to her guardian angel for protection. Jesus also appeared to her with the message, "My cross has conquered the world, but my light for some is darkness. My little ones, cast out all evil thoughts, evil actions, and act with peace and love, faith and hope."

Through divine intervention, Patricia was led to a place high up in the Andes Mountains called El Cajas, not far from the city of Cuenca, where the Virgin declared she would give her message to the world:

Children there is much sorrow in my heart for many natural catastrophes, and others created by man are coming. Hard times are already taking place. The third world war threatens the world.... Do not frighten your hearts because the peace of God is with you.... You must fill your heart with light.... Fast on bread and water at least once a week. Pray the Rosary daily. You, my little souls, do not forget that with prayer and fasting you can deter wars and natural catastrophes."

On February 3, 1990, the Virgin spoke to Patricia while 120,000 people spent the night in prayer at the mountain site. "Little children, do not be anguished. Sow happiness and give joy to the world. . . . We have begun the period of hard times. It will be ten very sad years. Time is short. I am expecting you the first Saturday in March. My physical presence among you will end this time. But I will always stay here to pour out blessings upon you."

Two months later the Virgin appeared with a final message: "Little children, I love you so much. Today is the day of my physical departure, but my spiritual retreat will never be. I will be with you. . . Remember the first commandment of my son: Love one another, and love God above all things. I ask you for peace, pardon and conversion . . . . Children, I give you the blessing of the all powerful God, Father, Son and the Holy Spirit. . . . Never abandon me little ones because I love you so much."

A book on the reported apparitions in Ecuador is being published by Franciscan University Press, Steubenville, Ohio, based on the records of Sister Isabel Bettwy.

All's Well

History tells of a certain high robber who gained remarkable fame for his custom of reciting a prayer to the Virgin Mary before expropriating the treasures of his victims. But alas, in due time, he was captured and condemned to death. On the day of his execution he was led to the gallows. When the hangman's noose was tightened around his neck, he made his final prayer to the Virgin. On this occasion, however, his prayer was answered with a miracle. At the moment of execution, two white hands appeared below his feet and supported him in the air for a period of two days. At the completion of the second day, the judges instructed the executioner to behead the prisoner. Lifting his sword to do so, he was turned away by the same pair of hands. Inwardly the executioner was compelled to release his victim. This being done, the highwayman quit his former ways, retired to a monastery, and ended his life in the odor of sanctity.

Middle Ages, Volume III, by Hallam.

Cloud Canopy

Peter of Verona liked to get involved, and usually did, with one protest movement or another. He once held a public dispute with the bishops from Milan. The assembly was held in the open air and the heat of the sun made it intolerable to continue the discussions.

Saint Peter prayed aloud saying, "O Lord, Thou hast promised that the sun shall not smite thy servants by day, nor the moon by night; bring now the clouds to be unto us a tabernacle for a shadow from this great heat." No sooner had he spoken than a gathering of thick clouds formed a canopy over the heads of the assembled bishops. There it remained until the discussions were brought to a close.

Saint Peter of Verona lived from 1206-1252 and was canonized one year after his death. Saint Peter's Tomb is considered an important pilgrimage for artists due to its many miracles connected with artistic inspiration. This account is taken from Life of St. Peter the Martyr.

Unburned Flower

Early sixteenth-century Europe was a period of corruption for both church and state. Leonard Keyser of Bavaria sought to reform the injustices enforced by religious and political administrations, and rallied many men and women to this cause. For this, he was arrested and condemned to be burned at the stake. He was taken to the burning fields, far from the city, and there he picked a tiny flower. Approaching his judge, he remarked, "My lord, I have plucked this flower. If you can burn me and this flower in my hand, then you have condemned me righteously. But if you can burn neither me nor the flower, then reflect on what you are doing and repent."

When the procession reached the appointed place, the judge gave instructions for extra logs to be thrown onto the fire. When the fire was consumed, the body of the martyr was removed from the ashes and found to be entirely unharmed.

A second fire was constructed to incinerate the body, but again, when removed, the skin was smooth and the flower in his hand was unfaded.

The judge who condemned Leonard surrendered his office in an act of redemption. The chief executioner did likewise and joined the Moravian brotherhood. It was from his mouth that this narrative is taken down.

Chronicle of the Roman Heresies, letter Z.

God's Favor

Scholastica was brilliant. She was the twin sister of Saint Benedict and abbess of a nunnery, five miles from her brother's monastery. Once a year she would visit her brother in a small meeting house between the two stations. During such a visit on February 7, A.D. 543, she engaged him in a discussion on the eternal happiness of the saints in heaven. The entire day was passed in this way, and when evening approached she pressed her brother to continue further. Benedict, however, was unwilling to transgress the rules of his order and informed her that he could not spend the night away from his monastery. Finding her brother resolved to leave, she placed her hands on the table and bowed her head in prayer. Instantly a downpour of rain, mingled with thunder, lightning and ominous winds, burst over the house. "What have you done sister?" said Benedict.

"I asked my brother a favor," she replied, "and he refused me. I asked the same of God, and He granted it to me."

Three days later, Scholastica died and undoubtedly entered the eternal happiness of the saints in heaven.

This story is given in Dialogues by Gregory the Great.

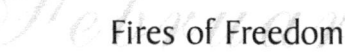

Fires of Freedom

When John of Matha was ordained a priest, a pillar of fire was seen. It appeared from nowhere and descended onto his head. His face was ablaze and his eyes were transfixed; a luminous glow encircled every part of his body. The bishops present asked the young priest if he had seen a vision and he replied, "I saw the angel of the Saviour sitting on a cloud of glory. His face was brighter than the sun, his robes were white as snow and he bore on his breast a cross of two colors, red and azure. At his feet I beheld two slaves laden with chains. One was a Moor and the other a Christian. The hands of the angel were crossed, the right hand towards the Christian, the left towards the Moor. That, father, is what I saw."

Two years later John formed an alliance with Felix of Valois and founded an organization to free the slaves imprisoned by the Moors during the Crusades.

Saint John of Matha lived from 1160-1213. He is celebrated on February 8th. Life of Saint John of Matha.

Seven Tiny Stars

Historic art shows St. Peter Nolasco portrayed with a clock at his feet and a beam of light emanating to heaven from seven stars, which rest on an image of the Virgin Mary. The account which inspired these works is as follows:

Peter Nolasco built the church of St. Mary del Puche in Spain at the direction of a divine architect. On four consecutive Saturdays, seven mysterious lights, resembling seven tiny stars, were seen at night in a particular place in a nearby field. They appeared to be dropping from the sky, and seven times repeatedly they entered the earth at a particular place.

Peter was certain these phenomena were announcements of some kind and accordingly had the spot carefully excavated. The ground was hardly broken when a discovery was made. It was a clock! An enormous clock! And on it was an image of the Virgin Mary.

Nolasco believed it was a gift from angels, and he later constructed an altar at the place of its discovery. When the altar was built, it was itself miraculous and was celebrated for the healings it bestowed.

St. Peter Nolasco lived from 1189-1256. Life of Peter Nolasco by R. P. F. Zumel.

Heavenly Nectar

From the time she could walk, Clare of Rimini was spirited, stubborn and always in motion. She was explosively angry at times and prone to be snobbish, but she had a genuine appetite to know what was true or false and was determined to figure matters out for herself. On one occasion she resolved to fast and drink nothing at all for forty days and forty nights. Brought almost to the brink of the grave by this abstinence, she prayed for guidance and for a higher understanding of the truth. At a moment when her breath seemed to be suspended between life and death, her prayer was answered. A goblet appeared before her. It was a golden goblet, filled with a celestial beverage. Partaking of the heavenly nectar, she was restored to full vitality. On the following evening, and every evening for the remaining twelve years of her life, she received the company of an angel who continually offered her this sweet beverage from heaven. She never again looked anywhere but to her God for understanding, and never again drank any earthly substance, with the single exception of the wine of the Eucharist.

Saint Clare of Rimini lived until 1334. She is celebrated on February 10th. Les Petits Bollandistes, Volume II.

Notre Dame de Lourdes

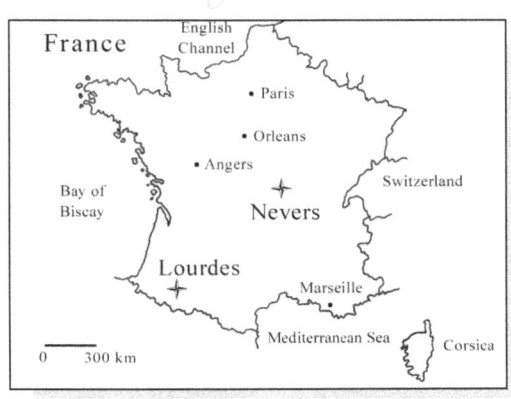

On February 11, 1858, in Shroventide, France, three girls gathering firewood near Massabielle had their lives transformed. Two of the girls crossed the river to continue their search, but the third, Bernadetta Soubirous, a fourteen-year-old, remained behind and sat resting at the bank of the river. As she stripped off one of her shoes, a sudden gust of wind caused her to raise her head. Not a leaf was stirring. The air was perfectly quiet. She dismissed the incident and continued to strip her other foot when another gust of wind arose. This time, something was stirring. A honeysuckle bush waved back and forth, drawing her attention to a recess in the hill.

Bernadetta knew a cave was there, but this time she noticed that the opening to the cavern was mysteriously lit up. Inspecting more closely, she was astonished to find, in the midst of the mysterious glow, a beautiful girl just slightly older than herself. She was a simple girl, but attractive, and arrayed in white. A long white veil fell from her head to her feet and a blue sash floated to her knees. Her feet were uncovered, and on the instep of each was a fully blossomed rose. Bernadetta rubbed her eyes and thought she must be dreaming. But the mysterious girl was still there in the mouth of the cave. "Come near," the girl asked her. In fear Bernadetta moved away, and shortly after wards the vision disappeared.

Later, she narrated the story to her mother who sternly disapproved and forbade her to return to that place. Three days later, a small party of Bernadetta's friends pressed obstinately for permission to return to the grotto. Reluctantly it was granted, but on the condition that they supply themselves with a vial of holy water, should their imaginings prove to overpower their common sense. When the party reached the grotto, there stood the girl as before, but only Bernadetta could see her. Her companions looked to Bernadetta's face and were astonished. It was beautiful and effulgent, like an angel's. Bernadetta sprinkled the water on the young girl's feet and unconsciously lowered herself to her knees. By sunset the entire countryside had heard of the event.

On Thursday, February 18th, in the early morning, Bernadetta returned to the grotto again. On this day the vision instructed her to come to the grotto every morning for fifteen consecutive days. The next day, and the following days, her parents, neighbors and people from the village accompanied her. Everyone saw the supernatural light which covered Bernadetta's face, but only she saw the vision. The crowds increased daily and numbered in the thousands. Every morning they watched as the child was transfigured in heavenly light.

For fifteen days this continued. Then unexpectedly, the police intervened. Dispersing the crowds, they banned further assemblies, but Bernadetta, disregarding their warnings, repeated her visits. During one visit, she dug a small hole in the earth beneath the grotto rock, and water issued forth and increased in volume every day. The waters proved to be healing, and the cures ascribed to them are endless.

In the following years the grotto was barricaded and no one was allowed to enter. Finally, after four years of scientific and ecclesiastic investigations, the Bishop of Tarbes proclaimed that the Virgin Mary had undoubtedly appeared to Bernadetta Soubirous. Accordingly he authorized the title "Notre Dame de Lourdes" (Our Lady of Lourdes).

Bernadetta was canonized in 1933. Her body remains miraculously incorrupt to the present day and may be seen in the chapel dedicated to her at Nevers, France.

Legend of Marina

Having been left a widower, Eugenius of Bithynia retired to a monastery and became a monk. After some time passed, the sweet memory of his little daughter, Marina, weighed so heavily on his mind he found it difficult to concentrate on his duties. He had left her in the good care of relatives, but separation from her was more than he could tolerate, so he told the abbot he had a son and obtained permission to bring "him" to live in the monastery. Marina willingly dressed as a boy, assumed the name Marinus, and was perfectly happy in her new life together with her father.

When she reached seventeen years of age her father died, but having enjoyed considerable spiritual progress, she continued to live as a monk. As such, one of her regular duties was to retrieve supplies from a nearby harbor. It was often necessary to spend the night in an inn and when the innkeeper's daughter was found to be pregnant, the fair and attractive Marinus was accused of being her seducer. The matter was brought to the abbot who questioned the boy, but Marinus would not deny the matter. He was asked to leave the monastery, which he consented to do, but lived at its gates, assuming the life of a beggar.

When the innkeeper's daughter had weaned her infant son, she left him with Marinus and told him to support his own child. This also Marinus suffered silently, caring for the boy and bearing the shame of false accusations. Five years later "his" example of patience and humiliation so impressed the monks and the abbot, that he was re-admitted to the monastery and given the lowest tasks of the house to atone for his sins.

Soon after, Marinus died and when the body was prepared for burial, its gender was discovered. The shame and gross injustices which had been hurled upon Marinus were now replaced with admiration for the heroism of this woman. The girl who had falsely accused Marinus confessed her lie, and the name Marina was raised to the status of a saint.

The story of Marina is found in the Greek calendar of saints. She is celebrated on February 12th.

Alphabet Lesson

The following narrative is from the original manuscripts edited from the Bible by its compilers, the Council of Nice (Fourth century).

CHAPTER 10: There was also at Jerusalem one named Zaccheus, who was a schoolmaster. 2. And he said to Joseph, "Why dost thou not send Jesus to me, that he may learn his letters?" 4. So he brought Jesus to that master; who wrote out an alphabet for him. 5. And he bade him say Aleph; and when he had said Aleph, the master bade him pronounce Beth. 6. Then the Lord Jesus said to him, "Tell me first the meaning of the letter Aleph, and then I will pronounce Beth." 7. And when the master threatened to whip him, the Lord Jesus explained to him the meaning of the letters Aleph and Beth. 8. Also which were the straight figures of the letters, which the oblique, and what letters had double figures; which had points, and which had none; why one letter went before another; and many other things of which the master himself had never heard, nor read in any book. 9. The Lord Jesus further said to the master, "Take notice how I say to thee;" then he began clearly and distinctly to say Aleph, Beth, Gimel, Oaleth, and so on to the end of the alphabet. 10. The master was so surprised that he said, "I believe this boy was born before Noah." 11. And to Joseph, he said, "Thou hast brought a boy to me to be taught, who is more learned than any master." 12. He said also unto St. Mary, "This your son has no need of any learning."

Valentine's Day

Though of quiet demeanor, Valentine was an observer and absorbed everything around him with great clarity and depth. Long before he made any moves he was sure to have thought out everything in advance. He was once brought before Asterius, the Roman judge, to be examined for heresy.

"All that I have spoken is the truth," stated Valentine. "There is no fault in the truth and it will surely cure all infirmity of body and soul."

"Support your words with proof," challenged Asterius. "I have a daughter who has been blind since age two. If your truth can bring light to her eyes, then who could possibly dispute your claims?"

Valentine placed his hands on the young girl's eyes and immediately her sight was restored. Asterius was struck with wonder, as was his wife and daughter. Together they knelt at his feet, whereupon he instructed them, and all the forty-six members of their household, in the teachings of Christ.

Saint Valentine lived during the third century. He is celebrated on February 14th. His patronage to lovers comes from the belief that birds choose their mate this day.

Innkeeper's Miracle

Jordan was a man of fierce individuality. His passions in life were three: peace, quiet and solitude. In pursuit of these he traveled much, and throughout his journeys the name "Jordan of Saxony" became akin to miracles. On one occasion, he stopped in an alpine village named Ursace. Hungry and tired, he and his three companions entered the village inn and appealed for food. The innkeeper declined since he had only three small loaves of bread which he had saved for his own family, but Jordan requested him to bring what he had available. When he did so, Jordan dispatched his companions to invite the poor folk in the neighborhood to join him. Thirty people gathered at the door and following a short prayer, he proceeded to distribute the loaves. First, he gave bread to the thirty poor folk, until all were full. Then to his three companions, until they were full. Next to his host and household and finally to himself. The innkeeper was stupefied and in a shout of great joy exclaimed, "This man is a Saint!"

Saint Jordon lived until A.D. 1231. Acta Sanctorum, Volume II, February 15.

Royal Escort

The son of Emperor Anselm of Rome and the daughter of King Ampluy were betrothed since early childhood. The time for marriage arrived and the princess was adequately prepared for her voyage to Rome and her espousal. During the voyage, a storm arose and the ship was driven onto the rocks, but the passengers and crew survived by clinging to the shipwrecked timbers. When the storm abated, all seemed well, but for the princess the danger had not ceased. Clinging to a floating timber, she was encircled, and then swallowed whole, by a pursuing whale. Struggling to survive, she slashed wildly with a knife and wounded the whale internally.

According to its instincts, it beached itself. In doing so, it was spotted by the Earl Pirris, who happened to be walking near the coast. He gathered a Party of men to harpoon the creature, but as they approached they heard cries of, "Mercy! Have mercy! I am the daughter of the king!" It took no time at all to unravel the mystery, and working with great haste they freed the princess, alive and unharmed. When her vitality returned, she narrated her remarkable tale to the earl. Messengers were immediately dispatched to inform her father and the Emperor Anselm. In the days that followed, the princess was again escorted to Rome, this time by land, and the wedding celebrations proceeded on time.

Recorded in the Gesta Romanorum, CIX MS.

Holy Cow

Saint Fritz was a sparkling swordsman. He was as effervescent as fine champagne and believed a warrior should die in battle. Accordingly, he died as he wished, mortally wounded in the battle of Lupiac. His body was never recovered.

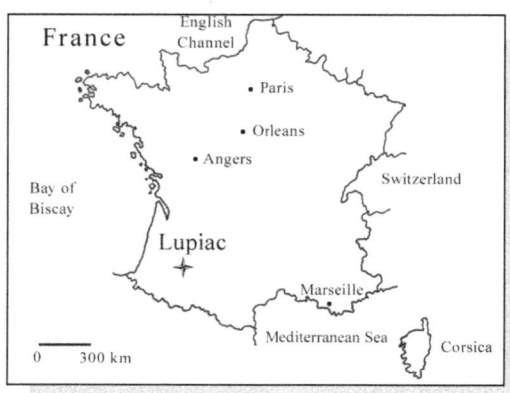

Years later, however, a herdsman living in the region was surprised when he found one of his cows licking a stone in the midst of some brushwood. He noticed that the cow repeated this ritual daily, and further, that she had assumed a sweet disposition and produced considerably more milk than any other in the herd. Curious as to the cause of this peculiarity, he gathered a group of townsmen and sought to examine the stone. They lifted it up and some of the men poked with shovels. Soon they came upon a body. It was a warrior in full armor. In time it was discovered to be the missing body of Saint Fritz from the battle of Lupiac. But no sooner was it raised from the ground, when a spring issued forth from the earth below. This spring, we are told, still flows and is locally employed for its healing properties.

Saint Fritz lived during the eighth century. La Chapelle de Saint Fritz was constructed on a nearby hilltop. This story is told in a brochure which was once sold to tourists on the chapel site.

Flaming Swords

Attila, King of the Huns, commonly referred to as "The Scourge of God," spread terror, violence and desolation wherever his appetite for conquest directed him. In A.D. 452, he sacked Milan and it was expected he would pass through Rome and lay it waste. Moving against Rome, he was intercepted by Pope Leo I, together with his ecclesiastical dignitaries who bravely advanced to plead for the city. To the astonishment of the entire Western Roman Empire, Attila forthwith removed his armies. Being asked the reason why, he replied, "While Pope Leo was speaking, I distinctly saw two shining beings of venerable aspect and manifestly not of this earth standing by his side. They had naming swords in their hands and menaced me with death if I refused to withdraw my army."

The Roman church has since held that the two celestials alluded to by Attila were the apostles Peter and Paul.

Pope Leo I, named "Leo The Great," was born in Rome and reigned from A.D. 440-461. He is celebrated on February 18th. This story is taken from Lives of the Popes, by Damasus.

Fresh Food

Andrew of Segni was a sensitive man who was curious about everything around him. He was a highly emotional individual, very much alive, with a riotous sense of humor. He cared more for the welfare of others than for himself. Being ill on one occasion, his brothers sought to cure him with a gift of freshly cooked meat. Two birds killed in a chase were finely roasted and brought to him. "Poor birds," said Andrew, "how I pity you who have been deprived of your life in order to give me pleasure!" Then making the sign of the cross over his dinner, the two birds were restored to life, full-feathered, and flew outdoors through an open window in his chamber.

Saint Andrew of Segni lived during the thirteenth century. The accounts of his life were recorded by Breviaire Pranciscain.

Bishop of Choice

The mother of Eucherius sat quietly in a church at Orleans, where she intended to spend the day in silence. Suddenly a man of distinct nobility, clothed in white, whispered quietly in her ear, "You are blessed, dear lady, for you are carrying in your womb a son who has been elected from all eternity to be the leader of this city of Orleans."

The mother was deeply moved and believed her visitor to be an angel. Whatever the case, as time revealed, the noble stranger spoke the truth. Eucherius was elected bishop of Orleans in A.D. 721 and proved himself to be an exemplary leader, deeply devoted to the citizens who loved and venerated him.

Eucherius was born in Orleans, France, but is more famous in Holland where he lived after being exiled by Charles Marrel. His relics are preserved in the monastery of Saint Trond, near Maastricht, where he died. He is celebrated on February 20th. Les Petits Bollandistes, Volume II.

Farmer's Rule

During the fifth century, the country surrounding Vienna was devastated by migrating locusts. Farmers and their families were powerless to resist this infestation and in desperation sought spiritual guidance from a holy man named Severin. Severin commanded them to remain in their homes and fast the next day. This they did wholeheartedly, for it seemed like a small price to pay for the safety of their crops. On the morning that followed, they were astonished when they entered their fields. Not only had the locusts completely disappeared, but not a blade of corn or a single tree leaf had been damaged.

The only exception was a single farmer who chose to confront the locusts and attempted to drive them from his fields. He had confessed his disbelief in the holy man, but now his produce was devoured. When Severin heard of the farmer's misfortune, he commanded the others to contribute to his support until his fields had time to recover. They obeyed willingly and Severin offered his counsel to the man, "Learn from the locusts this lesson. It is the Almighty who makes us poor and makes us rich. He will keep the feet of his holy, but the wicked shall be silent in darkness. For by strength alone, shall no man prevail."

Severin lived until A.D. 482. He is celebrated on February 21st. Les Petits Bollandistes, Volume I.

Two Lovers of Clermont

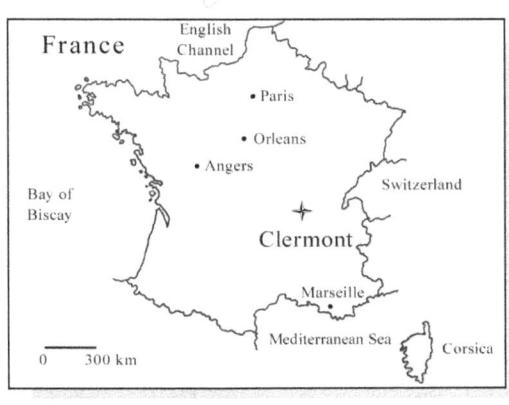

Injurieux, a noble senator of Clermont, France, fell in love, almost instantly, with a lovely girl named Scholastica who, feeling likewise, consented to be his bride. From the day of their espousal they vowed to love each other only with platonic love and mutually vowed to live together in chastity. Saint Gregory of Tours tells us that Scholastica died first, and Injurieux, standing over her tomb, spoke these words: "I thank thee Lord, for the loan of this treasure, which I return to your hands without spot, even as I have received it."

The dead wife replied from the grave, "What need to speak of such matters which concern no one but ourselves?"

Scarcely had the tomb been closed when the husband died. He was buried in a separate tomb, a considerable distance from his wife. The next day, however, it was found that Injurieux had left his own grave to repose in that of Scholastica. The couple remain undisturbed to the present day, and their tomb, popularly known as Two Lovers, has been the source of inspiration for countless writers, musicians and artists.

This tale was recorded by several writers including Saint Gregory of Tours in his History of The Francs, Book I. The subject is best known in its poetic form, The Tomb of the Two Lovers of Clermont.

Herbs and Roots

Saint Aibert was a secretive man with a somewhat dual nature, some times timid and meek, and sometimes dynamic and convincing. For twenty years he ate only a few herbs and roots and drank nothing at all. At the age of fifty-seven, when a great flood encircled his hermitage, leaving him without food for many days, the Virgin Mary appeared to him in a vision and placed a morsel of bread in his mouth. The heavenly bread was of such extraordinary virtue and provided him with such vigor that he never felt the need to eat again.

On another occasion Saint Aibert was consulted when Count Arnoul of Hainault was struck with a fever that his physicians were unable to cure. After confessing his sins to the hermit, the count begged to be cured of his illness. Saint Aibert replied, "There is nothing in the hermitage but water, which you may have." Then filling a cup for the count, he blessed it and bade him drink. Not only did the water cure the count's illness, but he affirmed that it had been converted to a wine, more delicious than any other he had known.

Aibert lived from 1060 to 1140. His life is recorded in Life of St. Aibert by Robert, Archdeacon of Ostrevand.

Bread Shovel

It was a day like any other day. The nursemaid of Honore was baking bread in her kitchen, as usual, when she heard the news that young Honore had been appointed bishop. In her amazement she exclaimed, "I don't believe it! Not Honore. It isn't possible!"

Poking her bread shovel into the ground, she continued, "When this shovel takes root and bears fruit, then I will believe that my boy is made bishop."

No sooner had she spoken, when the bread shovel rooted in its place, sprouted branches and leaves and was filled with magnificent mulberry fruit.

Honore lived during the sixth and seventh centuries. In reference to this miracle, he is represented in historic art with a bread shovel. Les Petite Bollandistes.

Physician's Dream

Sennadius was a physician and an intellectual who openly argued that "man was flesh and therefore after death, a future life could not exist." One night, in a dream, an angel appeared to him and asked him to follow. The angel took him to the outskirts of the city where he was ravished with celestial music. The angel told him that the music proceeded from the voices of spirits made perfect. When he awoke, Sennadius thought no more about the dream. A few days later the angel joined him in a dream again. The angel asked if Sennadius' earlier experience of the heavenly music had occurred to him while awake or asleep.

"During sleep," replied Sennadius.

"Just so," said the angel. "What you saw was not by your bodily senses, because your eyes and ears were closed in sleep."

"True," said the physician.

"Then with what eyes did you see, and with what ears did you hear?" asked the angel. "It must be evident that if you see and hear while sleeping, you must have other eyes and ears besides those of your material body. When, therefore, your body sleeps something other may be awake; and when your body dies, that something other may live on. Think of these things Sennadius." And the angel vanished.

This story is given by Saint Augustine in his Epistles.

Heavenly Dew

Victor of Plancy was a gentle hermit who built his home near Saturniac, in the district of Troyes, France. His reputation as a miracle worker induced King Childric to visit him. Victor received the king graciously and invited him and his party to stay for refreshments. The king accepted politely, but wondered what the hermit would serve. It seemed to them there was little more in the hermit's cell than a small quantity of water. Then Victor prayed, "Lord, bless this water and fill the vessel which holds it with heavenly dew." Making the sign of the cross over the vessel, it was immediately filled to the brim with an exquisite wine. Astonished at this display, the king applauded profusely. Then he, Victor, and all the king's companions drank heartily but reverently. They unanimously agreed that the quality was exceptional.

Victor lived during the sixth century. He is celebrated on February 26th. This account is found in Saint Bernard's Sermon on the Birthday of Saint Victor.

Native Revival

Abishabis (Small Eyes) was among the principle prophets of the Cree Indians who occupied the Hudson Bay region, from Churchill, Manitoba to Fort Albany, Ontario. His teachings were influenced by the Methodist missionary James Evans who translated pans of the bible into the Cree syllabic system. Abishabis and his brother disciple Wasiteck (Light), through mystical contact with the name Jesus, entered into the regions of heaven and realized themselves to be *children* or *sons* of God.

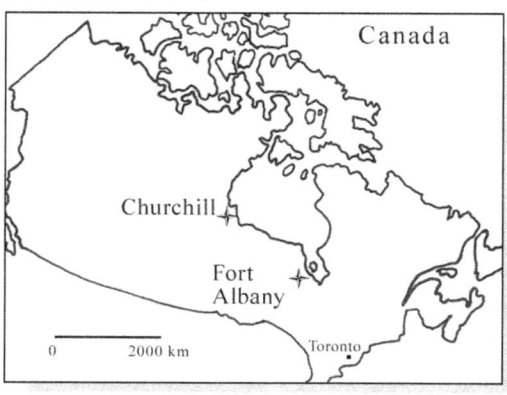

Abishabis changed his name to Jesus and the two men formed a revival of the Cree nation, teaching the people *The Track to Heaven* using a geometric chart they created to convey their prophetic message. They warned against the ways of the whites and inspired the Cree communities in "psalm singing and painting books" and "making the woods to ring. . . with music." The new religious revival was rooted in both native and non-native cultures, containing fragments of Christian observances, but its primary messages placed an emphasis upon returning to ancient native ways.

Aided by the efforts of an elderly woman referred to as a "priestess" the new movement carried its message eastward, from York Factory to Fort Albany. But the new revival and its prophets were short-lived because white opposition quickly mounted against it and an apparent conspiracy reduced its popularity. Abishabis was declared to be a madman and accused of robbing, killing and cannibalism. Cree punishment for cannibalism was death, and following the age-old pattern of persecution for the enlightened, Abishabis was burned at the stake. With him went the revival of the ancient Cree tradition.

Abishabis lived during the first half of the 1800s. His revival was documented by George Barnley, Methodist missionary to the James Bay area. Documents are also found in the Hudson's Bay Company Post records.

Antoinette of Florence

Antoinette of Florence could fly, or at least she could float. She tried to conceal her miraculous gifts but was unsuccessful. Frequently she was discovered, involuntarily rapt in an ecstasy, buoyed up from the ground and suspended in divine meditation.

On one particular occasion, a fiery globe appeared above her head, filling an entire cathedral with light. Free of personal motives, she would remain above the ground for as long as the heavens would have her.

Antoinette (Antonia) was blessed with many supernatural gifts such as clairvoyance and prophecy. She was greatly loved by the citizens of Florence and when she died, innumerable miracles occurred to those she had known. The phenomena attracted such large crowds to Santa Maria Novella, in Florence, it was impossible to proceed with the funeral for over a month. Antoinette lived until 1412. She is celebrated on February 28th. Her biography was recorded by her bereaved husband, following her death.

March

1 Little Things
2 Virgin of the Poor
3 Holy Captive
4 Angel's Bread
5 Ragged Old Habit
6 Canadian Sanctity
7 Laborer Bishop
8 The Will of Destiny
9 Catherine's Diary
10 Deacon's Command
11 Playful Child
12 Heavenly Dialogues
13 Visions of Handsome Lake
14 Legend of the Valley
15 Lone Soldier
16 Legend of Torello
17 Saint Patrick's Day
18 Lost and Found
19 Flowering Staff
20 Troop of Light
21 Burgeoning Bundles
22 Notre-Dame des Miracles
23 Healing Hands
24 Burning Bush
25 Saints Alive
26 Miraculous Rescue
27 Holy Oil
28 Iron Bridge
29 Morning Watch
30 Abundance of Prayer
31 Takes All Kinds

Little Things

David, known as Dewi, Patron of Wales, was a man of high morality and patient, enduring affections. Before his birth, while yet in the womb, miracles foretold of his enlightenment. An angel is said to have been his constant companion from birth, attending to his needs and playing a masterly role in his education of the divine mysteries. To the citizens of Wales, he is fondly remembered for transforming the freezing waters of the bathing pools and rendering them perpetually warm, soft and healing. Like Christ, he healed the sick and raised the dead. When he lectured, a snow white dove would perch upon his shoulder. Often enormous crowds would gather to hear him speak, and when the assemblies grew too large, the earth beneath his feet would rise to form a hill from which his voice was heard to best advantage.

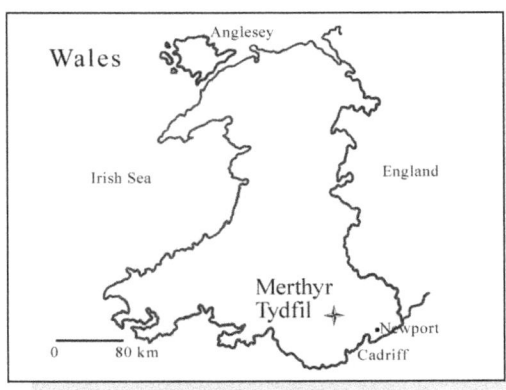

He lived beyond a hundred years and at the moment of his death, in A.D. 589, he spoke these final words, "Be joyful, brothers and sisters. Keep faith, and do the little things that you have seen and heard from me."

David, "the Waterman," founded fifty churches and twelve monasteries throughout Wales. His memory is kept alive in the principle abbey of Mynyw (Menivia). He is celebrated on March 1st.

Virgin of the Poor

March 2nd, in Banneux, France, will long be remembered. On that day in 1933, the Virgin Mary blessed the poor folk of France with miracles. It was the conclusion of many visions in which the Virgin appeared to children, in this case twelve-year-old

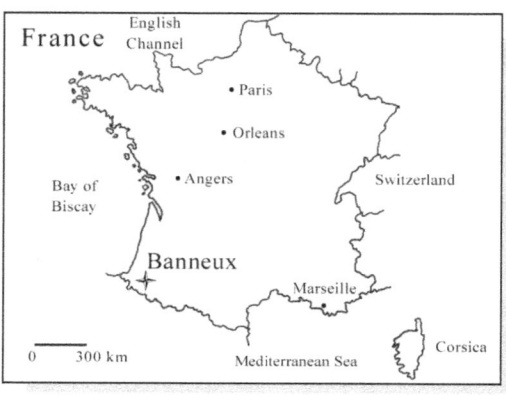

Marriette Beco, the only daughter of the neediest family of Banneux. Marriette enjoyed this miracle in a clearing between some pine trees, just beyond her family's home. The Virgin Mother was adorned in a long, white, pleated gown, which shone with soft-blue light. Her eyes were blue and her head was adorned with a crown of blue rays. Her smile was utterly disarming and no single detail lacked in majesty.

"I am The Virgin of the Poor," she said to Marriette, who swooned and fainted from the weight of this proclamation.

For months the Virgin appeared to the young child and on one occasion Marriette was led to a spring not far from her home.

"This spring is reserved for all nations," said the Virgin. "Use it to relieve the burdens of the sick. Here also, shall a small chapel be built. Proclaim to all, that I have come to relieve the suffering of the poor."

The Virgin Mother blessed the spring and to the present day it heals and comforts those with pain. It brings faith to those who lack it, hope to those who are poor, and restores peace to the troubled hearts of many.

In 1942, a chapel was constructed near the spring. The waters are used for remedial purposes.

Holy Captive

Pelerin was a holy man who believed in himself and in his natural Godgiven rights. The local authorities, however, held him in contempt and persecuted him, and thus, he was forced to endure a life of hiding in mountain caves. In time his hideaway was discovered by soldiers, and the man of God was taken captive. They marched him to prison chambers, seizing every opportunity to ridicule and dishonor him. One soldier felt that Pelerin moved too slowly and lifted his whip to lash him. But at the moment he did so, the whip flew from his hands and, before reaching the ground, was transformed into a writhing serpent, which quickly disappeared into the fissures of a rock. No further chastisement was attempted.

Pelerin lived until A.D. 303. The accounts of his life were recorded by Manager Crosnier, Vicar-General of Nevers.

Angel's Bread

A miracle had never happened to Avoya, but on the occasion of her capture by conquering Huns, that changed. She was confined to prison and sentenced to death because she would not marry her captor. On the evening of her arrest, her cell was filled with a celestial light. Unknown to the guards, an angel appeared which was perceptible to Avoya alone. The angel told her that he had been sent by Jesus to comfort her and bring news that her life would be spared. He also told her that the Queen of Heaven would be her fostermother for as long as she remained in prison. Accordingly, every week three loaves of bread "kneaded by the hands of the angels" appeared in her cell.

"The whiteness of this bread," we are told, "infinitely exceeded that used in the palace of her father Quintian, King of Sicily, and its sweetness exceeded in delicacy and flavor any food made by mortals."

Historic art shows Avoya receiving angel's bread from the hands of the Virgin in her prison cell. Martyrologe des Saintes Femmes.

Ragged old Habit

Saint John-Joseph of the Cross is favored among saints in that the richness of his spiritual ecstasies numbered him among the great wonderworkers of the Christian tradition. On many occasions he was lifted into the air where he remained suspended, sometimes for the entire night. During these and other ecstasies, he was subsumed in a heavenly bliss which rendered him insensible to all the world. He neither saw, nor heard, nor felt anything. He remained as motionless as a marble statue, his face aglow like burning coals.

His visions embraced an entire family of heavenly hosts: Mary, Jesus, the Apostles, the prophets of old and the saints. He healed the sick and multiplied food for the hungry. He caused objects to float in the air and read the thoughts of others as easily as if they were written words. On occasion, he perceived himself to be in two or more places at the same time.

When he traveled, crowds followed, often tearing or biting pieces from his ragged habit or grasping for a lock of his hair. Such was the life of this remarkable man who was utterly ignorant of evil. He lived only to teach others and care for their needs. He foresaw the day of his death and spoke freely of it to others. Yet on that day he continued his work as always, teaching others to live every precious day, as if it were their last.

Saint John-Joseph of the Cross lived from 1654-1734 and is celebrated on March 5th. His tomb remains a popular place of pilgrimage at Santa Lucia del Monte in Naples. The accounts of his life are recorded in Evangelic Demonstrations, Volume XVI, by Cardinal Wiseman.

Canadian Sanctity

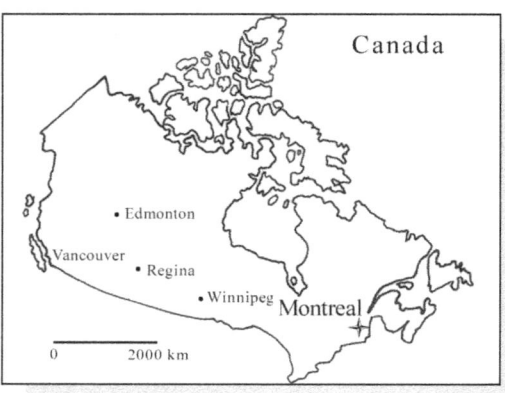

Georgette Faniel's life has remained hidden from the world until now. After seventy-two years of private revelation and intimacy with her God, she has been shown a new path which requires a public life. She was born in 1915 in Montreal, Canada where she continues to live today. At age six, she first heard the voice of the Eternal Father, which sounded in the depths of her heart (inner locutions) and in her ears (aural locutions). At first these dialogues were not clearly understood, but in time, the voices of God the Father, Jesus, the Holy Spirit and the Virgin Mary were clearly delineated. At first Georgette believed all children had similar experiences, however, when she discovered she alone received these dialogues she kept her spiritual life a secret.

Today, nearing the age of eighty, she is actively engaged in constant prayer for the peace of the world, sleeping only an hour or two every night. She ranks, unquestionably, as one of the great inspirations of our era and her life and revelations bring honor to both Canada and the world.

A deeper investigation into her life and teachings may be found in the book Mary Queen of Peace Stay With Us by Fr. Guy Girard, a member of the Society of Holy Apostles in Quebec.

Laborer Bishop

Once again the hand of God entered into the affairs of man, this time in Langres, France. A mysterious message to appoint Desiderius to the high office of bishop was conveyed through divine revelation to a delegation of religious officers. Who was this Desiderius, they wondered? No such person was known to any of them. Inquiries were made locally, but no one had ever heard of Desiderius. A deputation was dispatched to Rome for information, but no one in Rome had ever heard of Desiderius either. Who was this mysterious Desiderius? What manner of man must he be that the Almighty himself saw fit to honor and appoint him?

The deputation departed from Rome disappointed, however, along the road, nearing Geneva, they were passed by a laborer in an ox cart. As coincidence would have it, his name was Desiderius. It seemed unlikely that this laborer was the man they were seeking, but they asked to speak with him and he promptly dismounted. In doing so he struck his staff into the ground near his wagon and to the astonishment of everyone present it burst forth with leaves and blossomed with flowers. It was enough for the deputation. The sign was indisputable. Desiderius returned with them to Langres and was elected bishop.

Recorded in Saints de la Haute Marne (third century).

The Will of Destiny

Sir John Berry of Stratford was a knight of superb reputation. As fate would have it, he once passed near a servant's cottage and heard the cries of a woman in labor. Instantly he was struck with a vision that the newborn infant was destined to be his future wife. But for some reason, he was determined to elude this destiny.

In time, the child grew to a lovely young girl and he tried in many ways to avoid her, however, circumstances prevailed against his efforts. At last, when she was of marriageable age, he took her to a rocky seaside. Throwing his signet ring into the sea, he commanded her to never look upon his face again, unless the oceans themselves could return his family seal. Brokenhearted, the young girl accepted her fate and sought refuge as a cook in the house of a noble family. Two days later, while preparing a cod for dinner, she was struck with awe to find the exact signet ring of the Berry family lodged in the belly of the fish. Her joy was immeasurable, but it was still greater when Sir John, transformed by the event, implored her to be his wife.

As a record of this event, the Berry coat of arms shows a fish with a ring in the upper right-hand corner. This story was recorded at their marriage ceremony (seventeenth century).

Catherine's Diary

Catherine of Bologna aimed at a perfection so exalted she attained the undying admiration of all who knew her. More introvert than extrovert, the miracles that accompanied her were inner visions and ecstasies, which she recorded in her diary in the hope that they might help others at a later time. In her ecstasies she was wholly overcome with the realization of the unity of all things. She wrote, referring to herself in the third person as she always did, "Her sins, past, present and future, and the sins of her friends, neighbors and all peoples, were present within herself."

Her visions deepened her understanding of the connectedness of all things in life, but often during these moments she was oppressed by an overpowering inclination to sleep. It was useless to resist, for the force of sleep would overtake her. Ultimately, she was aroused one day when a vision of Thomas of Canterbury appeared to her clad in radiant, white robes.

"Catherine," he said, "do not wear yourself out, even with good deeds and generosity. You must now take rest and renew your strength so that you may return to your duties with greater vigor."

He gave her his hand to kiss, then vanished.

On that day she wrote in her diary, "And God entered into her soul like a radiant sunshine to establish there the profoundest peace."

Saint Catherine lived from 1413-1463. Her body was originally buried, but was later disinterred owing to the many miracles reported at the site. Her body was found to be incorrupt and may still be seen in the chapel of the convent church of Bologna. Catherine left many personal works of art which may be viewed at the Academy of Fine Arts in Venice. She was canonized in 1712. The accounts of her life are taken primarily from her own writings, which she kept secret until the time of her death.

Deacon's Command

Attalus was abbot at the monastery of Bobbio, in northern Italy. On one occasion the monastery mill was in danger of being swept away by flooding waters from the Bobbio river. Attalus gave his abbatial cross to Sinvaldus, his deacon, and instructed him to go to the river bank, make the sign of the cross and command the river to flow in another course. The deacon did as he was told and the river obeyed. Not only did the threatening waters leave the vicinity of the mill, but an entirely new river channel was formed. Struck with wonder at this miracle, he reported every detail to the abbot. Accordingly, Attalus commanded him to make no mention of it until he, Attalus, had passed into heaven.

Saint Attalus lived until A.D. 627. He is celebrated on March 10th. Life of Saint Attalus.

Playful Child

CHAPTER 15: And when the Lord Jesus was seven years of age he was, on a certain day, with other boys his companions about the same age. 2. Who when they were at play made clay into several shapes, namely, asses, oxen, birds, and other figures. 3. Each boasting of his work, and endeavoring to exceed the rest. 4. Then the Lord Jesus said to the boys, "I will command these figures which I have made to walk." 5. And immediately they moved, and when he commanded them to return, they returned. 6. He had also made the figures of birds and sparrows, which, when he commanded to fly, did fly, and when he commanded to stand still, did stand still, and if he gave them meat and drink, they did eat and drink.

This account is taken from the manuscripts which were edited from the Bible by its compilers, the Council of Nice, under the direction of Emperor Constantine (fourth century). It appears under the title "The First Gospel of the Infancy of Jesus Christ."

Heavenly Dialogues

Gregory the Great was the first monk ever elected pope. He was an outgoing man who was energetic, strong and able to persevere on sheer willpower. For years he worked as the chief civil magistrate of Rome, but drawn to an inner life at the age of thirty-five, he retired to a monastery. As fate would have it, fifteen years later he was elected pope. During his reign, he proved to be both a remarkable statesman at a time of great difficulty and disorder and a worker of many miracles. One of his most influential contributions to the people of his life and times remains with us in his book *Dialogues*. Peter, his deacon, salvaged Gregory's manuscripts and declared they were "written by Gregory while a heavenly white dove whispered in the ear of the saint."

In historic art Saint Gregory the Great is represented with a white dove whispering in his ear. He died on March 12, A.D. 604.

Vision of Handsome Lake

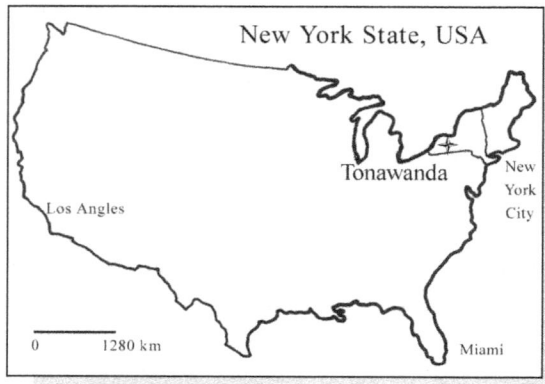

Handsome Lake, an Iroquois Indian born in the village of Seneca on the Genesee River, received his first vision during the summer of 1799. During the Strawberry Festival three messengers from heaven appeared before him and charged him with a mission: to speak out against alcohol, witchcraft, magic and abortion. The guilty should admit their sin, repent and amend their life style.

Two months later a vision of a *sky journey* occurred. Guided by heavenly spirits, Handsome Lake was lifted into the regions of heaven, then taken to the pits of hell. He was given knowledge concerning the moral plan of the cosmos and told that more visions would follow in the coming days.

His next vision came six months later and contained many details regarding the Great Spirit's concern for the Iroquois nation. Handsome Lake was made responsible for teaching his people that destruction would overtake the world if they did not turn from evil ways. Practices of meditation, confession and strict temperance were advised. Also a return to the ancient calendar of ceremonies and correct performance of ritual was emphasized, parts of which were restructured by Handsome Lake.

In other visions the messages were of peace, moral dignity and keeping land instead of selling it.

The practical wisdom and powerful words of Handsome Lake

soon gained him an enormous following. Thus, before his death in 1815 he formed a new religion, the *Code of Handsome Lake*, which he believed was a revival of the traditional religious observances. Others saw it as a combination of Iroquois and Christian belief.

The *Code of Handsome Lake* is practiced to the present day.

The headquarters of the religion of Handsome Lake are located on the New York Seneca Reservation at Tonawanda. His wampum strings are preserved here.

Legend of the Valley

Ulphia lived in a small hermitage in the midst of a marsh called the Paraclet, in France. One hot summer night, the frogs in the marsh kept up such an incessant croaking that the young woman was unable to sleep. When the morning sun arose, Ulphia did not. Domicus, her master, called for her at the usual time, with his familiar rap on the door with his staff, but there was no reply. Supposing she had already found her way to the morning service, he hastened on, fearing he was late. When he reached the chapel he discovered she was not there. Ulphia, meanwhile, was fast asleep. When she finally awoke and discovered what had happened, she wept, praying that God would impose silence upon the frogs. "All the biographies of the saint agree that ever after the frogs were mute, and even to the present day, no frog in the whole valley of the Paraclet is ever heard to croak." So ends the legend of Saint Ulphia.

Ulphia lived during the eighth century. The accounts of her life are recorded in the Hagiographie du Diocese d'Amiens.

Lone Soldier

Longinus was among the soldiers present at the crucifixion of Christ. He, under the order of Pilate, was stationed together with other centurions at the foot of the cross. It was he who pierced Christ's side with a lance and he whose face was splashed with blood from the wound. This drop of Christ's blood instantly healed him of incipient blindness and this miracle, together with the portents that followed (the darkening of the sun and earthquakes), transformed him so that he went to obtain initiation from the Apostles.

He later retired to Caesarea of Cappadocia and led a monastic life. For his service to Christ, he was arrested and condemned to death. Following many miracles associated with his sentence, he willingly surrendered himself to death, praying that his persecutors might be saved.

This account is recorded in the Acta Sanctorum, Volume 11. Longinus is celebrated on March 15th.

Legend of Torello

It happened that while a woman was washing linen in the River Arno, her child was seized by a wolf that dashed from a nearby forest. Torello, a local saint who was present at the time, immediately offered up a prayer and commanded the wolf to drop its prey. In obedience to the saint, the wolf obeyed and Torello, taking up the child, healed the wounds inflicted by the teeth of the beast. So done, he returned the infant safely to its mother. Reproving the wolves, he forbade them ever again to injure any inhabitant of Poppi. Those who reside there assert that this tale is no fantasy and further contend his command has been rigidly obeyed.

Torello of Poppi lived during the thirteenth century. He is celebrated on March 16th. In historic art he is represented with a wolf by his side.

Saint Patrick's Day

Saint Patrick, in his writings says, "I was profoundly ignorant and from boyhood hated study. A free and open life in the fields was my delight. But being made a captive and sent to tend the sheep, a desire for meditation came over me and I passed whole days and sometimes whole nights in communion with God. Six years was I in captivity, yet I was happy. One night an angel appeared to me and said, 'Thy meditations and fastings have come up for memorials before the angels. You shall return soon to your own land, for the days of your captivity are drawing to a close.' I now fled and arrived at the coast where I found a ship on which I embarked and arrived, in time, at my native land."

Saint Patrick lived from A.D. 385-461. He is celebrated on March 17th. His relics are preserved in Glastonbury and are the subject of popular pilgrimage. This narrative is taken from the Acta Sanctorum, Boffandists.

Lost and Found

Serenicus was a man of exquisite tenderness. He was a hermit at heart, but his dedication to others kept him constantly in the midst of crowds. Consequently, his sanctity and fame as a wonderworker kept him continually searching for greater seclusion. Eventually, his travels led him to the Sarthe River, and there his most notable miracles occurred. He arrived at the river without a boat, unable to cross. Kneeling at the riverside, he made the sign of the cross with his finger and immediately the waters divided leaving a dry passage. His young disciple, Flavart, was stupefied by this act, and as they crossed over the passage the bewildered boy, concerned that the water walls might collapse, unconsciously dropped his master's book on the river floor. When he later discovered his error, he threw himself at the holy man's feet imploring his forgiveness. Serenicus raised him from the ground and said, "Be assured Flavart, we shall find the book again, sooner or later."

Six years later the book was recovered. It was discovered by accident and lifted from the Sarthe river entirely uninjured. Two hundred years later, this same manuscript was examined by his biographer who authenticated the work and claimed no sign of water damage or aging of any kind had occurred.

Serenicus was born in A.D. 669 and lived for a hundred and eleven years. Acta Sanctorum, Bollandists, Volume II.

Flowering Staff

When the Virgin Mary was of marriageable age, the young men of Judah, who were of the lineage of King David, each took his staff and submitted it to the high priests of the temple. Should his staff be chosen by the priests, each acknowledged to take the vestal virgin Mary, prophesied to be the mother of the promised Messiah, as his wife. The staff of Joseph (a descendant of David through the House of Nathan, trained as builders of synagogues) miraculously budded and bore leaves. He was espoused to Mary with the prescribed formalities of the Jewish ritual. Shortly afterwards, he chose to divorce her quietly when he found she was with child. But an angel appeared to him and revealed that the child of Mary was conceived without the intervention of a man. He would be the "Holy One of God."

Joseph became the foster father of Jesus, raised him as his son and taught him his worldly trade.

Joseph is honored as Patron of the Universal Church. He is celebrated on March 19th.

Troop of Light

John Nepomucen was a man of sturdy morality. He refused to reveal the confessions of the queen and for this, by order of King Wenceslaus, was condemned to be drowned in the Moldau River. As fate would have it, this was done, but the moment John's body touched the water thousands of tiny stars encircled it and a fire played on the river's surface. A stream of light issued from the depths of the river, "reflecting the glory of the martyr's soul." His body drifted slowly downstream throwing off rays of light in all directions. A "troop of light" followed the body, as if to represent a funeral procession. The city was alive with excitement and everyone gathered to see the spectacle. Wenceslaus, however, terrified almost to death by the realization of his error, fled to the forest forbidding anyone to follow him.

John Nepomucen lived during the fourteenth century. This story is given in the Acta Sanctorum, Bollandists.

Burgeoning Bundles

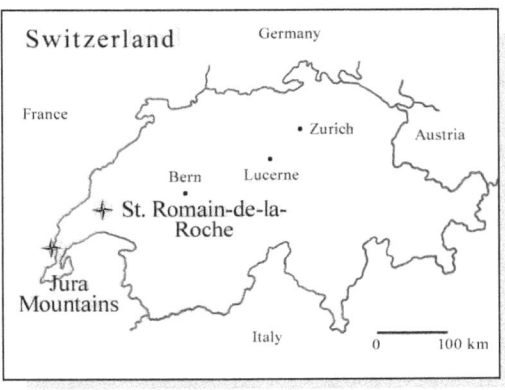

Lupicin multiplied food. A man of few words, he was particularly proud of the abbey over which he presided. At times, however, the soil of Lauconnem would not yield sufficient grain to supply its inhabitants with food. One year the abbey was unusually crowded due to a large number of clergy who sought asylum there. The result was a great scarcity of food. The steward informed the abbot that the resources would be utterly exhausted in fifteen days.

"Place the remaining sheaves in one bundle and they will not diminish," Lupicin remarked. The sheaves were bundled together and just as Lupicin had slated, after three months the sheaves were not depleted in the slightest.

Many have testified to this wonder and the matter is documented in the Acta Sanctorm, Bollandists, March 21. Lupicin, together with his brother Romanus, established many monasteries, including Saint Romain-de-la-Roche, in the Jura mountains, between Switzerland and France.

Norte Dame des Miracles

The year was A.D. 507. Why was there a mysterious light shining in the trees of Montselis' forest? This was the question that Theodechilde, the daughter of King Clovis, asked herself as she watched it from a distance, late into the night. Again the following night the mysterious light appeared. Curious about its cause, she formed a party and entered the forest to inspect it.

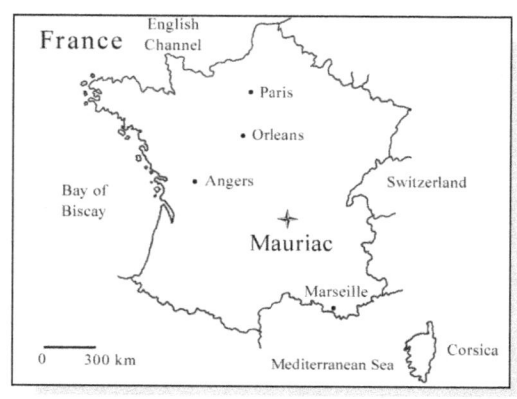

They came upon a huge orb of heavenly light. At its center was a wooden statue, "as black as coal." It was an image of the Madonna and Child. Nothing more was ever discovered about the origin of this statue, but Theodechilde, convinced it was a gift from angels, arranged for a chapel to be built at the site where the image was installed. In the years that followed, the miracles recorded there were so numerous the chapel was decreed Notre-Dame des Miracles (Our Lady of Miracles).

A pilgrim's town named Mauriac sprang up in the vicinity. Vies des Saints, Volume V, by Manager Guerin.

Healing Hands

Born in Barcelona, Joseph Oriol was renowned throughout Europe for his miracles. Eager for his healing touch, sufferers came from all parts of the world to be cured of their infirmities. Immense crowds would collect daily, waiting for his blessings and his touch. Miracle after miracle was reported. In time, the crowds that gathered to meet this holy man became so large that his confessor forbade him to perform such miracles in the church because of the disruption they caused.

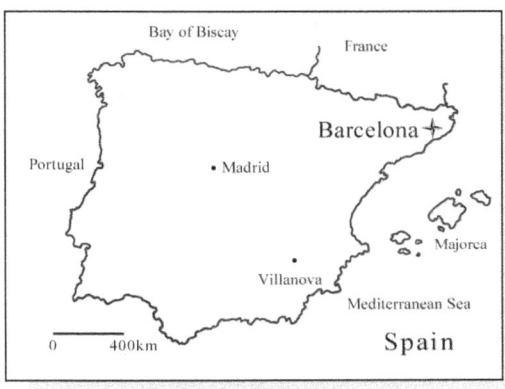

Joseph was also apt to float. While traveling from Marseille to Barcelona, the captain and crew of the ship observed him transfixed in an ecstasy and lifted several feet above the deck, "supported in the air upon nothing."

Like many wonderworkers before him, he possessed very little. He lived in tiny room containing only a crucifix, a table, a bench and a few books. It was all he needed.

Joseph Oriol died in 1702. He was canonized in 1909 and is celebrated on March 23rd. Miracles are still reported at his tomb in Barcelona. Les Petits Bollandistes.

Burning Bush

On March 24, 1400, a shepherd from a farm in Sainte Marie and another from Courtisol, observed a mysterious brilliant light radiating from what appeared to be a burning thorn bush. Though frightened, the two shepherds found the courage to move closer to look. As they approached, they were overwhelmed with rapture and ultimately fainted. Considerable time elapsed before they regained their senses, but when they did, they discovered the cause of the light was a tiny statue of the Virgin Mary with the infant Jesus in her arms. By sunset the news had spread to everyone. Every member of the community, young and old, attended the site of the miracle. The site was on a hill and the light was seen for thirty miles.

When the flames diminished and the light disappeared, the crowd of onlookers pushed closer. The bush, unharmed by the flames, was still covered with green leaves. The statue within (nineteen inches tall, made from grey earth and adorned with paint) was carried in procession by the neighboring clergy and the Bishop of Chalons. It was placed in the Chapel of Saint John the Baptist, where it remained until a new chapel was erected at the site of the miraculous bush.

The image remained in the church until it was removed to prevent destruction at the time of the French Revolution. This account is given in Vies des Saints by Manager Guerin, Chamberlain to Pope Leo XIII.

Saints Alive

Throughout her life Maria Esperanza Medrano de Bianchini has enjoyed charismatic graces. At sixty-five years of age, this farm-working mother of seven has been examined by scientists and clergy alike. Her gifts of clairvoyance, predicting the future, stigmata, transfiguration, healing and the mysterious emission of naturally flower-fragrant body odors are strikingly characteristic of bonafide saintliness.

She doesn't concern herself with what others think of her and concentrates on a mission that she claims to have received from the Blessed Madonna. Over one hundred people have sworn to have seen the Madonna at a grotto near a spring in Finca, Betania, Argentina, where Maria first spoke to her on March 25, 1976. The water from the waterfall that flows there is credited with a large number of medically documented miracles, including the disappearance of advanced kidney cancer and the sudden cure of duodenal ulcers.

On March 25, 1984 nearly a thousand people witnessed another public apparition. In 1987, after many years of investigation, Bishop Ricardo issued a pastoral letter declaring that the "apparitions are authentic and are supernatural in character."

As for Maria, her mission is one of service, sacrifice, kindness and fidelity.

Miraculous Rescue

King Gontran was well aware of the world around him and had a passionate tendency toward mysticism. Intrigued by the many miraculous stories of Saint Verulus, he decided to see for himself what manner of man he was. Together with his entourage, he journeyed to Marcenay and attended the mass of the saint. While celebrating the communion, Verulus suddenly became transfixed and remained entirely without motion for the length of an hour. At the end of this time, he unexpectedly continued the service precisely where he had broken off. When the ceremony had concluded, King Gontran approached the saint and inquired why the sacrament had been inexplicably interrupted.

Verulus responded, "A house at Mussy had caught fire and I was needed to rescue a child in grave danger."

Shocked at this reply, the king instantly dispatched a rider to inquire into the truth of this explanation. When the messenger returned, he reported that the town of Mussy was alive with excitement because Saint Verulus had risked his life to rescue an infant who was sure to be devoured by flames.

Saint Verulus lived during the sixth century. In historic art he is represented rescuing a child from a house on fire. The accounts of his life are recorded in Vie des Saints du Diocese de Dijon.

Holy Oil

"He can cure my blindness!"

These were the words uttered repeatedly by the wife of an Egyptian senator. She had lost her sight with age and was almost totally blind. Time and time again she petitioned her husband to usher her to the home of Saint John the Egyptian hermit. As the senator knew well, John was obligated by his vows never to admit a woman into his sight. Accordingly he approached the hermit and told him of his dilemma. The saint gave the senator a small quantity of holy oil and instructed him to anoint his wife's eyes with it. This being done, the cure was instantaneous.

Saint John the Egyptian hermit lived from A.D. 304-394. He is celebrated on March 21th. In 1901 the cell he had occupied was discovered near Asyut. The accounts of his life are recorded in Lives of The Fathers, Book II, by Ruffinus.

Iron Bridge

Gontran, King of Burgundy, was a man of extreme charitability and, as it happened, extremely good luck. While on a hunting expedition one day, he grew tired and stopping to rest, fell deeply asleep. Just then, a remarkable event occurred. An officer, who had accompanied him, was astonished to see a spirit-like weasel squeeze from the kings mouth and dart toward a nearby rivulet. As the weasel could not cross the stream the officer instinctively lay his sword across it. The creature swiftly spanned the bridge and disappeared into a mountain cleft on the opposite side. In a moment, the weasel reappeared, crossed the bridge again and reentered the king's mouth.

When Gontran awoke, he revealed to his officer that he had had a strange dream. He dreamt he had crossed over an iron bridge and come to a mountain where such a mass of money was hidden; he was dazed at its sight. The officer likewise recounted his tale and the unlikely coincidence induced the king to investigate the nearby fissure. In so doing, he discovered a treasure that exceeded his wildest imagination. With a portion of his newly-acquired wealth he founded the celebrated Abbey of Beaume-Les-Dames. With the remainder he indulged in his charitable ways without in any way taxing his subjects.

King Gontran lived from A.D. 525-593. He is celebrated on March 28th. The accounts of his life are recorded in the Hagiographic Annals of France.

Morning Watch

Then Moses stretched out his hand over the sea, and the Lord drove the sea back by a strong east wind all night and made the sea basin dry land, and the waters were divided. And the people of Israel went into the midst of the sea on dry ground, the waters being a wall to them on their right hand and on their left.

The Egyptians pursued, and went in after them into the midst of the sea: all Pharaoh's horses, his chariots, and his horsemen. And in the morning watch, the Lord in the pillar of fire and of cloud, looked down upon the host of the Egyptians and discomfited the host of the Egyptians, clogging their chariot wheels so that they drove heavily, and the Egyptians said, "Let us free from before Israel; for the Lord fights for them against the Egyptians."

Then the Lord said to Moses, "Stretch out your hand over the sea, that the water may come back upon their chariots, and upon their horsemen."

So Moses stretched forth his hand over the sea, and the sea returned to its wonted flow when the morning appeared. . . .

The Old Testament of the Bible: Exodus XIV, Verse 22.

Abundance of Prayer

Soon after Saint John Climacus was unanimously chosen as Abbot of Mount Sinai, hundreds of people from Palestine and Arabia gathered at the abbey entrance to petition his assistance. It was a time of great drought and they begged him to intercede with God on their behalf. John, kneeling in prayer, recommended their distress to the Father of all 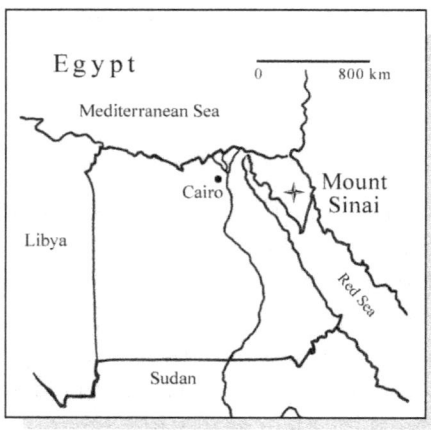 mercies and was immediately answered by an abundance of rain. Such was his reputation that Saint Gregory the Great, who then sat in Saint Peter's chair, wrote to John, asking for his prayers. In return the Pope sent beds and money for the numerous pilgrims who journeyed to Sinai seeking John's help.

John's prayer to obtain the gift of charity is as follows:

"My God, I pretend to nothing upon this earth, except to be so firmly united to you by prayer that to be separated from you may be impossible; let others desire riches and glory; for my part, I desire but one thing and that is to be inseparably united to you and to place in you alone all my hopes of happiness and repose."

Saint John Climacus lived until A.D. 649. He is celebrated on March 30th. The accounts of his life are recorded in Life of Saint John Climacus, by Daniel, a contemporary of Raithu Abbey.

Takes All Kinds

The personalities of saints are as vast as the ocean is deep. However, it would be difficult to conceive that there ever existed a more extreme religious zealot than Saint Angela Merici. It seems that only a medieval monk could have seen any merit in her unusual childhood.  Born on March 31, 1470, she was the youngest of five children in a well respected family of Desenzano. From the time she could walk, she conducted herself with the religious piety of a contemplative hermit.

As she advanced in years, she showed an unusual disregard for the finery and affectations usually resorted to by young girls to set off their personal advantages. She was a beautiful child with long, shiny, blond curls. Although she was greatly admired for her natural beauty, left to her own devices, she would wash her hair with soot and water saying, "If my hair is a temptation to sin, hide its beauty, lest it should feed vanity and wean the heart from God."

Although she was never renowned as a wonderworker, Saint Angela was favored throughout her life with heavenly visions and was, on one occasion, seen floating while in prayer. By obeying the messages given to her during her visions, she developed the order of the Ursuline Nuns which was founded on November 25, 1535. Her congregation continues to flourish today and is described as the oldest teaching order of women in the Christian tradition.

Saint Angela was canonized in 1807. Her body remains miraculously incorrupt and may be seen at Desenzano, near Lake Garda, Italy. The accounts of her life are recorded in Life of Saint Angela of Brescia, Montpellier, 1804.

April

1 Riotous Mob
2 Safe Sailing
3 Jonah's Mission
4 Anointed by God
5 Offstage Worker
6 Getting It Straight
7 Material Visions
8 Luke's Gospel
9 Bronze and Silver
10 Wonder of Egypt
11 Purity Named
12 Zeno's Protection
13 Bird Watchers
14 Mischief Backfires
15 Legend of Pamina
16 Shepherd's Double
17 Temperamental Cook
18 Breath of Air
19 Royal Receipts
20 Girl-Child
21 Lamprey for All
22 Nothing Lost
23 Virgin of the Rosary
24 Sunbeam Hangers
25 Good Council
26 Seeing is Believing
27 Serving Maid
28 Man with a Mission
29 Standing Guard
30 Mystic of Siena

Riotous Mob

It would be difficult to miss so striking a presence as that of Saint Valery. He was a tall, ascetic man who thought that being treated as ordinary was as bad as being treated like nothing at all. He was often quick to anger and would sometimes let loose before knowing all the details, but when he spoke, he seemed to spin a magic web that was both soothing and authoritative.

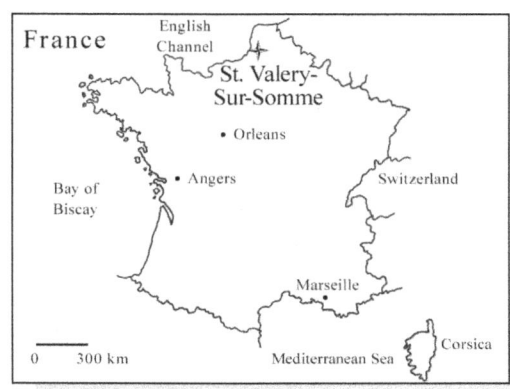

In one instance, while on an expedition near Bresle, he stopped to examine some images carved deeply into an oak tree. Subsequently, he instructed one of his young disciples to push the tree to the ground with one finger. The young disciple, who had witnessed many miracles performed by his master, did so, and the tree fell to the ground with a tremendous crash.

Many in the nearby community who witnessed this spectacle were filled with fear and hurried to arm themselves with sticks and hatchets, believing the saint to be a devil. Meanwhile, Saint Valery remained quiet and composed, waiting for something further to occur. And it did; a riotous mob approached with angry and threatening words. Valery did not budge. He stared at them head on and as they drew closer, their riotous fury was completely subdued. They stood quietly looking at him as if they had forgotten what had angered them in the first place. In a moment, Valery broke the silence. He spoke only briefly, but the power of his speech was evident. For when he left Bresle, the entire township was baptized.

Later a church was erected in the spot where the oak tree was felled. Saint Valery lived until A. D. 619. He is celebrated on April 1st. His relics are preserved at St. Valery-sur-Somme, at the site of the abbey of Leucomaus. The accounts of his life are recorded in Les Saints de Pranche Comte, by Besancon.

Safe Sailing

Saint Francis of Paola had no exaggerated illusions about what he could or could not do. On one occasion, en route to Sicily, he stopped at a ferry crossing near Messina and asked the ferryman to escort him and his companions across for free. The ferryman laughed at the request and turned him away. Without further ado, Saint Francis simply tossed his cloak upon the sea, climbed aboard, and bade his six disciples to follow. "Together, all seven sailed safely upon this cloak across the strait." We are told, "The sea trembled, but the saint did not tremble." When the seven voyagers reached the shores of Messina, an enormous crowd was assembled to see them disembark from their mysterious vessel.

This account is documented in the acts of his canonization (1519) by numerous witnesses including the ferryman. Saint Francis of Paola lived from 1416-1507. He is celebrated on April 2nd, as Patron of seafarers.

Jonah's Mission

Jonah, the biblical prophet, was commanded in a vision of God, to go to Nineveh and speak against its wickedness. But Jonah was afraid to go to Nineveh. Hoping to escape this undesirable mission from God, he set sail for Tarshish instead. During this voyage a great storm arose, tossing the ship to near wreckage. The mariners cast lots to ascertain which of the crew had provoked the gods to send this death upon them. The lot fell to Jonah.

The sailors were hesitant about what to do, but Jonah, acknowledging his guilt, commanded them: "Take me up and cast me into the sea, and so shall the waves be calm."

The sailors were unwilling to do so and rowed hard for land, but the storm was against them. At length, they obeyed the prophet and cast him into the sea. Immediately the storm subsided. Jonah was not drowned, however, for a great fish called a "whale" swallowed him. For three days and three nights he remained in the whale's belly wholly uninjured. At the expiration of the third night, he was vomited alive, safely onto dry land and was, ever after, thankful for this miracle.

The Old Testament of the Bible, Jonah 1, Chapter 11.

Anointed by God

Catherine of Vadstena, the child of a saint, was the coveted choice for marriage among Swedish aristocrats. She was a confident young girl, rather assertive and not easy to get close to. Nevertheless, her life was filled with continual turmoil caused by her many would-be suitors who schemed relentlessly to abduct her, but failed.

On one occasion, while en route to St. Laurent's Church, a cavalier about to lay his hands on her was instantly struck blind when a voice spoke to him, "Touch not Mine anointed and do My prophets no harm." Being so afflicted, the cavalier threw himself at Catherine's feet and begged to be forgiven. She offered up her prayers on his behalf and in a moment his sight was restored. The cavalier later narrated this occurrence to the Pope himself.

Not long afterwards, Catherine and her mother were entering Saint Mary's Church at Assisa when this miracle occurred again. A party of ruffians attempted to seize her, but were struck with instantaneous blindness.

Saint Catherine, daughter of Saint Bridget of Sweden, lived during the fourteenth century. Her life was recorded by Ulpho thirteen years after her death.

Offstage Worker

For those fortunate followers who traveled with Saint Vincent Ferrier, every day a miracle happened. Not once, but many times he multiplied a single loaf of bread and a single pint of wine so prodigiously that it easily provided sustenance for thousands. When the masses had quenched their thirst and satisfied their hunger, Vincent and his disciples would meticulously collect the remaining morsels so as not to waste even the smallest amount.

Vincent loved his freedom and had no desire for ecclesiastical grandeur. He refused even the cardinal's hat, preferring that his leadership take place behind the scenes or just offstage. He craved only simplicity and truth and blessed anyone who wished to find it. He single-handedly reformed nearly every province in Spain and taught uncountable numbers in France, Italy, Germany, Flanders, England, Scotland and Ireland.

At the moment of his death the windows of his chamber flew open of their own accord and hundreds of winged creatures, no bigger than butterflies, "very beautiful and purely white," filled the entire room. When the saint exhaled his final breath these winged creatures disappeared, leaving behind an exquisite perfume.

Though the Church was then divided by the great schism, Vincent was honored by all. Even Moslem factions invited him to speak. Saint Vincent Perrier was born in Valencia, Spain and is celebrated worldwide on April 5th. Thousands of miracles are recorded in the acts of his canonization, 1445.

Getting It Straight

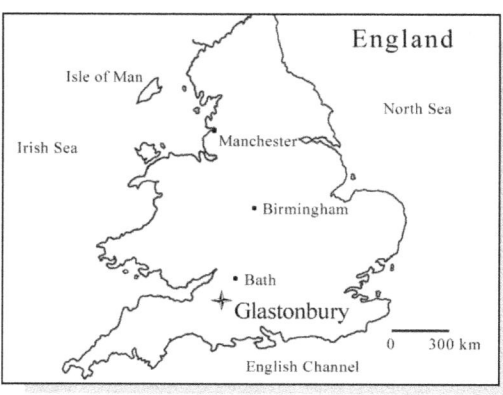

One of the most practical miracles on record comes from the life of Saint Dunstan of England. On one occasion during his travels, he observed a church which had been sited incorrectly, not due east and west. Adamant that the correction be made, he effortlessly pushed it with his shoulder into the true direction. By this and many other miracles he acquired such renown in England, that the king, prelates and peers hailed him as "Father of the Country."

Saint Dunstan was born near Glastonbury at Baltonsborough and lived from A.D. 909-988. He is regarded the most famous of Anglo-Saxon saints and is celebrated throughout England. His life is recorded in Life of Saint Dunstan, by Osbert of Canterbury.

Material Vision

Among the many German mystics of the twelfth and thirteenth centuries, special interest is given to Herman Joseph for the extraordinary nature of his visions. From his early years to his final day in extreme old age, he was in continual communication with the residents of heaven.

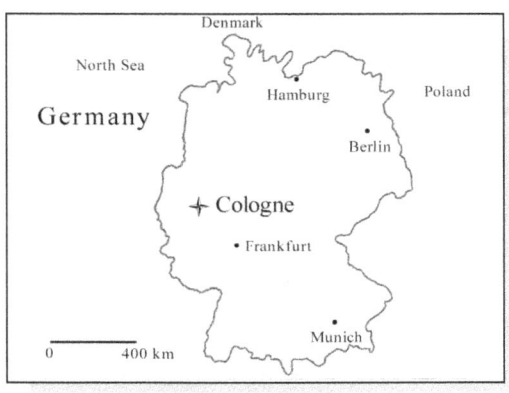

His life was so blameless and his innocence so genuine that he easily won the love of all he encountered. Even though he was a visionary, he had a practical side, and all his life he employed himself as a clever mechanic, traveling from monastery to monastery, adjusting or repairing clocks for the brothers.

His remarkable visions were evident even at the early age of seven. He once entered Cologne Cathedral and bore witness to a material vision of the Virgin Mary, the four evangelists and the infant Jesus. They were seated in the gallery above him which runs between the choir and the nave. All were conversing together in a charming manner and he anxiously longed to join them. However, the gallery was locked and there was no ladder to climb up. Presently the Virgin summoned him, "Herman, come up hither!" Since he was unable to do so, the Divine Mother assisted by stretching out her hand. Lifting him into the gallery, she placed him next to her son. He spent several hours in this divine society, his heart barely capable of containing the bliss.

When evening came, the Virgin lifted the boy down and he returned safely to his home. The proof that this was not a dream or celestial vision, but an actual material occurrence was manifest to the young saint by a wound he received from a nail in the balustrade.

Herman lived until 1241. The process of his canonization was introduced but never completed. His religious cult, however, has been officially sanctioned. The accounts of his life are recorded in the Acta Sanctorum, and he is celebrated on April 7th. His relics are preserved in Cologne, Germany.

Luke's Gospel

Now he was teaching in one of the synagogues on the Sabbath. And, look! There was a woman who had the spirit of infirmity for eighteen years, and was bowed together, and could in no way lift up herself. When Jesus saw her, He called her to Him, and said unto her, "Woman, thou art released from thine infirmity." And he laid his hands on her and instantly she straightened up and began to glorify God.

And the ruler of the synagogue answered with indignation because Jesus had healed on the sabbath day and said unto the people, "There are six days in which men ought to work: in them therefore come and be healed and not on the sabbath day."

The Lord answered him and said, "Thou hypocrite, doth not each one of you on the sabbath loose his ox or his ass from the stall and lead him away to watering?"

"And ought not this woman, being a daughter of Abraham, whom Satan hath bound lo these eighteen years, be loosed from this bond on the sabbath day?"

And when he had said these things, all his adversaries were ashamed: and all the people rejoiced for all the glorious things that were done by him.

The New Testament of the Bible, The Gospel According to Luke, Chapter 13: 10-17, written in Caesarea in A.D. 56.

Bronze and Silver

Saint Mylor was a prince, the son of Melianus, Duke of Cornwall, in Britain. The young saint was only seven when his father was ruthlessly murdered by his Uncle Rivoldus. Usurping the duke's power, Rivoldus further wished to permanently prevent

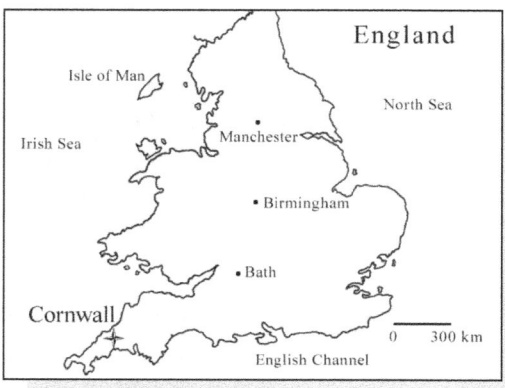

Mylor's succession. He severed the right hand and left foot of the young prince leaving him maimed and therefore, by law, disqualified from rulership. Accordingly the young prince was sent to a Cornish monastery. There he was furnished with a silver hand and a bronze foot. By the time he had reached the age of fourteen, his artificial limbs had begun to work as if they were natural limbs. He was seen picking nuts, handling them, clasping branches, throwing stones, and in every way functioning with fully operative limbs.

The abbot and monks of the monastery witnessed these events and recorded them. The entire description is found in Lives of the Saints, *by Baring-Gould.*

Wonder of Egypt

Saint Mary of Egypt was a wonder to behold. She often walked upon the waters of the Jordan River or was lifted into the air while absorbed in prayer. She lived as a hermit in the Egyptian desert and what is known of her life is given in her own words as recorded by Father Zozimus.

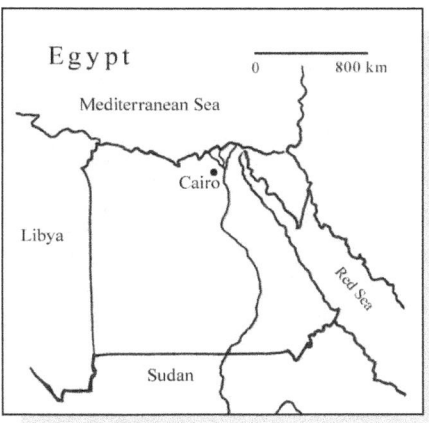

"At the age of twelve, I quitted my father's roof and went to Alexandria, where I abandoned myself to all sorts of licentiousness, having no fear of God or man. I lost my native modesty and lived seventeen years in the basest impurity. One day, seeing a number of persons embark for Jerusalem to solemnize the feast of the exaltation of the cross, I went on board too, with the intention of luring to carnal crime some of these pilgrims and succeeded by selling myself to pay my passage.

Reaching Jerusalem, I reveled deeper in sin than I had ever done in Alexandria, and when the day of exaltation arrived, I went with the crowd to see the holy tree. I intended to slip in unnoticed, but once at the door, I was unable to pass through. After using all my efforts over and over again to force my way through, I began to ask myself why it was that I alone should be unable to cross that threshold? Was I then too unclean to pass the way of holiness? My heart smote, tears ran in torrents from my eyes. Seeing an image of the Virgin Mary, I fell before it in passionate humility and cried with a broken heart, 'O glorious virgin, chaste and pure; pity me, pity me, base unworthy sinner that I am. Is there no balm in Gilead for such as me? Is there no physician for such as me? O glorious virgin, let me, let me see the cross of salvation; let me, let me look upon him who died for sin and suffered Mary Magdalene to wash his feet with her tears.'

I rose from the ground and again went to the church. I could enter it now. I saw the holy cross. I shrank into myself with shame. I ran back to the image of the Virgin and vowed henceforth, with God's help, to lead a new life. I heard a voice say to me, 'Mary, pass the Jordan and you will find peace for your soul.' I instantly directed my feet for the river, I washed my face in the water sanctified by the baptism of Jesus, I confessed my sins; received in the monastery of St. John the Baptist the divine mysteries which give life; entered this desert; and here have I lived for forty-seven years, hoping by penance to do away with the sins of my evil life."

Saint Mary of Egypt lived until A.D. 421. She is celebrated in Egypt on April 10th. The accounts of her life are recorded in the Acta Sanctorum, Volume IV.

Purity Named

Austreberta was called "the daughter of purity." Her biographers say that she was named by angels. The celestials announced to her mother that the heavens had heard her prayers and would grant her a child, "who will be a mother to many." At the moment of her birth the bedchamber was filled with a heavenly odor and a luminous dove hovered above the house. A short while later the resplendent bird flew into the chamber and settled on the head of the infant. "Austreberta will be your name," declared her mother, "given to me by the messengers from heaven."

Austreberta lived from A. D. 630-704. The accounts of her life are recorded in Analecta Bolandiana, Volume XXXVIII.

Zeno's Protection

Saint Gregory the Great and several other historians relate the following anecdote as indisputable historic fact.

On the feast day of Saint Zeno the people of the city of Verona assembled to celebrate his memory in the church where he had been buried almost two hundred years earlier. That same day, the Adige River overflowed and threatened to devastate the church.

"Though the doors to the church were open wide, the waters seemed afraid to enter," wrote Gregory.

The waters rolled up to the open doors, rose above the windows and menaced the assembly with death, not from drowning, but by starvation-for the walls of water encased the church and no one could escape. Wonder followed wonder because this water-wall provided the captive assembly with needed drink.

Saint Gregory tells us, "It served as drink, but made no attempt to enter the sacred edifice."

Even Alban Buder feels no reservation in the authenticity of this account and adds, "This extraordinary, wonder-filled event had as many witnesses as there were inhabitants in Verona."

Saint Zeno was Bishop of Verona during the fourth century. His relics are preserved in a subterranean chapel in Verona. He is celebrated on April 12th. This account is given in Saint Gregory's Dialogues, Book III, Chapter 19.

Bird Watcher

Although he seemed unfathomable to almost everybody, there was a firm direction in Medard's life. At times he may have seemed cold and unfeeling, but he was a man of deeds, not words, and one could faithfully depend upon his promises. He loved nature and was particularly fond of birds, to which many of his miracles are associated.

On one occasion, while still a young boy, he returned from the pastures with his royal father and attendants when a wild eagle appeared a few feet over his head and shielded him from a sudden burst of rain which lasted nearly thirty minutes. On other occasions witnesses claimed that Medard spoke to the birds and they obeyed his commands.

Even at the time of his funeral, in the presence of an enormous procession, two angelic doves descended from the sky and landed on his tomb. Moments later a third dove "whiter than snow" rose from the open mouth of the saint and accompanied the others as they flew upwards to heaven.

Saint Medard was born at Salency in Picardy and lived from A.D. 470-560. He is a favorite among the farmers of northern France and is invoked for protection against bad weather. The accounts of his life are recorded in the Acta Sanctorum, Volume II.

Mischief Backfires

Mischief was in the air. It happened that a small mob of Spanish libertines intent on mischief, hired a local harlot to deceive and seduce the king's chaplain, Friar Peter Gonzalez. Disguising herself as a woman of piety, she entered the friar's home and begged for council on a matter of great importance. When alone, she embraced his knees and pretended to weep. Then skillfully employing her arts, she attempted to seduce the holy man. Gonzalez rose to his feet and invited the woman to follow him to an inner chamber. There he lit a fire and stood in the midst of the flames.

The harlot screamed in terror, but the holy man who was untouched by the flames retorted, "What is this, to the hellfire that you would allure me?"

She was struck to the heart with these words and from that moment forward abandoned her former lifestyle. Fully transformed, she ever after reverenced the very shadow of Gonzalez.

Peter Gonzalez lived from 1190-1248. The Church proclaimed him worthy of public religious honor. He is celebrated on April 14th. His life is recorded in the Acta Sanctorum, Bollandists, Volume II.

Legend of Pamina

Legend tells us a story of two monks who, commanded by their superior, journeyed to administer the last rites to Pamina, a shepherdess who had fallen unexpectedly ill with fever. As they proceeded, one of the monks was overcome with a desire to take some rest. Doing so, a vision occurred to him, where three companies of virgins appeared.

The first company was magnificently dressed in gold brocade. The second was arrayed in dazzling white. The third wore robes whiter still and trimmed with royal purple. The first company saluted him, and he returned the salute. At the head of the third company stood a virgin who surpassed all the others in radiance. Her robe was entirely coated with white and red roses. He saluted the lady reverently and inquired her name.

"I am the Queen of Virgins," she graciously replied, "I accompany these troops from heaven. We are now seeking the soul of a young shepherdess, whom we will carry to paradise."

The monk knew well that the sought-after soul was that of Pamina and when the vision concluded, he spurred his partner to make haste for Paminas cabin.

When they arrived they knelt over the dying maiden and she spoke to them, "Oh, my fathers, that heaven would open your eyes to see the virgins from heaven that stand around me now."

The monks prayed that heaven would grant this favor, and they witnessed the Virgin Mary place a garland of flowers on Pamina's head.

This account is taken from Une Vie de Sainte par Jour.

Shepherd's Double

Drogo was happiest in his favorite setting, alone with nature. He was Flemish, of noble parentage, but preferred to do what he wanted, rather than what he was taught to do. He had little interest in the day-to-day business of commerce and chose to work alone in a pasture tending his family's sheep. Despite his humble aspirations, he soon came to be regarded with the greatest esteem by the inhabitants of the district, who respected him as a saint. On many occasions he was seen tending his flocks in the fields, while at the same time, was mysteriously observed assisting in the celebrations of the church. This afterwards gave rise to a local saying, "Not being Saint Drogo, I cannot be in two places at the same time."

At the age of thirty, stricken with a terrible affliction, he elected to finish his life in a monk's cell in the church of Sebourg, near Valenciennes. For forty years he never emerged from seclusion. Even when a fire devastated the church, he made no effort to flee. Both the church and his cell were burned to the ground, but not the slightest injury was incurred by the saint.

Saint Drogo lived from 1118-1189. He is celebrated as patron of shepherds on April 16th. His tomb continues to be a popular spot of pilgrimage due to the miracles which are reported to this day. His life is recorded in the Acta Sanctorum, Bollandists, Volume II.

Temperamental Cook

Saint Robert de Turlande, Abbot of Chaise-Dieu, lived in Allanche in the mountains of Auvergne. One particular occasion, during the celebration of mass, he was interrupted by the abbey cook who frantically insisted that all would go hungry that night, as there was nothing in the pantry for dinner.

"It's all right," said Robert, "we will first serve the mass and all else will be provided."

Robert had just begun the Preface when an eagle, passing over the abbey, let fall an enormous fish which landed only a few yards from the cook. That night, the abbot and his suite ate ample portions and, everyone agreed, the cook had once again outdone himself.

Robert of Chaise-Dieu lived during the eleventh century. He was canonized in A.D. 1095, seven years after his death. He is celebrated on April 17th. His life is recorded in the Acta Sanctorum, Volume III.

Breath of Air

Leo was a dynamo. He was self-confident, crusading and a born leader. Once during a visit to Bayonne, France, he preached in the temple of Mars and was very disturbed by the corrupt and licentious manner in which the temple deity was being honored. He delivered a sermon, aimed at abolishing these corruptions and in so doing, created an uproarious clamor in the assembly. He addressed the follies of inappropriate worship, but perceiving the people were no longer of a mind to listen, he ceased speaking and closed his eyes in silent prayer. When he later opened them, he walked directly to the idol of Mars and with nothing other than a single puff of breath, reduced the idol to powder. The assembly fell quiet, apparently stupefied, and the priest continued his sermon without the least interruption.

Saint Leo lived during the ninth century. His life is recorded in the Acta Sanctorum, Bollandists, Volume I.

Royal Receipts

King Gontran of Burgundy was fascinated by holy men. Nothing could prevent his traveling from place to place to visit wise men. Once he visited Aquitaine of Perigord and met with Sorus, a local saint who was much renowned for his ability to heal. He requested a cure for an ailment which troubled him and Sorus graciously obliged. After the cure had been effected, the saint invited the king and his suite to remain with him for dinner. Sorus instructed the steward to prepare a cable worthy of such honored guests, but the steward replied that the wine was depleted and none could be procured in time.

"Well then," said Sorus, "go to the vineyard and you will find three grapes plump and ripe. Pluck them and bring them to me." The steward did as Sorus instructed.

"Now," said the saint, "bring three empty barrels and squeeze a grape into each one."

This he did, and immediately the barrels overflowed with an exquisite wine. When the cable was laid, the king and his courtiers commended the wine, praising the hospitality of their host. In gratitude, King Gontran dedicated a new monastery for hosting travelers. The monastery was fully furnished and endowed with immense revenues. When a king acknowledges a benefit received, he acknowledges it like a king.

Sorus lived from A.D. 500-592. His life is recorded in the Acta Sanctorum, Bollandists.

Girl Child

In 1268, in the little Tuscan village of Gracchiano-Vecchio, three miles from Montepulciano, a girl was born named Agnes. She was a simple and playful child, like any other, and no one would have guessed that she would one day be numbered among the great women wonderworkers of the world.

At age nine, her life was already rich with miracles. By fifteen, she was herself a miracle. She would draw people close to her with an almost magical magnetism and if lucky, they would see her lift from the ground, "five feet or more," absorbed in heavenly ecstasy.

In the presence of all the inmates of the Convent del Sacco, she freely hovered in the air, subsumed in divine meditation, oblivious of her surroundings. At sixteen, she was elected abbess in the convent of Monrepulciano. A special dispensation was obtained from Pope Nicholas IV, who authorized the appointment of one so young to so high a post.

Her life was filled with visions and healings and miracles of every kind. At on time, her fellow sisters observed her covered with "manna" from head to toe and all around "as if she had been outdoors in a heavy snowstorm." Miracle after miracle accompanied her life. After death countless miracles continued in the vicinity of her tomb. Thousands of pilgrims journeyed there, among them Catherine of Siena. When Catherine stooped to kiss the foot of Agnes' incorrupt body, it graciously raised to meet her lips. Such were the miracles of Agnes of Montepulciano.

Saint Agnes lived from 1268-1317 and was canonized in 1726. Her body remained whole and incorrupt until the sixteenth century. After it had been placed inside the walls of the main altar of the church, parts of it decomposed due to excessive humidity. Today her incorrupt body, cosmetically adjusted, may be seen at the Sanctuary of St. Agnes in Montepulciano, Italy. She is celebrated on April 20th. Her life is recorded in The Life of Saint Agnes, *by Raymond of Capua.*

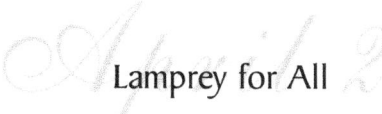

Lamprey for All

From time to time, Saint Hermenland would retreat from his duties as abbot to a small island in the estuary of the Loire. It was there that a monk spoke to him of a little fish called a lamprey—a particularly sumptuous variety which he had tasted only once in the bishop's palace in Nantes.

Saint Hermenland remarked, "Do you suppose that God cannot send such fish here?"

As he spoke a lamprey leapt from the Loire and threw itself on the bank where the monk was sitting. Saint Hermenland divided the tiny fish into three parts. One he kept for himself and the other two, distributed by him, were multiplied to such an extent, they fed the entire community of monks.

Hermenland lived until A.D. 720. His life is recorded in the Analecta bollandiana, *Volume XXIX.*

Nothing Lost

Gerard was a man of great will and equal patience. He had a calm and unhurried way and possessed a keen sense of unfettered observation. One day he was summoned for a council by Emperor Otto II. While traveling by ferry on the Mosel River from France to Germany, an unfortunate accident occurred. One of his clerks, attempting to wash his hands, leaned over the side of the boat and caused a highly valued reliquary to fall overboard. The casket sank quickly and everyone aboard feared it was an omen of some great misfortune, but Gerard and the ferryman were untroubled and continued their passage according to schedule.

Arriving safely in Germany, Gerard met with the emperor, accomplished his mission satisfactorily and returned home to France by the same route. When the ferry reached the site where the casket had fallen overboard (near Dommartin), Gerard asked the captain to stop the boat. After a short prayer, he placed his hand into the river and to the astonishment of everyone present, the lost reliquary buoyed to the surface of the water, where he drew it out with little ado.

Gerard lived until A.D. 994. He was canonized by Pope Leo IX in 1050. This account is given in Life of Saint Gerard by Father Benedict.

Virgin of the Rosary

On April 23, 1991, over 100,000 people witnessed *The Miracle of The Sun* in Sabana Grande, a small agricultural village on the southeast corner of Puerto Rico. The history of this miracle dates from April 23, 1953, when the Virgin Mary appeared to three small children, guiding and instructing them for a period of thirty-three days. Juan Angel Collado was an eight year old second grader. Ramonita Belen was seven and in the first grade. Her sister, Isidra Belen, the oldest of the visionaries, was nine years old and in the third grade.

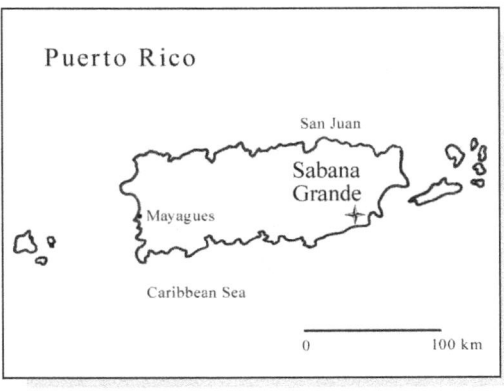

Their adventure began when Juan and one of his playmates were sent to the pocito to fetch two buckets of water. Juan's playmate was pouring water into one of the buckets when his hand suddenly froze in midair while a stream of celestial rainbow colored water issued from the tin cup he was using.

"Juan! Juan!" the boy yelled loudly, then dropped the cup and ran back to the school in fright.

Juan claims that he tried running, but his body would not move. Everything was motionless as if all creation had melted into one profound silence. Suddenly, a young lady appeared. She stood on a cloud and was clad in a beautiful long white gown with a mantle of blue covering her head which reached almost to the bottom of her feet. She held a rosary in her hand and above her head was a crown of seven stars, each one more brilliant than the sun. When she looked into

Juan Angel's eyes, he was transported into a peace and joy which transcended any human experience he had ever imagined.

The next day, April 24th, Juan returned to the site of the miracle. The two Belen sisters, the only children brave enough, accompanied him. Again the lady appeared, this time to all three children, and again peace and joy, beyond any they had ever known permeated their souls.

The children told their experience to their teacher who disbelieved them and forbade them to return to the well. But in the days that followed the children felt compelled to gather at the same spot and the visions continued daily, just before 11:00 a.m.

"Be not afraid," spoke the vision. "I am the Virgin of the Rosary."

After the fifth day, crowds of people began to gather at the miracle site making teaching clearly impossible. The children were no longer allowed any where near the well and from that day forward, at 11:00 a.m., the Virgin of the Rosary walked from the well to the schoolhouse, where she assumed the role of teacher to the three visionaries. The entire class participated in the lessons when the visionaries told the others what they saw and heard. The teacher herself felt powerless to resist an urge to get up from her chair. She stood quietly in a corner of the room, where she watched and listened.

By the end of the first week, thousands of people had gathered at the school to participate in the event. The excitement and chaos frightened the children and a police officer named Dario Garcia was assigned to protect the children from the jostling crowds. He later became a witness to many of the reported miracles. Once, while carrying the children on his shoulders to protect them from the crowds, he fell and cut his index finger very deeply. Juan Angel responded, "Don't worry the Virgin says she will make it well." Then Ramonita shouted, "Look, look. She is putting something green on his finger!" The bleeding stopped immediately and the cut was gone.

The reports of miracles during these first thirty-three days are too numerous to mention but include everything from objects floating in the air to healings, which are continuing today. The most dramatic miracle of all happened in the presence of almost 100,000 people. On May 25, 1953 they witnessed a miracle of the sun similar to that of Fatima. A magnificent rainbow appeared similar to that of the rainbow seen by Juan on the first day of the Apparition. As the people watched the celestial phenomena they began to look at each other and shout, "Look at your hands, your head, your shoulders!" Everyone was saturated with the colorful rainbow waters. Some claim they still possess the clothing they wore on that day and that it remains vibrant with rainbow hues.

Thirty-eight years later, on April 23, 1991, this miracle recurred in the presence of over 100,000 witnesses at Sabana Grande. This phenomenon, no longer subject to doubt, contains many messages from the mouth of the Virgin of the Rosary, conveyed by her visionaries. These messages, too lengthy to mention in such a brief account of the event, may be found in the visionaries' own writings or from the Pittsburgh Center for Peace.

Sunbeam Hangers

Saint Robert of Casa Dei was preaching at Avignon when two mischievous teenagers began tossing their gloves over the heads of the audience. They succeeded in distracting the assembly until, in the midst of one of their tosses, Robert caused the gloves to "catch on a sunbeam" and hang in the air too high for the pranksters to reach. The gloves remained suspended, we are told, until the service was over.

Saint Robert of Casa Dei (Chaise-Dieu in Avignon) lived until 1067. He was renowned for his enthusiastic zeal and devotion to the sick and poor who would throng to his hermit's hut seeking his mastership. People came forward with donations and buildings arose which formed the great abbey of Casa Dei. Saint Robert's biography was recorded within thirty years of his death by Marbod, Bishop of Rennes.

Good Council

The families of Scutari, Albania, had diligently defended themselves for years, against relentless attacks from Turkish forces. Finally, in 1467, it was apparent that defeat was imminent. Like the majority of the city's inhabitants, Jorge and Sclavis prepared to abandon their homeland in search of protection in a neighboring country. Before their departure they met in the chapel to pay final honor to the portrait of the Madonna and Child, a practice they had cultured all their lives. As they stood before the image, they were filled with an ecstasy, and it seemed as if they were paralyzed.

Then unexpectedly, each heard a mysterious voice from within, "Tomorrow you will leave Scutari."

They had no idea what this message meant, but each arrived early the next morning and prostrated before the holy image. Then without warning, the sacred painting miraculously detached itself from the wall and transported itself by means of a small cloud which formed at its base.

Again the mysterious voice was heard, "Follow Me."

Led by this floating portrait, the two men followed faithfully over mountains, rivers, valleys, for hundreds of miles, until they reached Italy. There the portrait vanished and despite endless searching, they could not locate it.

Meanwhile, in another part of Italy, a lady named Petrucia was busy soliciting funds to construct a chapel to be completed by April

25th of that same year. By divine revelation, she was told that on this day in April, the Madonna would sanctify and inhabit the newly-erected church. Despite her sincere efforts, when April 25th arrived, the chapel was unfinished.

At the appointed time, the donors flocked to the chapel site. Seeing it less than complete they began to denounce Petrucia as a fraud and a heretic. It was at this moment that the air was filled with ethereal music. The bells of the chapel rang of their own accord and a gushing sound, like a waterfall, suffused the atmosphere. Then a very small cloud descended from the sky holding the portrait of the Madonna and Child of Scutari. It glided slowly downward, carrying its sacred cargo, and mounted itself to one of the unfinished walls of the chapel. We are told it remains miraculously suspended there to the present day.

This miracle has received the sanction of the highest order of ecclesiastical rank. Pope Pius IX and Leo XIII were especially fond of this portrait, titled Our Lady of Good Counsel. Pope John XXIII selected this location in Genzano, southeast of Rome, for prayer before the opening of the 2nd Vatican Council.

Seeing Is Believing

Saint Marcellinus was a natural salesman. He was a missionary with extraordinary tact and diplomacy. He was a self-taught, self-made man with a gusto for theatrics and a high sense of personal honor, which he loved to defend. As Bishop of Embrun, he was a box office hit and succeeded in converting every member in his diocese. Everyone, that is, except one man, a powerful and well known aristocrat. The bishop hosted a banquet celebration and this man was invited. Marcellinus expressed his desire to see the man follow the example of his countrymen and ally himself to the Almighty.

The man replied, "I have heard speak of your miracles, Marcellinus, but have never witnessed one. Nor have I seen anything yet to induce me to leave my present philosophies."

At that moment the bishop's cupbearer dropped a valuable glass goblet which broke into a hundred pieces.

"There," said the man, "mend that goblet and give me reason to believe."

Marcellinus groaned in spirit but prayed that God would bring assistance and not confirm this doubter in his disbelief. At the same moment the broken glass pieces came together and the goblet was restored to its original form. Struck with wonder at this miracle, the new convert confessed that he could not doubt what his own eyes could see.

Saint Marcellinus lived during the fourth century. This record is given in Hagiographie de Gap.

Serving Maid

What would the Fatinelli family have done without Zita. She was a beautiful young girl of twelve when she joined their household in Lucca as a serving maid. She perfectly exemplified simplicity and innocence and had a natural way of making everyone feel loved.

The miracles she preformed at the entrance to the Fatinelli house were so numerous that the citizens of Lucca named it "The Angel Door." On one occasion, she was visited by a pilgrim parched with thirst, begging to be relieved of the burden of his travels. The household was entirely without wine at the time, but at Zita's request he remained at the door. From a nearby well, she retrieved a vessel of water and handed it to the pilgrim. Putting the jug to his lips, he was astonished and delighted, for as the water entered his mouth it changed to a wine of exquisite quality which he drank with relish.

Gradually the Fatinelli household realized what a treasure they possessed in Zita. They tried to raise her position, but Zita would not have it. Indeed, her work was her religion. She would say, "A servant is not good if she is not industrious. Work-shy piety in people of our position is sham piety."

She died at age sixty, but she lives on in the hearts of thousands she embraced as her children. That was the miracle she hoped for.

Zita, the Patroness of maid-servent, lived from 1218-1278. Her incorrupt body may be seen enshrined in a glass reliquary, in the Basilica of san Frediano at Lucca, Italy. Her story is given in the Vitae Sanctorum.

Man with a Mission

Saint Aphrodisius had a destiny. He was a man with a mission who tended to lead causes against social injustice. However, he lived at a time when the rewards for questioning the conventional way led to certain death. He was the object of great condemnation and was often persecuted by those who believed him a madman or a devil, but he believed in himself and in the power of the Almighty.

On April 28, A.D. 69, following the conclusion of one of his public addresses, an angry group of disapproving activists put an end to his leadership, roughly shoving him about from one to another, and finally finishing their sport by cutting off his head. However, the severed body of Saint Aphrodisius then rose to its feet, took its head between its hands and walked through the midst of the crowd. We are told that hundreds bore witness as the severed body of the holy man carried its head to a chapel just beyond the town.

This story is recorded in Vies des Saints, Volume V by Manager Guerin, Chamberlain to Pope Leo XIII.

Standing Guard

It's very unlikely that Saint Odilo would start something but not finish it. He was a serious, sober man with a quick, sarcastic wit who preferred work over social activities. At age twenty-nine, he assumed the position of abbot of the great abbey of Saint Mayeul and from there many stories of his miracles are told.

Pillage and looting were common in the eleventh century, due to the lawful right for every man to settle his own affairs. Consequently, one night a petty thief made the unfortunate mistake of attempting to steal Saint Odilo's horse by sneaking into the abbey stables. No sooner had he reached the outer gates of the monastery, when both he and the horse were petrified and utterly powerless to move.

Throughout the night they stood like living statues. At daybreak, Odilo greeted them remarking, "Friend, you have put yourself to a vast deal of trouble to stand guard here all night."

Then tossing the thief a coin, he dismissed him and returned his horse to the stable.

Odilo lived from 962-1049. He was canonized in 1063. He is celebrated on April 29th. Acta Sanctorum, Volume I, Bollandus.

Mystic of Siena

On the eve of Lent when the whole world seemed mad with folly, the great Italian mystic, Catherine of Siena, was alone in her room crying in fervent prayer. "Dear Saviour, give me grace that nothing may separate me from Thy great love."

Her cry was not in vain, for the voice of her Saviour replied, "Be at peace, Catherine. I will never leave thee or forsake thee."

With these words her room was suddenly filled with heavenly visitors. There was Mary, patroness of virgins in heaven and on earth; John the evangelist, with the eyes of an eagle and the purity of a dove; Saint Paul the victorious; the learned and angelic Dominic; and King David, the model of penitent love. Mary, placing the right hand of Catherine in that of her son's, asked him to give her his mystic ring. The ring was gold with a large diamond and four precious stones around it.

He placed the ring on the maiden's finger with the words, "I, with My Father in heaven—I, thy Redeemer and thy Spouse—will preserve thee pure, till that day when I come to claim thee as my heavenly bride."

The vision vanished, but the ring remained on Catherine's finger, visible to some but not to all. Throughout her life, these visions continued without interruption.

Catherine lived from 1317-1380. She was canonized in 1461. Many of her belongings are preserved at her house in Siena where a surviving early portrait reveals her remarkable natural beauty. Her visions were recorded by Raymond of Capuain, her confessor, in Life of Saint Catherine of Siena. In addition, her many written works including Dialogue of Saint Catherine have survived. Her body remains incorrupt. She is celebrated on April 30th.

May

1 Open Air
2 Guardians
3 Tried by Fire
4 Motherhood
5 Reformer Pope
6 Like Mother Like Daughter
7 The Mystery of Golgotha
8 Gift of Sight
9 Forewarned
10 Farming Angels
11 Street Preacher
12 Second Wind
13 Mysterious Lady
14 Nocturnal Edification
15 Slander Disproved
16 More Apparitions
17 Two Angels
18 Desert Fathers
19 Pena de Francia
20 Something New
21 Holy Candle
22 Breaking the Rules
23 Espoused
24 Odor of Sanctity
25 Coat Hanger
26 Heart
27 Humble Opinion
28 Legend of Saint Bernard
29 Our Lady of Deols
30 Joan of Arc
31 Perfect Balance

Open Air

Saint Aldebrand, Bishop of Fossombrone, possessed a particularly fond love for the creatures of the field. He abstained from meat throughout his life and his great love for birds and beasts was demonstrated by the many miracles he performed in their favor. Such an instance occurred at a time when an illness had overcome him. Being greatly reduced in weight and in failing health, a roast partridge was brought to him at his bedside. It was believed that his illness was caused by the absence of meat in his diet; therefore, if he would only eat the meat, his health would be regained.

Without a word to anyone, he bade the bird, "Flyaway."

The bird recovered its life and flew from the dish through an open window to join its companions in the fresh air.

Saint Aldebrand lived during the twelfth century. His life is recorded in the Acta Sanctorum, Bollandists, May 1.

Guardians

No collection of miracles could be complete without mention of the proverbial guardian angels. Almost every saint from every conceivable background has confirmed the presence of these celestial companions, assisting us in unseen ways every day, for our whole lives. The following narrative, taken from the writings of Sister Rosana is just one among millions of testimonies.

Rosana, called "Sister Humility," had two guardian angels, one named Sapiel and the other Emmanuel.

"When I think," says Rosana, "of the exalted rank of my celestial guardians, my heart is exalted. When I muse on their incomparable beauty, I am utterly ravished. But when I call to mind that they too stand before the throne of the Supreme Almighty, my joy is ecstatic. With two such guardians, I can fear no evil. They are a fortress, a buckler, a rock of defense. They direct me with their council, protect me with their love, and keep the keys of my heart and the door of my lips. O Emmanuel, O Sapiel, my angels, my beloved, conduct me into the presence of the queen of heaven, and place me in the arms of the divine Almighty."

This narrative from Sister Humility is given in the Acta Sanctorum, Volume V. May 2.

Tried by Fire

In 113 A.D., Aurelian, one of the magistrates of Adrian, sentenced Alexander and Eventius to be bound together and cast into a blazing furnace for refusing to denounce their religious beliefs. Alexander (possibly the sixth successive pope) was thirty years of age, and Eventius eighty. Bound together, they were thrown into the midst of the flames but remained unharmed.

Theodulus, a fellow captive, was held nearby and Alexander called to him from the flames, "Come brother. Come to us. The angel who walked with the Hebrews is with us now and keeping a place for you."

On hearing these words, Theodulus broke from his guards and dashed into the furnace, where all three stood on their feet singing aloud.

Having defeated Aurelian in the fires, these three martyrs were later beheaded. They are celebrated on May 3rd. This account is recorded in Life of Pope Alexander, *by The Roman Notaries.*

Motherhood

Motherhood certainly ranks among the most trying and wearying of spiritual practices. No doubt the rewards are great, but the sacrifices require immense compassion, understanding and flexibility. It is these qualities that best exemplify Monica, the mother of Saint Augustine. Although in his later years Augustine proved himself to be worthy of his title, as a child, he was a walking, talking nightmare for his mother. Monica was a model of motherhood, forever gentle and patient as she guided the restless and confused spirit of her son. In time, the son came to love his mother as though she were the source of life itself, but it took nearly a lifetime of patience to do so.

Monica was gifted in may ways, but only near the end of her life did Augustine realize her sanctity. Often he would discover his mother, rapt in prayer, so inwardly absorbed that she remained like a statue for the entire day. On other occasions during prayer, she was seen lifted three or more feet into the air, where she remained freely floating, subsumed in a heavenly ecstasy.

Monica never ceased in her efforts to raise her child with a healthy understanding of how the human spirit can participate in divine regions. She literally stormed heaven with her prayers, her tears and fasting. Near the end of her life, she had the satisfaction of seeing her son take the path of holiness under the mentorship of Saint Ambrose. At the moment of her death she addressed Augustine thus:

"Son, nothing in this world now affords me delight. I do not know what there is left for me to do or why I am still here; all my hopes in this world being now fulfilled. All I wished to live for was that I might see you as a child of Heaven. God has granted me more than this."

Monica was born in Tagaste, sixty miles from Carthage, North Africa. She lived from A.D. 332-387 and is honored universally as the Patron of Mothers and Married Women on May 4th. The accounts of her life were recorded by her son, Augustine, in his famous book Confessions.

Reformer Pope

From the moment he was elected pope in December, 1565, Michael Ghislieri (Pius V) began to reform the church under the guidelines recommended by the Council of Trent. Among his reforms were the direction of church funds away from the treasuries of cardinals and other dignitaries, and into hospitals, homeless shelters and convents in the city. He enforced strict laws against prostitution and bull fighting. He was particularly firm with clergy members and the penalties for breaches were so severe that he was accused of wanting to turn all of Rome into a monastery.

To no one's surprise, an attempt to assassinate him was perpetrated. The plan was cleverly devised, using a deadly poison which was secretly applied to the foot of Christ on the cathedral crucifix. According to custom, upon entering the church, the pope would be the first to kiss the crucifix. The poison was instantaneous and the plot seemed diabolically ingenious. However, when Pope Pius lowered his head to kiss the foot of Christ, the image came to life and drew back its poisoned limb. Panic filled the church, but in time the crowd settled and the assassination plot was uncovered. True to his nature, Pius exercised even greater vigor and conviction to generate reforms in the Church. This he did until the day of his natural death, in 1572.

Pope Saint Pius V lived from 1504-1512 and was canonized in 1712. He is celebrated on May 5th. History of Saint Pius V.

Like Mother Like Daughter

Catherine of Sweden was the fourth of eight children of Saint Bridget. Not unlike her mother, many miracles occurred around her. In one instance, while traveling by carriage, one of her attendants was overtaken with sleep and fell from his coach-box. The unfortunate man landed on his head. The horses could not be stopped in time and the poor man was trampled underfoot. When told of the accident, Princess Catherine hurried to where the man lay. She touched his hand and he quickly rose to life, wounds healed, safe and sound, as if nothing whatsoever had happened.

Catherine of Sweden lived during the fourteenth century. Numerous miracles are accredited both to her and to her mother. Acta Sanctorum, Volume III.

The Mystery of Golgotha

On the seventh day of May in the year A.D. 356, at nine in the morning, a magnificent ethereal cross appeared in the open sky just above the township of Golgotha. It stretched out as far as the Mount of Olives, about two miles distant. This miraculous event was witnessed not by a few but by the entire city. Many wept in the streets, some knelt in prayer, some held hands or embraced, while others simply marveled, but all bore witness. It continued to float above the city for several hours and, we are told, the light from it blazed more brilliantly than the sun. Why it appeared, we may never know.

This event occurred immediately following the inauguration of Saint Cyril as bishop and is documented in his letters to Emperor Constantine. Acta Sanctorum, Volume II.

Gift of Sight

During his life, Peter II, Archbishop of Tarentaise, was renowned throughout Western Europe as a worker of miracles. His reputation won him an audience with King Henry II of England and King Louis VII of France, and he had hopes of bringing the two nations together.

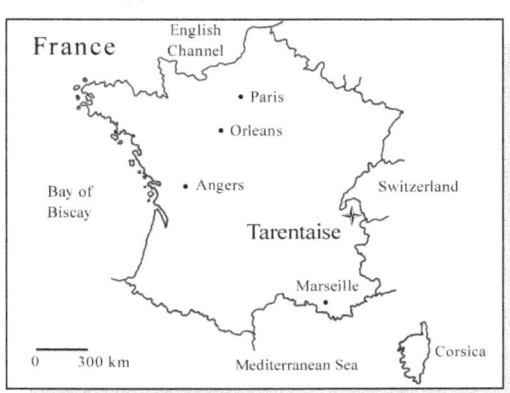

Amidst the immense crowd that gathered to see the celebrities was a woman leading her blind son by the hand. She found it impossible to force her way to the front of the crowd and in this dilemma, bellowed at the top of her voice imploring the saint to heal her son. Peter requested the boy to come forward. Then wetting his fingers with spittle, he rubbed them across the boy's sightless eyes. The kings and princes watched anxiously for the result and were not disappointed.

With a burst, the boy exclaimed, "Hurrah! Hurrah! I see my mother! I see the trees! I see men and women! I see everyone!"

The crowd was enraptured; the mother, in an ocean of tears, fell at the saint's feet and kissed them; while King Louis VII, likewise, fell prostrate. When he rose, he embraced the child and kissed his forehead, eyes and cheeks. Further still, with tears in his eyes, he gave the boy the promise of a kingly donation.

Peter lived from 1103-1174. He was canonized in 1191. He is celebrated on May 8th. This story is given in The Life of Peter II. Written nine years after his death by order of Pope Lucius III.

Forewarned

Three officers, Nepotian, Ursus and Herpilion, were falsely accused before Emperor Constantine and condemned to death. The evening before the execution an apparition of Saint Nicholas appeared to both Constantine and his judge, Ablavius.

Nicholas declared, "The men you have condemned are innocent. Unless they are released by morning, war shall desolate the land and your kingdom will perish by the sword. I, Nicholas of Myra, forewarn you."

Then he vanished. When the emperor met with the judge the next morning, each confirmed the other's vision. The emperor promptly ordered the release of the prisoners and dispatched them to Nicholas with gifts consisting of four gospels in letters of gold and a gold incense burner.

Further, he commanded the party to deliver this message: "The emperor begs Saint Nicholas not to threaten him but to pray for him."

Nicholas of Myra lived during the fourth century. He is celebrated on May 9th. The accounts of his life are recorded in the Analecta Bolandiana, Volume I.

Farming Angels

Isidore loved the simple life. He was a farm laborer who was employed under the charge of a wealthy landowner from Madrid (a position he held for his life time). He once roused the anger of fellow employees, who continually griped that his long meditations in the morning made him late for chores. After much public grumbling, the workers finally approached their employer, John de Vergas, and accused Isidore of wasting his time in meditation. The employer agreed to watch him and if he found him neglecting his duties to rebuke him sharply or dismiss him.

Early the next morning, the landowner secretly went to the field where Isidore had been sent to plow. When he arrived, he expected to find less work done than required, but instead he found three times as much was accomplished, and done admirably well. Moreover, half the work was being done by angels who guided their plows in step with Isidore. The angels were "snow white oxen led by unknown figures of similar composition." The farmer was ravished, and falling to his knees, craved the pardon of his servant for listening to false reports.

Isidore replied, "Master, no time is ever lost by prayer, for those who pray are workers together with God."

Isidore lived from 1070-1130. His body remains miraculously incorrupt and may be seen at the Cathedral of Madrid, in Spain. He was canonized in 1622 and honored as patron of Madrid, his celebration being set for May 10th. Acta Sanctorum, Volume III.

Street Preacher

It was impossible to keep Francis di Girolamo off the streets. He was a man of wit and character and had a distinct sense of humor. He once chose to do his preaching at the entrance of a notorious brothel in Naples. Amused by his showmanship, an enormous crowd gathered to hear him, making the streets virtually impassable. His preaching was in prime form when a carriage, with a team of horses, tried to force its way past the unrelenting crowd. The gentleman within ordered the coachman to disregard the commotion and drive through.

Hearing this, Francis held out his arm and cried aloud, "Holy Lord, if these infidels have no respect for Thee, then let their horses teach them better."

As he spoke, the horses fell to their knees and remained there, unable to be coaxed upward, until the sermon was over.

Francis di Girolama lived from 1642-1716. He was canonized in 1838. He is celebrated on May 11th. The accounts of his life are recorded by Cardinal Wiseman.

Second Wind

Maybe Audaldus wasn't meant to be a hermit. Youthful idealism first encouraged him to settle as a hermit in the Pyrenees mountains. In time, he grew weary of a solitary life and resolved to abandon his efforts and return to the world. He proceeded to bid adieux to Saint Pancras, his master, and informed him of his decision but while his hand was on Pancras' cell door, he heard the old man praying,

"Give him strength my Lord, that he may not fail and may finish his course with joy."

Instantly a peal of thunder burst over the cell and a brilliant light, like a star, settled on the head of Saint Pancras. Terrified, the young hermit abandoed his plans for a worldly life and threw himself to the ground, imploring the heavens for guidance. Filled with newfound joy, he retired further into the desert and disciplined his silent life with even greater vigor.

This story is given in the religious historic records of France, May 12.

Mysterious Lady

Nothing was different about this fine spring morning of May 13, 1917. Just another routine day tending sheep for Lucy Abobara, age ten, and her two cousins Francisco and Jacinta Marto, age nine and seven. Then, unexpectedly, out of a clear azure sky a brilliant flash of light appeared. Fearing a storm might be forming, the children hurried to gather the grazing sheep into the shelter. Then another flash erupted, this time closer and more intense. Suddenly above the branches of a tiny oak tree, an angel materialized, "the most beautiful lady they had ever seen."

"It was," writes Lucy, "a lady dressed all in white, more brilliant than the sun, shedding rays of light clearer and stronger than a crystal glass filled with the most sparkling water and pierced by the burning rays of the sun."

Their first impulse was to run, but the lady beckoned, "Do not be afraid, I will not hurt you."

After a long pause, as the children gazed in silence, Lucy found the courage to break the spell. "Where do you come from?" she asked.

The beautiful lady had now won their hearts with her smile.

"I come from heaven," she replied.

"Why have you come down here?" asked Lucy with the directness of a child.

"Because I want you all to return here on the thirteenth day of each month," said the lady. "In October, I will tell you who I am and what I want you to do."

"Do you really come from heaven?" asked Lucy. "Shall I go to heaven too?"

"Yes, you will go there," the lady replied.

"And Jacinta and Francisco?" she asked again, growing more confident with each passing moment.

"Yes, Jacinta will go to heaven and Francisco too, but first he will have to say many rosaries."

They spoke for some time further, until the heavenly lady insisted, "Go my children, and say the rosary as you have done in the past. Come again on the thirteenth day of next month."

So saying, she hovered over the ground, moving toward the east, then melted into the sunlight.

On the thirteenth day of every month the children came to the spot again and met with their new heavenly friend. In October, as she had promised, she revealed her identity (see October 13th). On that day, in the presence of forty thousand witnesses, the miracles of Fatima were documented.

Nocturnal Edification

Day by day, little by little, Saint Arey, Bishop of Gap, waxed in spiritual strength and wisdom. Probus, his contemporary and biographer recorded his observations. During the hours when all the others slept, Saint Arey would remain ravished in meditation before the church altar. During these vigils he was lifted high into the air by a gathering of angels. Here he would remain suspended, until the time he chose to break off his divine meditation. Probus further adds that at such moments, the whole church was ablaze with celestial light.

Arey lived from A.D. 535-604. His life is recorded in Histoire Hagiologique du Diocese de Gap.

Slander Disproved

Why would anyone want to criticize Mary Toribia? She was a beautiful woman, with an almost magical glow around her and a seemingly endless capacity to love. She was the bride of Saint Isidore (See May 10th), and was, on one occasion, falsely accused of unfaithfulness at a public assembly.

Looking to her husband, she remarked, "I perceive, my beloved, by your countenance that this slander distresses you, but I am innocent. In proof whereof I am ready to pass over the River Xamara, trusting in God to clear me of this foul imputation."

So saying, in the presence of her husband, several ecclesiastics and hundreds of her neighbors, she spread her cloak upon the river, sat upon it, and crossed over and back again in perfect safety, without getting a bit wet.

Isidore and his wife Mary (Santa Maria de la Cabeza) are celebrated together on May 15th. Acta Sanctorum, Volume III.

More Apparitions

"My children, I, your Most Holy Mother, have come to ask for peace and for that purpose, I speak in many places over the entire world."

These were the words received by three children from Terra Blanca, Mexico who have reputedly seen apparitions of the Virgin Mary since as early as 1987. The children belong to the same family and the two girls, Elba (age 14) and Zendia (age 11) record the messages themselves, on paper, despite the fact that they have received almost no education.

The Mexican people of Terra Blanca are isolated from the rest of the world and live in extreme poverty. However, there the apparitions have been occurring and, thus far, indications lead to their full authenticity. The messages are similar to those of Medjugorje and other modern-day apparitions. The Mexican people are being urged to pray, particularly the rosary, go to confession, read the Bible and fast. As there is great malnutrition in the area, the Virgin has limited the requirements for fasting to an abstinence from salt rather than daily food.

This account is one among numerous similar accounts occurring throughout the world in over thirty countries.

Further information may be obtained through the writings of Fr. Rene Laurentin or the Pittsburgh Center For Peace.

Two Angels

The Second Book of Hermes, called Commands:

Command VI. 7-12: And now, says he, understand first of all what belongs to faith. There are two angels with man: one of righteousness, the other of iniquity. And I said unto him: Sir how shall I know that there are two such angels with man? Hear, says he, and understand. The angel of righteousness, is mild and modest and gentle and quiet. When, therefore, he gets into thy heart, immediately he talks with thee of righteousness, of modesty, of chastity, of bountifulness, of forgiveness, of charity, and of piety. When all these things come into thy heart, know then that the angel of righteousness is with thee. Wherefore hearken to this angel and to his works. Learn also the works of the angel of iniquity. He is first of all bitter, angry, and foolish, and his works are pernicious. . . When, therefore, these things come into thy heart; thou shalt know by his works, that this is the angel of iniquity.

The foregoing narrative is taken from the manuscripts edited from the Bible by Its compilers, the Council of Nice. In the early days of the church, the book from which this excerpt is taken was read aloud publicly, along with the other works of the New Testament.

Desert Fathers

"Fetch the cloak given to you by Athanasius of Alexandria!"

These were the last words Antony ever heard from Paul, the Egyptian hermit. Antony at once obeyed his command and set out to retrieve the cloak, expecting that at any moment the hermit might depart from this world. He returned with the cloak in hand, and, as he neared the entrance to Paul's cave, he was suddenly transfixed by a vision. The sky above him was filled with angels and prophets. They were carrying to heaven the spirit of Paul which "was shining like the sun and of pure white hue."

Antony, who was over ninety years of age, raced like a young child and entered the cave where he found the hermit's body kneeling with his hands stretched out. Full of joy and supposing him yet alive, he knelt to pray with him, but by his silence soon perceived he was dead. Wrapping the cloak around his dear friend, he stood perplexed for a moment. Then without warning, two lions suddenly entered the cave. Responding to the danger, Antony stepped away, but the wild beasts showed that they meant him no harm. They sniffed the hermit's dead body, then retreating a small distance, and proceeded to scratch a deep hole in the ground.

When the hole was large enough to act as a grave, the industrious beasts twisted their tails around the body, transported it to the hole and covered it with earth. When their task was complete, they moved mournfully to Saint Antony, lowered their heads and licked his hands and feet. Antony gave them a blessing and they returned from whence they had come.

Saint Paul the hermit lived for a hundred and thirteen years, until A.D. 342 This account is given in a biography by Saint Jerome.

Pena De Francia

Simon Vela was the only son of a wealthy and prominent family in France. Though endowed with all the privileges of aristocracy, he was disinterested in the turmoils of politics and business and would frequently sink into sadness or depression, being bored with life.

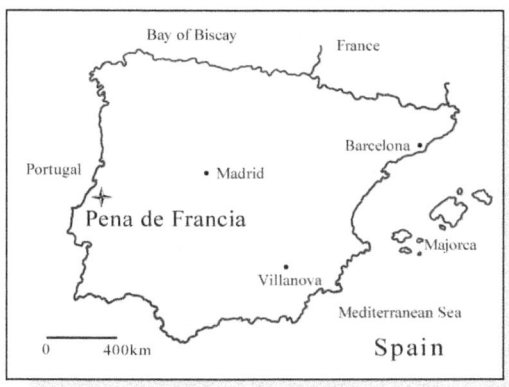

But this was not to last. One evening, which was like any other, he was aroused from his bed by a celestial voice:

"Simon do not sleep. Go to Pena de Francia. In that area where the sun sets, you will find an image of the blessed Virgin. This holy image will be the object of great devotion."

Bursting with zeal, Simon lost no time. He had never heard of this region, Pena de Francia, but he was sure it must be in the western slopes of Spain so it was there that he directed his steps.

For five long and weary years, he continued his quest, but there was nothing to be found. He began to believe he had hallucinated and finally, with his hopes exhausted, he abandoned his mission.

Then again, unexpectedly, the divine voice aroused him during the night:

"Simon, do not stop. A great reward awaits a great sacrifice, and yours will he great."

Simon's enthusiasm had been renewed and his search continued. This time he covered more territory, asking everyone he met for knowledge of a spot called Pena de Francia. Nothing. Always nothing.

He had covered the entire region of western Spain and still, nothing. Again he thought to abandon his quest. But the voice was so real. How could he ignore it?

It was May 1534, when Simon reached Salamanca. He was on his way to visit the professors at the university when he encountered two vendors arguing about the quality of the coal they were selling. One claimed his products were superior because they had been taken from the slopes of Pena de Francia.

At last! It was real! Pena de Francia did exist!

He followed the man to his home, a village at the foot of the slopes of Pena de Francia. That night he dreamed. In his dream he saw a vision of the spot where the image of the Virgin was buried. The following morning he made his plans. He could hardly wait to reach the area when suddenly the divine voice spoke again. This time he was told to proceed to the mountain with witnesses. So Simon returned to the village and employed the assistance of four prominent men including the Notary Public.

Finally, on May 19, 1534, the five men removed a large stone from the spot which Simon had seen in the vision. There it lay. The beautiful image of the *Virgin of Pena de Francia*. Each man was instantly ravished with blessings and could hardly contain his cries. Each was restored from bodily infirmities or weaknesses to health. One man regained his hearing, another recovered from defects of birth. Their rapture was inexhaustible. But for Simon, only one thing mattered. His heart was at peace. His mission was completed.

The miracles accredited to this image are too numerous to mention. This account is given in the original documents preserved in the archives of San Martin de Castanar, the village at the foot of Pena de Francia.

Something New

Saint Bernardino loved to travel so much that he practically walked the whole of Italy. Throughout his journeys the people he met spoke of him as a priest with a "new knowledge," which captured the spirit of life rather than its laws.

Nevertheless there were those who took exception to his teaching and accused him of superstitious practices. He was denounced to Pope Martin V, who, for a time, commanded him to keep silent. However, an examination of his doctrine and conduct led to a complete vindication, and he received permission to preach wherever he liked. The same Pope, in 1427, urged him to accept the bishopric of Siena, but he refused on the claim that his true calling was the life of a missionary.

Not unlike Christ, Bernardino walked upon the sea. Once needing to pass over a waterway in order to arrive at Mantua, he threw his cloak on the surface of the water and standing on it, was conveyed across without getting wet.

In the spring of 1444, near his sixty-fourth birthday, though obviously dying, he continued his travels and set out for Naples. He never reached there. However, for his strength gave out and he died on May 20th, while teaching his "new knowledge."

Saint Bernardino was originally buried in the church of Saint Francis, but twenty-seven years later was transferred to a newly erected church dedicated to him. His body was discovered to be perfectly preserved and was put in a crystal reliquary and later placed inside a silver sarcophagus. His body has been examined as recently as 1968 and declared to be incorrupt. Saint Bernardino was canonized in 1450. He is celebrated on May 20th. His life is recorded in Life of Saint Bernardino, by Barnaby of Siena, his contemporary.

Holy Candle

In 1105 a frightful disease called the "Fire of Ardent" broke out in Arotis, France. It was a terrible scourge, similar to the Black Plague of the fourteenth century, and decimated a major part of western Europe. It visited equally the mansions of the rich

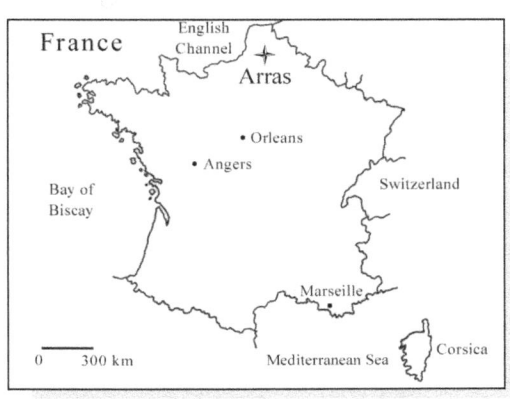

and cabins of the poor, old and young, male and female. The disease attacked body parts which grew black as coal and fell into powder. Hands rotted from wrists and feet from ankles.

In the midst of this epidemic, on May 21st of that year, a mysterious event occurred. An apparition of the Virgin Mary appeared to two men named Itier and Norman who were sworn bitter enemies. She appeared only long enough to instruct them to contact the Bishop of Arras and command him to meet with them in the church that same evening. They were told to remain fully awake in prayer until the cock crowed the following morning, at which time she would appear again. They did this, and at the appointed moment the Virgin appeared. She descended through the roof of the church carrying a lighted candle.

"I confide this taper to your charge," she declared. "Take it as a gauge of my compassion. It shall be for the healing of the people."

She then gave them the candle and vanished. In the days that followed, the three chosen ones gathered three large vessels of water and let fall a single drop of wax into each one. As instructed, the water was distributed for the healing of the sick. It was taken internally or used as a lotion and by the end of the first day, one hundred forty-four medically unexplainable cures were recorded. Later, Itier and Norman founded the society, "The Charity of Our Lady of Ardents," whose duty it was to distribute the holy water. Soon after this time, the plague was arrested.

The miracle of the holy candle is celebrated throughout Europe. Apparently this relic has survived the passage of time, including two world wars, and is presently enshrined in Arras, France.

Breaking the Rules

Magarita de Cascia (Rita) lived a simple respectable domestic life and it was all she really wanted. However, her married life proved disappointing. Eighteen years of sorrowful submissions to a veritable brute of a husband finally ended in widowhood. With

no one to care for her, she applied for acceptance to the local convent of Saint Mary Magdalene. Unfortunately she was refused, because it was contrary to the rules of the convent to admit any but virgins.

Three times she applied, begging to be admitted in any capacity, but three times the prioress reluctantly refused. However, on the evening of her third refusal, an unusual event occurred. An apparition of Saint Augustine (A.D. 430), Saint Nicholas de Tolentino (1306), and John the Baptist appeared before the convent sisters aiming to reform their conventions. With full pomp and ceremony, they threw open the convent doors and announced her introduction, "Magarita de Cascia." Needless to say, all rules and formalities were dismissed and she was wholeheartedly accepted.

Forty-four years later, on May 22, 1457, Rita died. Her body has remained miraculously incorrupt until modern times.

Magarita de Cascia is celebrated on May 22nd. This story is given in the Acta Sanctorum, Volume V.

Espoused

Born in 1027 at Troyes, Saint Robert Champagne was the founder of the great monasteries of Molesmes and Citeaux. We are told that shortly before his birth, his mother, Ermangarde, was blessed with a vision of the Virgin Mary.

The Virgin gave Ermangarde a mystical gold ring and instructed, "I wish the son which you now carry in your womb to be betrothed to me. Take this ring and be assured that he will be my spouse."

Hence, throughout his life Robert was called the "Spouse of Mary."

Robert Champagne lived until 1111. He was canonized in 1222. The accounts of his life are recorded in the Acta Sanctorum, Bollandists.

Odor of Sancity

May 24, A.D. 727, marks the passing of Saint Hubert of Liege, the principle disciple of Saint Lambert of Maastricht. It was on that day, at the same moment his soul lifted from its body, that an intoxicatingly sweet odor diffused the entire countryside of Brittany. His biographers describe this fragrance as being "so sweet, it seemed God had combined all the perfumes of all the sweet-scented flowers of spring to symbolize the depth of his internal sanctity." This account and many more like it fill the volumes of the *Acta Sanctorum*.

This phenomenon, common at the death of a saint is called "The Odor of Sanctity." Acta Sanctorum, Volume VII.

Coat Hanger

Saint Leonorus of Brittany is well remembered for the many divine favors granted him. Among them, the following account is most popular:

It once happened that King Childebert requested Leonorus to celebrate the divine mysteries before him and his court. The king's servant graciously consented and prepared to do so. Before robbing himself with the priestly ornaments, he pulled off his cloak and searched for a place to hang it. As circumstance would have it, nothing was available. However, in the moment that followed, a ray of sun burst through the window of the vestry. To the astonishment of the entire royal assembly, he hung his cloak on the ray as if it were a coat hanger. We are told it remained suspended by the beam of light until he put it on again later.

Saint Leonorus of Brittany lived from A.D. 509-560. In historic art, he is depicted hanging his cloak on a sunbeam. This account is given in Lives of the Saints of Brittany, *by Dom Lobineau.*

Heart

Philip Neri was bored to death with commonplace life. As far as he was concerned, life was shallow and material. So at age eighteen he set out for Rome, without money or plans, trusting entirely in divine providence.

In Rome he lived like a recluse for two years, spending whole days and nights in meditation. Later he took up classes in philosophy and theology and worked with such diligence that he was regarded as a promising scholar. But in time he outgrew his books and, giving them up, took to the streets of Rome to live among the common man. It was there that a series of mystical experiences occurred to him.

One evening, while fervently praying, a globe of fire appeared before him. It entered his mouth and a moment afterwards he felt his chest dilating.

Instantly he was filled with such paroxysms of divine love that he rolled upon the ground exclaiming, "Enough, Lord, I can bear no more!"

When he rose and was more composed, he discovered a swelling as big as a man's fist in the region of his heart. This swelling remained with him for the rest of his life and, at times, the emotional fervor which it ignited was so consuming it obliged him to bare his breast to relieve the heat it generated. In those moments he prayed that God would lessen his blessings before he died of excess love. His face would shine with a mysterious light, and often he was transfixed in heavenly bliss and unable to lower his arms. Occasionally in these ecstasies he was seen lifted off the ground, his body weightless and buoyant. On other occasions, not only did his face shine with light, but real sparks of fire flew from his eyes.

Finally, at the age of eighty, he laid down his body to die with the words, "Last of all, we must die."

After Philip's death it was discovered that two of his ribs were broken and had formed an arch, enlarging the normal space for the heart. He lived from 1515-1595 and was canonized in 1622. His body rests in the Chiesa Nuova where it remains miraculously incorrupt. He is celebrated on May 26th. His life is recorded in Life of Saint Philip of Neri, *by Father Antony Galonio.*

Humble Opinion

Richard of Wyche was a man of firmly resolved principles. He was literally addicted to study from childhood and retained this avocation throughout his life. Although renowned for his gift of miracles, he maintained the humblest opinion of himself

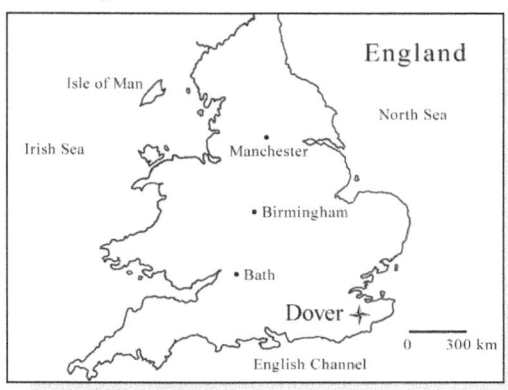

Never would he consider asking God for any personal benefit.

With regard to the many miracles he performed, the majority were conducted at the request or suggestion of other people. One such miracle occurred whenever Richard was asked to distribute food. Be assured that a single loaf of bread, distributed by Richard, would satisfy in excess of three thousand people, which it did on more than one occasion. Despite his modest opinion of himself, he was emulated and revered by many. And although he was regarded as a saint in his own time, it was a reputation he preferred to live without.

At the early age of fifty-five, he died in the humblest of places, a house for poor pilgrims on the shores of Dover. Nine years later he was canonized.

Saint Richard lived from 1197-1253. The accounts of his life are recorded in The Legends of England by J Capprave.

Legend of Saint Bernard

Bernard of Montjour was an Italian priest to whom numerous Alpine travelers owe their lives. He lived during the eleventh century and visited the most remote regions of the Alps, establishing guest houses along the passes which subsequently bore his name. Later, the famous breed of dog trained to rescue travelers from avalanches was named after him. His legend is as follows:

Together with nine other pilgrims, he ascended a mountain in the Alps which was feared to be inhabited by a dragon-like creature called "The Giant." When the company neared the cave of the creature, it charged, terrifying the pilgrims who fled for their lives. Bernard, however, stood firm. When the monster approached to devour him, he swiftly encircled its neck with his scarf. Instantly the cloth scarf was transformed into an iron chain. Yet the two ends held in the hands of the saint remained as cloth. The moment the monster was subdued, the pilgrims rushed in and finished its life. The body was later transported to a cave near the abbey of Saint Maurice-en-Valais where it is buried. There also, the two ends of the scarf are preserved.

Richard de la Val d'Isere, successor of Bernard of Montjour, was a witness of the event and has declared it to be one of sober historical fact.

Saint Bernard lived from 996-1081. He is celebrated on May 28th, as patron of mountaineers. His legends are recorded in the Acta Sanctorum, Volume III.

Our Lady of Deols

During the twelfth century, France was overrun with highwaymen and cutthroats, many of whom were peasants who had been called away as soldiers. On May 29, 1187, a number of these aimless peasants were gambling outside the gates of the chapel of Deols where a statue of the Madonna and Child stood. One of the gamesters, having lost his money, likewise lost his temper. In a rage, he flung a rock at the image, which broke off the arm of the child. No sooner had he done so, when a stream of blood poured forth, forming a pool on the earth below. At the same moment the infamous gamester was struck with instantaneous madness.

John Lackland and Adhemar, Viscount of Limoges, ran to the scene, having heard the commotion. Though greatly disturbed they carefully collected the blood to the best of their ability. After a brief investigation of the event, the blood was taken to a chapel in England and dedicated to the Madonna. The number of cures effected by this blood are too numerous to calculate and before the year had ended, a confraternity was established to commemorate *Our Lady of Deols*.

This account was recorded by Rigord, an historian and contemporary.

Joan of Arc

Jeanne la Pucelle, or Joan of Arc, as she is known to the English speaking world, accomplished what no woman before her had done. She was born in Domremy, January 6, 1412, to a family of farmers, so there was little practical need for the children to learn to read or write.

"In sewing and spinning I fear no women," said Joan proudly.

She was conscientious, loved by everyone in the village but was as ordinary as any child her age. Yet this simple girl, in her fourteenth year, received by divine revelation a mission so great, it would have seemed too ambitious for the greatest military general of that time. She, a simple peasant girl, was to save France!

The first of her revelations appeared to her as a single voice emanating from a blaze of light. But afterwards, the voices increased in number and she was able to see and identify her celestial companions. Saint Michael, Saint Catherine and Saint Margaret were a few of the many who entrusted Joan with the mission of leading the French military forces to victory against the oppressive English battalions.

Many times Joan protested against this mission saying, "I am a poor girl who can neither ride nor fight!"

But the voices gave her no rest, "It is God who commands it," they would say.

Unable to resist this call, she secretly left home and sought council with the heir to the throne of France. Clothing herself in male dress to protect herself, she pressed the royal court until at last she gained audience with Prince Charles. It was not easy to communicate the supernatural nature of her mission, but she succeeded.

Six weeks after her first meeting with the king, she mounted his charger clad in white armor and led the troops to victory against the English at Orleans. Each event transpired according to the prophesies she had foretold. Her second encounter was equally successful, the

English forces suffered a crushing defeat at Patay. On July 17, 1429, Charles VII was solemnly crowned King of France with Joan standing at his side, her standard in hand.

Her mission was complete. Her celestial companions informed her that soon she would be with them in heaven. And so it was. In less than two years, with the most ignoble betrayal and ingratitude from both church and state, she was abandoned and allowed to be sold to the English leaders who sought only to publicly denounce and humiliate her. Her execution was a foregone conclusion, and she was sentenced to be burned at the stake as a witch. She was not yet twenty years old.

It is the opinion of this author that no crime against humanity is worse than the persecution of saints. On that execution day the people of the city of Rauen cried out, "We are lost! We have burned a saint!"

Joan of Arc was canonized on May 16, 1920. She is celebrated on May 30th. This story emerges from the text of the original documents of her trial.

Perfect Balance

Over fifteen hundred years after Christ first established his Holy Church, the first teaching order of women, the Ursulines, was established by Angela Merici. She was a remarkable woman, a perfect balance of romance, practicality, creativity and discipline, who was favored with miracles throughout her life.

On one occasion, having returned to Brescia, Italy after the treaty of Cambrai in 1529, she attended the "Holy Sacrifice" and was suddenly and involuntarily entranced. She was elevated high above the ground, in plain sight of everyone present and remained suspended there for a "great length of time."

The sheer delight of this miracle enraptured the crowd, but it was no surprise to the citizens of Brescia, for they had long before venerated her as a prophetess and saint.

Saint Angela Merici lived from 1474-1540. Her incorrupt body may be seen in the Casa S. Angela in Brescia, Italy. She was canonized in 1807 and is celebrated on May 31st. Her life is recorded in Les Petits Bollandistes, Volume VI.

June

1 Thomas' Gospel
2 Saint Elmo's Fire
3 Unburned Candles
4 Danger Averted
5 Brothers
6 Healing Touch
7 Pastoral Staff
8 Mark the Boundary
9 Vision of Moses
10 As You Sow
11 Our Lady of Aranzazu
12 Outspoken
13 Rimini Linguist
14 Remarkable Encounter
15 Angelic Companion
16 Unreasonable Request
17 Coast of Dunbar
18 I Shall Not Speak
19 Hide and Seek
20 A Hero
21 Every Bit of Silver
22 Hermit's Dwelling
23 Chief Cook
24 Medjugorje
25 Tears of Love
26 Fountain of Saint Firmatus
27 Arms of Angels
28 Love Story
29 Doubting Peter
30 Fisherman and Knight

Thomas' Gospel

II. Infancy. Chapter I.

I, Thomas, an Israelite, judged it necessary to make known to our brethren among the Gentiles, the actions and miracles of Christ in his childhood, which our Lord and God Jesus Christ wrought after his birth in Bethlehem in our country, at which I myself was astonished; the beginning of which was as followeth. 2. When the child Jesus was five years of age and there had been a shower of rain, which was now over, Jesus was playing with other Hebrew boys by a running stream, and the water running over the banks stood in little lakes. 3. But the water instantly became clear and useful again; he having smote them only by his word, they readily obeyed him. 4. Then he took from the bank of the stream some soft clay and formed out of it twelve sparrows, and there were other boys playing with him. 5. But a certain Jew seeing the things which he was doing, namely, his forming clay into the figures of sparrows on the Sabbath day, went presently away, and told his father Joseph, and said, 6. Behold, thy boy is playing by the river side, and has taken clay, and formed it into twelve sparrows, and profaneth the Sabbath. 7. Then Joseph came to the place where he was, and when he saw him, called to him, and said, "Why dost thou do that which is not lawful to do on the Sabbath day?" 8. Then Jesus clapping together the palms of his hands, called the sparrows and said to them: "Go, flyaway, and while ye live remember me." 9. So the sparrows fled away, making a noise. 10. The Jews seeing this, were astonished and went away, and told their chief persons what a strange miracle they had seen wrought by Jesus.

What is transcribed here is taken from the original manuscripts edited from the Bible by its compilers, the Council of Nice, under the direction of Emperor Constantine (fourth century). It is deemed apocryphal.

Saint Elmo's Fire

Saint Adelem (Elmo) possessed the spirit of a warrior. He was an extremely determined and outgoing man who demanded as much from himself as he did from his disciples. The famous legend of Saint Elmo's Fire is as follows.

Saint Elmo set out to visit Ranco, Bishop of Auvergne, on a violently stormy night. Unable to see in the darkness he lit a candle, which he handed to his disciple and requested, "Lead on!" The disciple was more than a little surprised. Did Elmo really expect an unprotected candle to remain lit in such a storm, he thought? But despite his many doubts, the howling gusts and torrents of rainfall, the candle remained inextinguishable and unaffected by the storm. Thus began the legend of Saint Elmo's fire—the inextinguishable light which conquers the darkness.

Saint Elmo's fire was later associated with the electric lights seen above the mastheads of ships before and after thunderstorms. This account is given in Life of Saint Adelem, by Saint Rudolf A.D. 1130.

Unburned Candles

John Grande seemed to be born a monk. He was a native of Carmona in Andalusia, Spain, but he was unlike the playful boys of the field. In early childhood he was a volunteer in the parish church, whose duty it was to light the candles on the altar. Though still in his early boyhood he would often spend many hours sitting in silent meditation after the celebration of Mass. It was a terrible inconvenience to the sacristan, whose duty it was to clear the altar, so one evening he scolded the young boy for wasting the candles with his long meditations.

"Blame me not," said the boy. "Do you not see that the candles, though they burn, diminish not?"

The sacristan observed closely and finding the boy to be right, called others to witness the spectacle. Time after time, they kept watch on the candles, and time after time, even the most skeptic among them was forced to admit that the candles did not diminish. Thereafter, John Grande was regarded a young saint.

John Grande lived from 1546-1600. His life is recorded in Les Petits Bollandistes, Volume VI.

Danger Averted

Lutgardis was hardly twelve years old when the Virgin Mother first appeared to her. She was lifted in spirit and found herself at the feet of the virgin Mother. But to her surprise the Blessed Mother looked sad. Her garments were neglected and black, as if soiled by soot. Young Lutgardis demanded to know how the queen of heaven, bright as the sun and fair as the moon, was so cast down.

"My affliction," replied the Holy Mother, "comes from those who speak blasphemies against my son. They crucify him afresh and breed unheard-of evils on this earth. I come to tell you, Lutgardis, you must fast for seven years to avert these dangers for mankind. Take no nourishment but bread and water and let your eyes never be dry of tears."

So inspired, Lutgardis observed this fast, during which time she was frequently visited by the Divine Mother. When the seventh year concluded, she was compelled by a vision of Jesus to continue her fast for seven more years.

"This fast I enjoin for the sins of the world, to reconcile God," said Christ. Thus divinely inspired, she observed this fast with ease. Such was her merit for delivering souls, that in the midst of her prayers, her doubtless confidence was revealed with the command, "Either erase my name from the book of life, or rescue this man from sin at my intercession." We are told her prayers were granted.

Lutgardis lived during the thirteenth century. This account is given in Life of St. Lutgardis by Thomas de Cantimpre.

Brothers

Faustinus and Jovita were brothers, nobly born and natives of Brescia, Italy. According to tradition, they were initiated in the name of Christ, fearlessly, while their bishop lay in hiding. For those were the days when Emperor Hadrian had renewed the Christian persecutions begun by Trajan. The zeal of the noble brothers excited the fury of the Romans who arrested them and locked them away. Refusing to renounce their beliefs, they were sentenced to be devoured by lions in the public arena.

The amphitheater was filled to capacity when four lions, leopards and bears were let loose against the brothers, but the expected execution did not occur. The beasts assumed an attitude as gentle as sheep and lay down beside the brothers, licking their feet. Soldiers were dispatched to enrage the beasts by burning their flanks, but as they approached, the animals became wild again and devoured their tormentors. The unshakable constancy of these two noble men, and the mysterious power which calmed the beasts in their favor, so impressed the court officials, that they, along with twelve thousand other citizens of Brescia, sought out Bishop Apollonius in hiding and begged to be instructed in his teaching. Many of these new converts were also persecuted but refused to renounce their faith.

Faustinus and Jovita lived until A. D. 121. This story is given by Saint Calocerus, later martyred, who was present in the amphitheater as a guest of Emperor Hadrian.

Healing Touch

Saint Galla was particularly renowned for her healing touch, but she would not heal everyone who came to her for help. She once entered a house filled with sick and lame folk who were patiently waiting with hopes of being healed. Among the gathering was a child both deaf and dumb. Saint Galla was compassionately moved by the sincerity of the young girl, so requesting a glass of water, she blessed it and gave it to the child to drink. In the words of those present, "Her ears were immediately opened and the string of her tongue let loose."

Saint Galla lived until A.D. 550. Her life is recorded in the Acta Sanctorum, Volume III.

Pastoral Staff

After the battle of Hastings, William the Conqueror seized rulership of England, and in an attempt to control its people, he filled the religious seats of dignity with his own loyalists. In so doing, he ordered Wulfstan, Bishop of Worcester, to yield his pastoral staff and ring to Gundulf, whose loyalty he trusted. Wulfstan had been appointed by King Edward the Confessor.

When he heard of his deposition, he rose from his seat and walked to the tomb of the deceased king declaring, "Thou knowest, O my master, how reluctantly I received this staff at thy bidding, but now we have a new king, a new law and a new archbishop, who found new rights and declares new sentences. They convict thee, O saintly king, of error for appointing me to the See of Worcester, and me, in presumption, for accepting the dignity. Not to them, but to thee only can I resign my staff. Not to those who walk in darkness, but to thee who has escaped the region of ignorance and error."

So saying, he struck his pastoral staff into the sepulchral stone and laying aside his episcopal robes, seated himself among the common monks. The assembly was astonished to see that the pastoral staff had pierced deeply into the solid stone as though it were made of soft clay.

The news reached the archbishop almost immediately, but not believing the report, he dispatched Gundulf to retrieve the staff. However, try as he might, Gundulf could not budge it. On hearing the report the king and archbishop themselves came to the chapter house to wrench out the staff. But they, likewise, could not remove it.

Convinced of the miracle, the archbishop addressed the assembly saying, "Verily, God resisteth the proud, but giveth grace to the humble and meek. Thy simplicity, brother, was scorned by us, but thy righteousness is exalted. Keep the bishopric over which God himself has made thee the overseer, for God hath sealed thee by miracle to the holy office."

Approaching the archbishop, Wulfstan placed his hand on his familiar staff and without the slightest resistance, removed it from the stone.

Wulfstan lived during the eleventh century. He was canonized in 1203 and is celebrated on June 7th. This story is given by Wendover and Caprave.

Mark the Boundary

Saint Medard, Bishop of Vermandois, was a man of deeds and not words. He could be trusted to get the job done, and, with his remarkable mind for details, he was a fair and honest judge. It happened that two farmers from Picardy, bitterly quarreling about the boundaries of their respective lands, applied to Saint Medard to settle their dispute. Medard patiently reviewed their various complaints, then resolved the matter by having a large stone brought to mark the boundary. To give greater authority to his judgement, he set his foot on the stone and a deep impression remained there as if it were made of wax. There it remained for the world to witness.

Saint Medard lived during the sixth century. He is celebrated on June 8th. The accounts of his life are recorded in the Acta Sanctorum, Volume II.

Vision of Moses

1. Now Moses kept the flock of Jethro his father-in-law, priest of Midian, and he led his flock to the west side of the desert, and came to Horeb, the mountain of God. 2. And the angel of the Lord appeared to him in a flame of fire out of the midst of a bush, and he looked, the bush was burning, yet it was not consumed. 3. And Moses said, "I will turn aside and inspect this great sight, why the bush is not burned." 4. And when the Lord saw that he turned aside to see, God called to him out of the midst of the bush, "Moses, Moses!" And he said, "Here am I." 5. And the Lord said, "Come not near; put off thy shoes from thy feet, for the place whereon thou standeth is holy ground." 6. Moreover he said, "I am the God of thy father, the God of Abraham, the God of Isaac, and the God of Jacob." And Moses hid his face; for he was afraid to look upon God. . . . 10. "Come, I will send you to Pharaoh that you may bring forth my people, the sons of Israel, out of Egypt." 11. But Moses said to God, "Who am I that I should go to the Pharaoh and bring the sons of Israel out of Egypt?" 12. To this God said, "Because I shall prove to be with you, and this is the sign for you that it is I who have sent you. After you have brought the people out of Egypt, you shall serve God upon this mountain." 13. And Moses said unto God, "Behold, when I come unto the children of Israel, and shall say unto them, The God of your fathers hath sent me unto you, and they shall say to me, What is his name? what shall I say unto them?" 14. And God said unto Moses, "I AM THAT I AM," and he said, "Thus shalt thou say unto the children of Israel, I AM hath sent me unto you."

The Old Testament of the Bible, Exodus III.

As You Sow

It was common for miracle seekers to find their way to the home of Bridget, the Patron saint of Ireland. Her reputation had reached all parts of the country and much of her day was spent attending to those who had journeyed to receive her blessings. On one such visit, she was unexpectedly confronted by two lepers beseeching to be healed of their leprosy. Moved by their pleas she consented to do her utmost but warned that they must have faith in the goodness of God. Then making the sign of the cross over a basin of water, she told each leper to wash the other therewith. The first, washed by his companion, found that his leprosy had entirely disappeared. But in fear of recontamination, he refused to render the like service to his still leprous friend. Instantly his leprosy returned to him, and likewise, his unwashed companion was instantly made clean. If there could be a moral to this story, certainly it would have to be, "As you sow, so shall you reap."

Saint Bridget lived from A. D. 453-523. This account was recorded by Cardinal Baronius, in the Roman Martyrology.

Our Lady of Aranzazu

It happened on Saturday, June 11, 1469. Rodrigo de Baltaztequi, a young shepherd, the son of a carpenter from Onate, was tending his sheep in the mountains of Alona, Spain. It was like any other day, when suddenly a shining image of a beautiful lady holding an infant in her arms, appeared before him.

The vision was only momentary but lasted long enough for the Lady to say, "My son, tell your father to build on this site a tiny shrine of five thin boards and seven tiles. You will call this shrine Aranzazu. I assure you it will be famous in time and a great number of my children will come here to honor me with songs of praise and attend Holy masses."

Overjoyed, Rodrigo did as he was told, and his father obeyed also. But in a few days, while again tending his sheep, a second event occurred. He was startled by the mysterious sound of a bell ringing. "What person could possibly have found his way to this mountain place without my noticing," he thought. He followed the mysterious sound and was led to a thorn tree with a strangely curved trunk. The bell was hanging from the trunk and ringing of its own accord. Further, on top of the tree was a magnificent stone statue of the Madonna and Child, just as Rodrigo had seen them in his earlier vision.

He took the beautiful statue to the tiny shrine erected by his father and just as the vision had foretold, Aranzazu (which means "a hidden mountainous place with thorny plants") grew to be a famous spot of pilgrimage.

After years of investigation, the statue discovered by Rodrigo was sanctioned under the title Our Lady of Aranzazu.

Outspoken

Saint John of Sahagun was a man who spoke his mind, a characteristic which didn't win a large following of friends. He was glorified by many miracles, both during his life and after death. He had a remarkable talent for reading the thoughts of others and employed it admirably to end many social feuds—the bane of society at the time. His biographers tell us that during his residence in Spain he flew. He would lift high in the air and remain suspended in prayer until the time that he chose to return to the ground. Occasionally the entire evening would pass and the saint would remain afloat. However, John's life was not free of worldly complications. His outspokenness resulted in many enemies, and it is believed that his unnatural death by poison was the work of a promiscuous woman, vexed by his interference in her love life. It was but one of many assassination attempts on his life.

John of Sahagun lived from 1430-1419. He was canonized in 1690. He is celebrated on June 12th. Acta Sanctorum, Volume III.

Rimini Linguist

Saint Antony was born in 1195. The documentations of this remarkable saint are vast, and it was known to many of his contemporaries that he possessed a truly miraculous gift of speech. On many occasions thousands of people, representing numerous nations, gathered to hear him preach. What language he spoke we may never know, for every faction reported that he was "notably eloquent" in their native tongue. Among the many miraculous accounts of this saint, the following remains most unforgettable.

While preaching in Rimini, the saint found the hearts of the people obstinately closed to his message of love.

Rising from his chair he cried, "Let those who like follow me to the sea shore."

Here he cried aloud over the waters, "Ye fishes of the sea, hear! For man, though the image of his Maker, is like the deaf adder and refuses to harken to his God. To you, therefore, I announce the gospel of salvation."

Instantly, from the depths of the sea, schools of fish, from the miniscule to the gigantic thronged to the shore. From every side they arrived in countless numbers, crowding thick upon each other, their heads above the water and their eyes turned toward the preacher who spoke the following words:

"What acts of thankfulness, O fishes, ought you not to render to Him who has given you to live in this mighty ocean? It is to God you owe those deep retreats, which protect you from the raging storm. When the great flood destroyed the families of men, God preserved you. It is you who saved the prophet Jonah. It is you who brought the gold to Saint Peter and the Lord of glory. You receive your life, your food, your protection from God and God alone. Praise Him seas and magnify him forever. Praise him ye whales and all that move in the waters. Bless ye the Lord. Praise him and magnify him forever."

At these words the fishes seemed restless. Flapping their tails and opening their mouths, in a thousand ways they demonstrated their recognition and willingness to respond to the words of the saint. The crowd on the shore were likewise caught up in unrestrained excitement. They cried, danced and hollered, "Magnify God! The Maker, Redeemer and Sanctifier!"

"Praise Him, children of men," cried Antony.

"Praise Him, and magnify Him forever! Let the fishes of the sea teach man to praise the Lord, should man, the image of his Maker alone, be mute in his praise!"

Hundreds fell at Antony's feet, refusing to rise until they had received his blessing. Hundreds more came to witness the spectacle. Before the passing of the day, this miracle was known to all of Rimini.

The remembrance of this moment is perpetuated throughout Italy and France. A chapel was constructed at the site of this miracle, but today it no longer stands. Antony died in 1231. He was canonized one year later. He is celebrated on June 13th.

Remarkable Encounter

At the early age of thirteen, Saint Mary of Egypt was a much desired prostitute on the streets of Alexandria. For seventeen years she reveled in carnal Lusts, but through a miracle was called to a life of repentance (see April 10). Thereafter she retired to the deserts of Palestine, living on dates and berries and remaining entirely unclothed.

Father Zosimus, who was searching the deserts in a study of the recluses who lived there, came upon her by chance. At Mary's request he gave her his cloak as a covering, so they might converse with greater comfort. From her own narration he learned of her history and when the time had come for Mary to resume her daily prayers, he watched as she retired a short distance from him and turned to the East in prayer. During this interlude she was lifted from the ground, a distance of five feet or more, where she remained suspended for hours. Father Zosimus says he was more than half afraid and thought at times that what he saw must be a ghost.

It had been forty-seven years since Mary had entered the desert when the father came upon her. He confirmed many stories rumored about a miraculous lady in the desert and further confirmed that this lady, once the celebrated instrument of carnal pleasure from Alexandria, was now a celebrated object of veneration and sanctity.

Mary of Egypt lived until A.D. 421. Father Zosimus witnessed many other miracles, which to her were nothing other than conveniences of life. What is known of her life was recorded by Father Zosimus and is entered in the Acta Sanctorum.

Angelic Companion

As an infant Saint Francisca was fortunate to have the companionship of an angel watching over her, day and night. The angel never left her side for a single moment and sometimes, by special favor, she could see the splendor of his person.

She writes, "He was of incredible beauty, his countenance being whiter than snow and redder than the blush rose; his eyes were always uplifted towards heaven, his long curly hair was the color of burnished gold, his robe which extended to the ground was sometimes white, sometimes blue, and other times a shining red. From his face proceeded a radiance so luminous I could read my matins by midnight."

On one occasion her skeptical father requested the honor of introduction to this imaginary creature. She took her angel by the hand, led him to her father, and introduced them, as requested.

Francisca lived from 1384-1440. Several months after her death, following the opening of her tomb in Rome, it was discovered that her body remained miraculously incorrupt. Further, it exhaled a ravishing perfume which was familiar to those who had known her while she lived. The accounts of her life are recorded in the Acts of her Canonization, 1606.

Unreasonable Request

Saint John Francis Regis was no idiot, but sometimes Margaret Baud thought otherwise. He kept a granary of wheat for distribution to the poor and accordingly gave custody of it to Margaret, a reasonable woman, who acted on his behalf. On one occasion a poor woman arrived at the granary and informed Margaret that Regis had sent her to acquire a sack of grain for her family. Margaret was surprised to hear that Regis had sent the woman, for she had informed him only that day that the granary was completely empty.

Margaret returned to remind him of that fact, but Regis remarked, "Oh yes, I quite remember, but please fill the sack which this woman has brought to us."

Margaret persisted, "But there is not a single grain left sir!"

"Please, do as I bid you," commanded Regis.

Not happy with this request, Margaret returned to the granary and found the woman still waiting there. She paused a moment to consider what Regis had told her, then checked the granary again. It was filled to the top with wheat. This happened on several occasions. However, Margaret never again doubted the words of Saint Regis.

Regis lived from 1591-1640. He was canonized in 1113 and is celebrated as patron of social workers on June 16th. His life is recorded in Life of Saint John Francis Regis by Father Daubenton.

Coast of Dunbar

Edward I founded his claim to the lordship of Scotland on four petitions. Three were the presentations of ancient chronicles and charters. The fourth was taken from the biographical records of Saint John of Beverley. They stated that during the reign of King Adelstan, the Scots attempted to invade England. King Adelstan determinedly set out to drive the Scots back, but on reaching the Tyne river, found that they had retreated.

That midnight the celestial body of Saint John of Beverley appeared and spoke to Adelstan. The saint instructed him to cross the river at daybreak, at which time he would discomfit his foe. Adelstan obeyed, and his victory was decisive.

On his homeward march, Adelstan thanked God for the messenger he had been sent and prayed that some lasting sign might be granted that the ages would know of this conquest. Then, with sword in hand, he struck the basaltic rock near the coast of Dunbar and the blade sank deep into the solid stone, "as if it had been butter," cleaving it asunder a depth off our feet or more. As the cleft remains to the present day, it is difficult to dismiss the justice of this claim.

This account was recorded by Rymer in Foedera, Volume I.

I Shall Not Speak

San Sebastian de Garabanal is a small village wedged within the northeastern mountains of Spain. Its only access is a narrow dirt road and the town itself does not appear on most maps. However in 1961, news spread across Europe that four young visionaries were seeing repeated apparitions of the Virgin Mary.

The apparitions began on June 18, 1961, when four young girls skipped out of their Sunday services to steal apples from a neighbor's orchard. As they enjoyed their booty on the side of the road, they were suddenly entranced by a vision of an angel. The angel was male, about eight years old, had pink wings, wore a blue robe and was "surrounded by a great light that did not dazzle my eyes," said one of the children.

This account is similar to other apparitions of the Virgin Mary. After a few preliminary meetings with angels, the visionaries are often introduced to the Virgin herself. However, there were a few interesting twists in Garabanal. During the visions the children simultaneously experienced almost violent ecstasies and fell to the ground. The villagers present tried to lift them to their feet, but their weight became so great, no amount of effort could budge them. One of the visionaries, in particular, would rise up while still prone as if beginning to levitate. On other occasions, while caught up in an ecstacy, the girl would suddenly begin to run backwards at impossible speeds without tripping or falling, their eyes fixed to the sky. These bizarre occurrences, which often lasted several minutes, were filmed for documentary purposes.

Although there are many unique characteristics surrounding this particular apparition, one of the strangest occurred on August 4, 1961. One of the spectators had brought a tape recorder to record the mumblings the children made when they spoke to the Virgin. When Mary Loly, one of the visionaries, came out of her trance the spectator explained its use. Suddenly Mary slipped back into a trance holding the microphone in her hand. The onlookers could hear the girl ask the Virgin to speak into the microphone. Then just as suddenly, she awoke from her brief ecstacy. The observers could hardly wait for the tape to be rewound.

When it was, the crowd clearly heard a sweet female voice say, "I shall not speak."

The assembly surged with excitement at the discovery and the tape was replayed several times. The voice of the lady was heard twice more then it mysteriously vanished from the tape.

There are numerous unique characteristics concerning this apparition and many astonishing written testimonies, but the entire matter is published in Father Joseph Pelletier's book Our Lady Comes to Garabanal (1971).

This book offers a precise chronology of the case, being drafted from one of the visionary's detailed diary of the appearances. The ecstasies and experiences of Conchita, Mary Cruz, Mary Loly and Jacinta continued for five years, ending in 1965.

Hide and Seek

During the reign of Nero in A.D. 64, Saint Protase and Saint Gervase were martyred together, but their bodies were never recovered. Three hundred years afterwards, Saint Ambrose, Archbishop of Milan, was favored with a vision of the Apostle Paul who informed him of the whereabouts of these holy bodies. Paul instructed him to find, along with the bodies, a manuscript containing their names and history.

Saint Ambrose wrote: "I then called together the bishops of the cities thereabouts, told them what Saint Paul had said to me, and we went together to the place indicated. I was the first to ply the mattock and throw up the earth, but the rest joined in and at length we came on a stone chest (twelve feet underground) in which were found the bodies of the two martyrs, whole and perfectly sound, as if they had been laid there only that very day. Further, they emitted a divinely sweet odor which spread throughout the city. At their heads was a book containing their lives and martyrdom."

In honor of this miraculous discovery, Saint Ambrose elected to have a church constructed on the spot where the ground had been sanctified by the bodies of the saints. In time, this was done.

Saint Gervase and Saint Protase are celebrated on June 19th. This narrative is taken from Saint Ambrose's Epistle 22.

A Hero

Gilles was the first disciple of Saint Francis of Assisi. He was a military hero, fearlessly courageous, with a powerful sense of who he was and what he wanted in life. Near the turn of the thirteenth century he traveled to the solitary home of Saint Francis and begged to be admitted into his society. Saint Francis wholeheartedly consented but requested from him one thing, obedience. Gilles agreed joyfully, but on that same day was put to the test. As he and Francis journeyed on the road, they encountered a beggar. Saint Francis asked Gilles to give the unfortunate man his cloak and Gilles instantly obeyed. To his surprise, however, when the beggar wrapped the cloak around his shoulders, he rose upwards to the clouds, then vanished from sight. This was only the first of Gilles' tests. Many more were to follow, but he passed them all.

The lesson he learned was: "When you give to My poor, you give to Me."

This account is recorded in the Acta Sanctorum, Bollandists.

Every Bit of Silver

The following narrative is given in the words of Anseald of Brabancon, a famous twelfth-century highwayman.

"Four years ago in an expedition under Count Richard, I was wounded in the upper jaw by an arrow. The doctors could not remove it and, the pain I felt was horrible. On June 21, 1187, suffering like those of hell, I made my prayer to Our Lady of Deols and said to the image, 'If you will heal me and extract this cursed arrow, you shall be my queen, and I will give you every year a bit of silver.' Scarcely had I uttered this vow when the arrowhead began to move; it then fell out of my jaw into my mouth without producing the least pain. I called for my horse, and with a little help, for I was weak, I got into the saddle and went to fetch my tribute. The monks requested me to deposit the arrowhead with them as a memorial of the 'miracle,' which of course I did willingly. Mounting the steps with the help of two comrades, I made my offering and instantly my full strength was restored. I attended the next service and told this story to the people assembled, showed them the arrowhead and handed it to the priests. I have renounced the highroad and mean to take Mary for my suzerain."

Hermit's Dwelling

Saint Godrich was born in Norfolk during the twelfth century. Like many from the town of Norfolk, he spent his early adult life lost in the reckless squanderings of privateering. However, following an expedition to Jerusalem, he lost his taste for a ruthless life and resolved to live the life of a hermit. With this intent, he settled in a forest near Durham and dedicated himself to prayer until the end of his days.

It happened one year that the river passing near his hut overflowed, inundating the countryside for miles around. The occupants of Durham, concerned for Godrich's safety, ran to the vicinity, but could see neither hermit nor hut. Everyone believed the hermit was drowned and the hut swept away by the flood, yet when the waters subsided, not only was the hut still standing, but it was occupied by Godrich who was wholly uninjured. When questioned about the flood, Saint Godrich expressed surprise, declaring that no waters had come anywhere near his dwelling. And apparently, it had not.

Saint Godrich lived during the twelfth century. His biography was recorded by Reginald of Durham, a contemporary.

Chief Cook

Saint Benet the Black, a Moor, was the son of Negro slaves who were taken from Africa to San Fratello, Sicily. He was chief cook in the convent of Saint Mary, near Palermo. It happened one winter that heavy snowfall trapped the convent occupants and Benet was unable to make his usual excursion for supplies. Concerned for the welfare of the convent residents he applied to God to help him. Assisted by his brother cooks, he filled several large kitchen tanks with water and asked his companions to pass the night in prayer with him. When the morning came, the convent was buzzing with excitement. All the tanks of water were abundantly stocked with live fish. There was no passage to or from the convent and it seemed apparent a miracle had occurred.

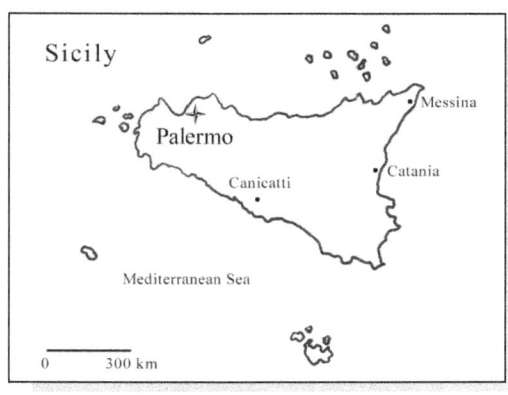

"Miracles of this sort were often repeated in favor of Saint Benet," wrote his biographers. And no less were his talents as a cook.

Saint Benet lived from 1526-1589 and was canonized in 1807. His body remains miraculously incorrupt, but a little dry and hard, and is exposed for public veneration in a shrine at the church of the convent of Saint Mary, near Palermo. This story is taken from the Acts of his Beatification.

Medjugorje

On June 24, 1981, the first of an ongoing series of apparitions of the Holy Virgin appeared to six children from Medjugorje, Yugoslavia. She appeared on the hill Podbrdo, behind the village of Bijakovici. Within days the news had spread throughout the country and pilgrims numbering in the thousands, flocked to the site of the apparitions. Both church and state strongly denounced the validity of these claims and Mount Crnica, the apparition site, was declared off-limits under police supervision.

It was of little consequence, however, for the visions continued in private homes and fields, and currently on a regular basis, in the parish rectory of Medjugorje. What the visionaries are telling us is simple. First, the apparition is unquestionably the Virgin Mary, mother of Christ. Second, her main message, given in three words, tearfully and emphatically is, "Peace, peace, peace." In subsequent visions she described herself as the "Queen of Peace."

In all the apparitions of Mary in the last two centuries, especially Fatima and Lourdes, the message was one of penance, prayer and recitation of the rosary. But in Medjugorje, it is fasting that receives priority. Fasting promotes a readiness for meditation and prayer. Some have even suggested global fasting for peace on earth.

When news of the apparitions reached the scientific community, it wasn't long before the visionaries were subjected to a variety of medical examinations. In addition, during the actual period of the vision, the children were monitored by means of electrodes attached to their eyelids, for simultaneity of focus. Moreover, they were exposed to blinding lights, piercing sounds through headsets, their bodies were elevated, pricked, poked and pinched in every conceivable manner. In every instance, no evidence of discomfort, tensing of muscles, or abnormal behavior was evident.

It appears that as we near the twenty-first century, apparitions of the Virgin Mary are multiplying. During the past fifty years, more than two hundred and fifty have been worthy of investigation and recorded. Still none have received ecclesiastical approval. Nevertheless, the news of the apparitions and the messages of the Holy Virgin have been circulating throughout the world, generating a growing response and bearing good fruit among thousands.

This account is taken from the writings of Fr. Tomislav Pervan, O. F.M, ThD., pastor of St. James Parish in Medjugorje.

Tears of Love

After one of his many missionary tours, Saint James of Tarentaise journeyed to visit the tomb of a dear friend who had died during his absence. His biographers tell us that the saint wept so bitterly over the grave, that the dead man could not resist the force of his deep, deep grief. And just as Lazarus had come from the grave at the voice of Christ, so this friend returned to life at the tears of Saint James.

James of Tarentaise lived during the fifth century. Many miracles of this magnitude have been credited to him. The above account is recorded in Life of Saint James of Tarentaise, *by Pope Callistus II.*

Fountain of Saint Firmatus

Saint William Firmatus of Tours spent much of his life as a hermit in the woods of Laval, in Mayenne, France. But he suffered from the ignorance of his neighbors who frequently accused him of sorcery. In time, these false accusations led to his arrest, and he was jailed. But there was little reason to keep him locked up. When he was released, he returned to his home in Brittany.

On the way, he rested in Vitre for two days then traveled to Dardenay. There his sanctity was first recognized because his miraculous powers were publicly displayed. At a time of great drought, seeing the citizens of Dardenay in need of water, William poked his staff into the dirt and relieved their burden by producing a clear spring of water. In honor of this miracle, the spring was named "Fountain of Saint Firmatus" and has ever after been celebrated.

Saint William Firmatus lived during the eleventh century. His life is recorded in the Acta Sanctorum, Bollandus, Volume III.

Arms of Angels

Saint Marcellinus, venerated as the first bishop of Embrun, was an African priest. His message of faith made him especially unpopular with the followers of Arius who denied the divinity of Jesus. They perceived him to be their most formidable political adversary.

It once happened that a militant group of Arians captured and carried him to the top of a steep rock, where they intended to push him to his death. However, as they did so, angels appeared and bore Marcellinus in their arms, carrying him safely to the ground below. No injury was incurred, but the miracle infuriated the militants.

In concern for the safety of his followers, the aged bishop escaped to the Auvergne Mountains where he lived a life of silence and prayer. He remained there until his death, making only occasional visits by night to advise and encourage his faithful devotees. In A.D. 374, he gave up his soul to God.

This event is recorded in Hagiographie de Gap, by Mons. Depery. A short record is also printed in the Acta Sanctorum, Volume II.

Love Story

Saint Gerasimus was standing on the banks of the Jordan River when he looked up to discover a fully mature lion, limping on three paws, following a course directly towards him. Not the type to run from danger, Gerasimus watched the creature and soon determined why it was limping. When the lion reached him, he grasped its enormous right forepaw and holding it firmly in his hand, removed a large thorn lodged deeply in the soft pad. This being done, he pushed the creature away. But unexpectedly, the lion affectionately attached himself to Gerasimus.

Love begets love, and surely this tale must be a love story. For, we are told, they lived together in the monastery, the lion following faithfully behind Gerasimus like a devoted servant, neither molesting nor threatening anyone in the least.

Saint Gerasimus lived until A.D. 475. The stories of his life are recorded in Vies des Peres des Deserts d'Orient.

Doubting Peter

Jesus, having fed five thousand men, women and children with five barley loaves, bade his disciples to pass over the sea. And when the ship was in the midst of the sea, it was tossed with the waves, for the winds were contrary. In the fourth watch of the night, Jesus went unto them, walking on the sea. And when the disciples saw him they were troubled, but Jesus spoke unto them saying, "Be of good cheer, it is I. Be not afraid."

Peter then got out of the boat to join him, but his courage failed him. When he began to sink, Jesus caught him, saying, "O thou of little faith, wherefore didst thou doubt?"

The New Testament of the Bible, Matthew: 14: 24-32.

Fisherman and Knight

The history of Spain includes many visions of the apostle James guiding the destiny of its citizens during times of crisis. The following account explains the unique characteristics of these apparitions.

When King Fernando lay waiting to conquer Coimbra, Bishop Estiano arrived at Santiago from Greece. While the bishop prayed in the church he overheard the townsfolk gossiping about a vision of the apostle James. Many times James had been seen as a knight mounted atop a white charger coming to the aid of the Spanish soldiers. Having thus overheard them, the bishop issued his rebuke, saying, "Friends, call not Saint James a knight but a fisherman."

Later that day Bishop Estiano fell into a deep sleep in which the apostle James appeared to him, clad in bright armor and holding a number of keys in his hands.

"You think it a fable, bishop, that I come to assist the Christians in their battles? Know that I am a knight. A knight in the army of Christ Jesus."

Then mounting a white horse he declared, "Tomorrow I will help King Fernando who has lain waiting for seven months before Coimbra. With these keys I will open the city gates and deliver Coimbra into his hands."

The following morning the gates of Coimbra were opened at 9:00 a.m. and the victory was decisive.

This account is documented in the Chronicles of the Cid, Book I by Southey.

July

1 Protection
2 Man with the Angels
3 Humble Master
4 Time for a Change
5 The Admirable Life of Peter Celestine
6 Baby Talk
7 Apparitions in Italy
8 Angelo
9 Different From the Rest
10 Our Lady of Caravaggio
11 Valet
12 Vengeance
13 Good Friends
14 Freshman
15 Multiply Yourself
16 A Promise Given
17 Protected
18 Crucifix of Martres
19 Mother of All
20 Voice of the Unborn Prince
21 Barefoot
22 Sacred Heart
23 Esteem Each Other
24 Christina the Astonishing
25 An Open Mind
26 A Miracle to Come
27 Duel of Strength
28 Fiery Personality
29 Hostess
30 Angelo's Flood
31 Defending Heaven

Protection

One should never feel alone and unprotected because guardian angels are everywhere and watch over us constantly. Some protect us personally while more powerful ones care for societies and nations, even the world. The following story mentions the guardian angel of Barcelona.

Angels were common company to Saint Vincent Ferrier. His eyes were ever opened to them and he had as many friends from heaven as he did on earth. Once, quite by accident, he discovered a young man "environed in light," keeping watch just outside the city gates of Barcelona. In one hand he carried a naked sword; in the other, a shield. Vincent asked him who he was and what he was doing in that place, armed in that way. The angel replied, "I am the guardian angel of Barcelona. This city is under my protection."

Later that evening Vincent delivered a sermon to the citizens of Barcelona and told them what he had seen at their city gates. He congratulated them on their good fortune and advised them to render themselves worthy of such an honor. For a city whose citizens were healthy in body and spirit would strengthen their guardian and render him invincible to all evil forces.

In time, an enormous statue of the angel was erected at the city gates, where it remains today.

This story is given in Vies des Saints, Volume IV, by Manager Guerin, Chamberlain to Pope Leo XIII.

Man With The Angels

As a child Antoney shied away from social gatherings. He preferred a quiet atmosphere and lots of time to reflect and develop his inner life. He seldom found it, though, for his ecstasies and miracles often occurred in the presence of many witnesses, making him a famous and much sought after curiosity.

Near the end of his life of silence, he offered up mass for the first time, following his initiation into the priesthood. A celestial light encompassed him and hundreds of angels formed a circle around him, assisting in the particulars of the ceremony. This was known to everyone in Cremona, as the young priest was affectionately dubbed, "The Man with the Angels."

Antoney Mary Zaccaria of Cremona lived from 1502-1539. Following his death, his body was kept above ground and remained miraculously incorrupt for thirty-three years, at which time it was buried under the soil. In 1664, what remained of his body was removed to Milan, where it is exposed in a crystal case in a crypt beneath the main altar of the Church of Saint Barnaby. His life is recorded in Life of The Venerable Zaccaria, by R.P. Teppa.

Humble Master

Saint Germanus of Scotland was not one to follow the orthodox methods of the world. For him the gift of miracles was simply a means to an end. He once began a pilgrimage to France to visit with his namesake, the Bishop of Auxerre. Having arrived at the Scottish coast, he found no vessel available to carry him across to France. Without wasting a moment, he knelt in meditative prayer, taking recourse to a miracle. While he prayed, a chariot from heaven, driven by white horses, appeared on the sea directly before him. He entered the chariot, was lifted in the air and was transported across the channel to Flammenville, close to Dieppe.

The residents of Dieppe were astonished and shouted their praises to the heavens, hailing that it must be Neptune who had come to bless them with abundance of fish. However, Germanus convinced them he was no God of the sea but rather a simple man like themselves. His sincere humility proved to be more influential than his miracles. Before he left the village of Dieppe, five hundred of its citizens embraced him as their spiritual master. This being done, he continued on his pilgrimage to Auxerre.

This story is given in the Hagiographic Records, by Corblet (Fifth century).

Time For a Change

History has reviled many cultures who offered human sacrifices to their gods. Among them were the Frisians, whose executions were made by fire, water or sword. Appalled by this inhuman behavior, Saint Wulfram sought to abolish these senseless practices. When the lottery fell to two young children, five and seven years old, Wulfram implored King Radbod to prohibit this cruelty. But Radbod replied he could not violate the laws he had sworn to preserve.

The children were taken for execution to a spot where two rivers emptied into the sea. A large crowd had assembled there and among them was Wulfram, who was kneeling in prayer. When the children were thrown into the rushing rapids the waters suddenly parted and formed a wall around them. Wulfram then walked on the sea, entered the children's premises and lifted them safely into his arms. This event was seen by all who had assembled there, including families of the children who were watching from the shore.

Saint Wulfram lived from A. D. 647-720. The accounts of his life are recorded in the Hagiography of the Diocese of Amiens.

The Admirable Life of Peter Celestine

In the year 1274, Peter Celestine journeyed to Rome to petition the Pope for approval of a new order, the Order of Celestines. On arrival he was ordered by the pope to say mass, and naturally he obeyed. The officers who waited on the priests, offered him magnificent robes and ornaments suitable for this honored occasion, but he requested permission to use only his hermit's cloak. This he was granted, but no sooner had he received consent when angels, appearing from nowhere, surrounded him and covered his cloak with heavenly ornaments. A moment later, he started mass and was lifted high in the air where he remained suspended until the service was concluded. The pope did not hesitate to confirm the new order and accordingly granted the required documentation.

Twenty years later, on July 5, 1294, Peter Celestine was elected to lead the church as pope. His new station, however, was one of great dissatisfaction to him personally. Five months after his ordination, he became the first pope in history to voluntarily abdicate, asking pardon for his mistakes.

Peter Celestine lived from 1215-1296. Following his abdication he retired to a monastery, where he hoped to remain in hiding, but was later captured by the new pope, Boniface VIII, and kept in honorable captivity. He was canonized in 1313. The accounts of his life are recorded in The Admirable Life of St. Peter Celestine.

Baby Talk

Rusticus, Bishop of Treves, was a jealous man. He hated Saint Goar and deeply envied his reputation as a worker of miracles. Saint Goar, on the other hand, was a simple hermit, entirely unassuming and ambitious only for his silent life. Rusticus sought to discredit Goar's reputation and ordered him to his palace on church business. He secretly assembled a congregation of clergy to witness his denouncement of the recluse, on the grounds that he had violated the rules laid down for the observance of hermits.

When Goar arrived in the city of Treves, he first stopped at a chapel to commend himself to the Almighty. He then continued to the bishop's palace. Before the assembly, the bishop accused Goar of practicing magic and dabbling in demonology. Surprised by these accusations, Goar appealed to God to vindicate him from this charge. Suddenly a clerk entered the palace. He was holding in his arms an infant whom he had found abandoned in the baptismal font.

The bishop seized the opportunity to challenge the hermit and said, "Let us see what divine powers you possess. Tell us who are the parents of this founding. If you cannot you will be cast out of the church."

Saint Goar addressed the babe of three days, "Dear child, in the name of justice, please tell this company who are your father and mother." The baby pointed to the bishop and spoke distinctly, "My father is Rusticus and my mother Flavia."

The bishop, enraged by this unexpected revelation, declared it was an infamous lie. But in time, being unable to bear the sin in his heart, he confessed that the infant had spoken the truth.

This story is recorded in the Acta Sanctorum, Bollandists, July 6.

Apparitions in Italy

"My dear children, God sends me to earth to save all because the whole world is in danger."

These were the words spoken to the children visionaries of Oliveto Citra, Italy, during the winter of 1986. The visions began eight months earlier when reports of mysterious apparitions circulated in the small town of Oliveto Circa. Over one hundred sworn affidavits were submitted to the local parish office stating that they had seen the Virgin Mary appearing at a gate entering into an old local castle.

Many others, tourists, businessmen and people from nearby towns have spoken out, declaring that they have seen the apparition as well. Since the time of the first sightings, many children of Oliveto Circa have become messenger visionaries who communicate the Virgin's message to the world. The apparitions and messages continue to the present day.

"I have come among you to bring peace to your hearts. God wants peace to reign in the hearts of all mankind. . . . Therefore, my dear children, pray, pray, pray; if you do not pray you will receive nothing . . . . . Dear children, when God comes among you with some manifestation, he does not come as a joke. He does not joke, and he is not afraid of men, so take this message seriously. . . . People should not bow only before God but also toward their own brothers and sisters who suffer, fighting hunger in the world. . . . Peace on earth is about to end, the world cannot be saved without peace, but the world will find peace only if mankind returns to God. I will engage in the final struggle against Satan which will conclude with the triumph of my Immaculate Heart. . . . Those who refuse God today will go far from him tomorrow. . . . Have this message read to priests, and I want it to be communicated to everyone as soon as possible.

Do not be ashamed of my message, but say it to everyone you meet. For the speaking of my message is a great apostolic work, because with information about the apparitions and with knowledge of the messages, many people will pray more.

Now my children I bless you all. Remember: prayer and penance, and pray for the conversion of all mankind."

The messages given at Oliveto Citra are recorded in Mary Among Us, by Father Robert Faricy and Luciana Pecoraro.

Angelo

During the consecration of Gregory XV as Pope (1621), a terrible pestilence devastated Rome. Gregory attempted to restore the morale of the city by organizing a grand celebration with a procession, which carried in its forefront a painting of *The Glorious Virgin* (apparently the work of the apostle Luke). As the procession marched forward, a thick cloud of corrupt air hovered in front of the painting. Those present attested they had heard a choir of angels singing joyfully "Regina Caeli loetare, Alleluja!"

Pope Gregory declared he had witnessed a vision of an enormous angel standing above a nearby castle. From that day on this angel is referred to as Saint Angelo, in remembrance of the purging of the pestilence of Rome.

Saint Gregory reigned as pope until the day of his death, July 8, 1623. The accounts of his life are recorded in Lives of the Saints, by Edward Kinesman.

Different From The Rest

Saint Catherine was endowed with a natural grace and beauty which was the envy of her twenty or more natural brothers and sisters. As a child, she was different from the rest, preferring solitude and often refusing to wear fine clothes, "bravely flattering herself

according to her station in society." Her obstinacy in this matter often earned her a reprimand from Mrs. Benincasa, her mother, who would relegate her to the kitchen for punishment.

One day Catherine's father entered the kitchen and saw her kneeling on the floor, absorbed in prayer. To his astonishment he saw "a heavenly dove, whiter than snow," seated on her head. He approached the child, but the dove took flight and soon disappeared. When he asked his daughter to explain, she replied, "I know of no dove, Father, but my heart is full with holy spirit."

Saint Catherine lived from 1347- 1380 and is celebrated as the principal saint of Siena. Following her death, her body remained miraculously incorrupt. She was canonized in 1461 and declared a Doctor of the Church in 1970. This account is given in Lives of the Saints, *by Laurentius Surius, 1570.*

Our Lady of Caravaggio

The apparitions of Our Lady of Caravaggio began in 1883. In the same year the Court Journal wrote: "The number of pilgrims who have visited the shrine this year exceed a hundred thousand." The narrative which follows comes from an eyewitness.

"Every day at noon, the vision of the Virgin Mary rises from a dark recess behind one of the pillars, and thousands of eager devotees struggle to catch a glimpse of the apparition. Those who cannot approach near enough to the shrine throw handfuls of copper coins against the iron grating which encloses it, and the shock of metallic sound, amid the deep monotonous intoning of the priests, seems to produce a frenzy in the crowd, many of whom rush wildly about, shrieking and tearing their hair. . . .

The village church, which is capable of containing only a few hundred people, is made to hold ten thousand, who, although packed, suffocating, and trembling beneath the stifling atmosphere, contrive to howl out their invocations. Outside on the piazza, the scene is still more astounding. Around the fountain stand groups of devotees. This year (1883) the pilgrimage has been swollen by many families of the highest rank in north Italy. . . and when the dismal howlings of the pilgrims within the church announce the appearance of the misty vapor which precedes the apparition of the Virgin, the whole crowd falls to the ground and shrieks forth the litany composed for the occasion. . . the litany is succeeded by a dead silence."

Valet

Saint Benedict, Abbot of Monte Cassino, authored the Rule which bears his name. He was a hermit who later became the Patriarch of Western Monks, due to the large number of followers who traveled to the desert seeking his mastership. The following account is a story of his disciple *Brother Exileratus:*

A French nobleman once sent an offering to Benedict of two flasks of wine. He ordered his valet to deliver the gift and thought no more of it. The valet, however, stole one and concealed it for his own consumption.

When he delivered the other to the abbey, Benedict remarked, "On your way home my man, don't forget the stolen flask. But before you put it to your mouth, look well into it. Adieu."

The attendant was frightened by the words of Saint Benedict and almost abandoned his stolen treasure, but when he returned to the spot where he had concealed it, he looked into it carefully. Instead of wine, he found a deadly asp. This miracle so thoroughly transformed the young valet that he joined Saint Benedict's monks and was affectionately named *Brother Exileratus* by his master.

Saint Benedict lived from A.D. 480-547. He foretold the time of his death to his disciples and had them prepare his grave six days before. He is honored as Patron of Europe on July 11th. His relics remain in the abbey of Monte Cassino.

Vengeance

Saint John Gualbert solemnly vowed to avenge his brother's death. He was the son of a prominent officer in the Italian army, and his brother Hugo had been unjustly slain in battle. He pursued the murderer to Florence and cornered him in a place where there was no hope for escape.

Drawing his sword, he attempted to run it through the murderer when the man extended his arms and cried aloud, "In the name of God, please spare my life!"

Gualbert's arm was arrested as if by some invisible force, and he replied to his foe who lay helplessly on the ground, "I cannot refuse what you ask in the name of the Almighty. I not only give you your life, but also my friendship. Go in peace."

Gualbert continued on his way until he reached the chapel of Saint Miniat's abbey. He fell before the altar with tears in his eyes and prayed to be forgiven for his vengeful anger. Then, a miracle occurred. Looking up at the crucifix, he saw the image of Christ come to life and bow his head approvingly, thanking him for having accorded pardon to his enemy so heroically. The miracle was enough to transform his life. He quit his position with the army and committed his life to unconditional conquest over his own soul.

Saint John Gualbert lived during the eleventh century. He is celebrated on July 12th. This story is given in the Acta Sanctorum, Volume III.

Good Friends

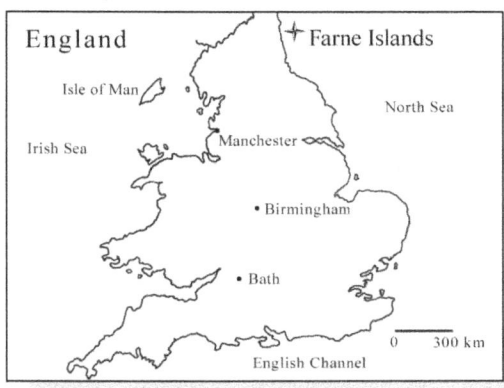

Saint Cuthbert always had a friend when he needed one. And why not? He had a sparkling personality, which seemed to spill over and enlighten those around him. In the Abbey of Rippon, it was his responsibility to entertain all newly arrived guests. However, no one would have guessed that many of the new arrivals were angels who had come to enjoy the sanctity of the monastery.

On one occasion, in the execution of his office, Cuthbert entertained an angel, who, in return for his hospitality, left three large loaves of bread on a table as a gift. The whiteness and taste were of such exquisite quality that there was little doubt it was "bread from heaven." Saint Cuthbert's heavenly friends often came to the monastery for conversation and frequently left him these gifts of bread. On another occasion, before he entered the priory of Mailros, he was healed of an abscess in the knee by an angel. And again, an angel nursed him to health when he was stricken with the plague.

Saint Cuthbert lived from A.D. 634-687. His body remained miraculously incorrupt for several centuries after his death. The Fame Islands where Cuthbert lived are now a sanctuary for birds, seals and other wildlife under the protection of the National Trust.

Freshman

Little is known of the life of Saint Maurus, but he is notably remembered by the stories of his obedience to his master, Saint Benedict. Once, while Benedict was absent from the abbey, a dumb and lame child was brought to be healed. When Benedict returned, he was disappointed by the lack of self-confidence his disciples displayed. Wanting to put them to the test he said angrily, "Am I God, to make alive and to heal?"

Saint Maurus understood his message and instantly fell to his knees. Then rising to his feet, he approached the child and touched her, saying, "In the name of all that is Holy and through the merits of my master Saint Benedict, I command you to rise up in perfect health."

The child, fully restored to health, obeyed and rose to her feet, much to the delight and wonder of her household.

On another occasion, Maurus walked on water, without realizing it, to save a boy from drowning.

Saint Maurus lived from A.D. 512-584. The accounts of his life are recorded in the Acta Sanctorum.

Multiply Yourself

A true master of miracles, Saint Philip of Neri was often discovered in two or more places at the same time. Once, while visiting the house of Saint Jerome, he was simultaneously seen actively engaged in the Church of Santa Maria in Vallicella. On another occasion, while in Rome, he appeared to Catherine, a nun of the order of Saint Augustine, in Tuscany. On a third occasion, one of his penitents, en route to Naples, was overtaken by pirates, and to avoid capture threw himself into the sea. He called the name of Saint Philip to save him, and at once the saint appeared, caught him by the hair and drew him safely to the shore. All this occurred while Philip conducted his public duties in Rome. After thorough investigation by the church, these and many other events formed the official edict given by Pope Gregory XV at the canonization of Philip of Neri in 1622.

Saint Philip Neri lived from 1515-1595. Four hundred years after his death, his body remains miraculously incorrupt and is exposed, in its entirety, for public veneration under the altar of his chapel in the Chiesa Nuova, at the Church of Santa Maria in Vallicella, in Rome (see May 26).

A Promise Given

It is said that a vision of the Virgin Mary appeared to Saint Simon Stock and promised him that whoever died wearing the brown scapular of the Carmelites would be guaranteed a place in the heavens. This vision occurred shortly after he was promoted to the dignity of General of the Order of Carmelites. The Virgin appeared adorned in the uniform of the Carmelites and presented Simon with a scapular (shoulder cloth). She instructed him to institute the *Confraternity of the Scapular*, its aim being to unite all her devotees into a single regulated observance. This apparition occurred on July 16, 1251, and Saint Simon set aside this day as the anniversary of the confraternity. This association invited all its members to wear a small emblem, a scapular, and practice certain spiritual exercises, together with prayers, for the remainder of their lives.

This tradition is kept alive by the Carmelite Friars. Saint Simon Stock lived until 1265. The accounts of his life are recorded in the Acta Sanctorum.

Protected

Saint Clams, Abbot of St. Ferreol, was famed for the marvels of his healing touch. He was so calm and relaxed at times it may have seemed that he was just waiting for life to pass while enjoying its tastier moments. Although there are many miracles credited to him, the following is one which is more memorable.

The River Rhone was full to overflowing and one of the monks of St. Ferreol had fallen in. He was in imminent danger of being carried away by the rapid current, but fortunately Saint Clams had witnessed the incident. Remaining perfectly calm, he made the sign of the cross over the river whereupon the waters lifted the man upward and guided him safely to the nearest bank.

The monk returned to the abbey without injury.

Saint Clams lived until A.D. 660. The accounts of his life are recorded in the Acta Sanctorum.

Crucifix of Martres

One evening Vincent Ferrier sat in silence before the Crucifix of Martres. Meditating on the unjust persecutions of the innocent child of Mary, he was moved to tears and cried out involuntarily, "O my Saviour, how great was thy suffering on the cross!"

Then suddenly the image of Christ on the cross rose to life and turned his head over his right shoulder. Gazing directly at Vincent he addressed the saint's outpouring of emotions with the words: "Yes Vincent, I have suffered all you say, and more."

So saying, the crucifix solidified, retaining its position with the head turned to the right. Today this crucifix is held by the Roman Catholic Church as a greatly valued relic.

Saint Vincent Ferrier lived from 1350-1419. This account was recorded by Father Teoli, Book I.

Mother To All

July 19, 1831, marks the first of a long series of apparitions of the Virgin Mary as they appeared to Saint Catherine Laoure. This narrative is given in the indefinable charm of Catherine's own words:

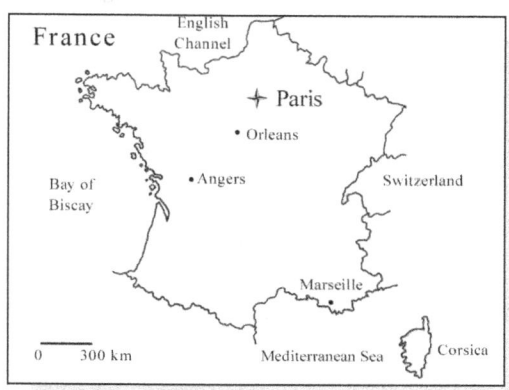

"Looking toward the blessed Virgin, I flung myself toward her, and falling upon my knees on the altar steps, I rested my hands in her lap. There a moment passed, the sweetest of my life. I could not say what I felt. The Blessed Virgin told how I must conduct myself with my director and added several things that I must not tell. . . . I asked her the meaning of everything I had seen, and she deigned to explain it to me. . . . I could not say how long I stayed with her. When she left, it was as if she faded away, becoming a shadow which moved toward the tribune, the way she had come."

This apparition was a prelude to the great apparition of the Miraculous Medal (see November 27). Having often predicted that she would not see the year 1877, Catherine died on December 31, 1876. Her body was exhumed half a century afterward and found to be miraculously incorrupt. "Even her hands were white and natural looking." Her body may be seen under the side altar of Our Lady of the Sun ill the motherhouse chapel of the Sisters of Charity, in Paris.

Voice of the Unborn Prince

During the seventh century, Ireland was divided into six kingdoms, and Gelges, daughter of King Edfind, was the ruler of one of the divisions. Against her father's wishes, she secretly married Prince Fintan of Momonia, rumored to have been baptized a Christian. Within a year Gelges began to show the signs of child bearing, and their secret was revealed. When King Edfind discovered that his daughter had married a Christian he was blindly enraged and ordered that his own daughter be burned at the stake at once—he himself overseeing the sentence carried out.

When Gelges was led to the fires, the voice of an infant suddenly sprang from her womb, filling the air with a reprove for the king. With a loud voice and intelligible words the unborn prince declared that no flames would ever harm his mother. The king was deeply shaken by the incident but ordered that the execution continue. When the fires were ignited, a torrential downpour extinguished the flames, saturating the logs and everyone present. The sign was enough to convince the king of his error, and he returned his daughter to her husband.

When their child was born, he was named Fursa (Fursey). At an early age he constructed a monastery at Rathmat and gained fame as the greatest spiritual visionary of Ireland.

The details of his visions are common knowledge in Ireland today.

Saint Fursa was born on the island of Inisquin, near Lough Corrib. He died in A.D. 648 and was canonized shortly afterward. He is celebrated throughout Ireland, where the details of his visions are known to all, thanks to such writers as Bede and Aelfric.

Barefoot

Saint Hermann seldom wanted anything. His innocence seemed, at times, to be just shy of chronic gullibility, but the simplicity of his heart won true favor from his mother in heaven. Once, while still a boy, he entered the cathedral in Cologne, Germany, barefoot in the depth of winter. The Virgin Mary appeared to him and asked how it came to be that he walked barefoot through the snow.

"Alas, the poverty of my parents constrains me," said the boy.

The Virgin pointed to a stone and told him to go and see what he could find there. He went and found four pieces of silver, and returning, thanked the Virgin for her benevolence.

She kissed him and said, "When in want, return to the stone. You shall always find sufficient for your daily bread."

This occurred frequently and what makes this miracle especially interesting is that other boys accompanied him from time to time, but none could find the deposit.

Saint Hermann lived during the eleventh century. The accounts of his life are recorded in Les Petits Bollandistes, Volume VI, *by Cardinal Wiseman.*

Sacred Heart

Few women have met with as much ridicule as Margaret Mary Alacoque. Her many visions were for years frowned upon as whimsical dreams or the delusions of a madwoman and challenged the essential fabric of Church dogma. But in time, through self-honesty and perseverance, she advanced the evolution of Christian thinking and formed the confraternity of *The Sacred Heart of Jesus*, sanctioned by Pope Clement XII in 1732. Her biographers tell us that Jesus would often appear to her to comfort and instruct her. On one occasion he tenderly placed a crown on her head saying, "My daughter, take this crown in token of that which will be given you in the Church triumphant."

The visionary crown remained on Margaret's head but caused great pain as if someone was constantly pricking her head with sharp pins. "To carry My cross in your heart," Jesus told her, "is to be purified entirely."

When the period of Margaret's headaches came to an end, she began to experience *The Holy Hour*. Every Thursday and Friday throughout the year, spontaneously she rose from her bed to recite five *Paters* and five *Ave Marias*. Afterwards, she would fall prostate five times in adoration to the earth and in respect for Jesus, her master and teacher. Although unknown to her, these experiences marked the beginning of what would one day be known as the *Devotion of the Sacred Heart of Jesus*.

It took twelve years of spiritual purification and repeated mystical experiences, but one glorious day, her master Jesus revealed the secrets of his sacred heart. "My sacred heart," said Jesus, "is full of love to man in general, but to you especially, whom I enjoin the privilege of making known the treasures of love which it contains—those treasures of sanctification and salvation which alone can free everyone from the depths of hell."

Then taking His heart, he put it into hers. She saw it with her eyes and described it as an atom heated red-hot in the midst of a furnace. Every Friday her master Jesus repeated this ritual until the sacred heart appeared to her as the blazing sun, shining in all its glory, with its rays falling on her own heart, setting it on fire and utterly reducing it to ashes. In times of difficulty He would comfort her, saying, "I promise that My heart shall shower abundant grace on all those who honor this day in the prescribed manner."

Despite the indignities thrust upon her from the leaders of the Church, Margaret Mary Alacoque persevered. Her enthusiasm proved infectious, and in time many religious houses adopted the new office and built chapels dedicated to the *Sacred Heart of Jesus*. Seventy years after her death, on June 24, 1864, Margaret Mary was beatified.

Margaret Mary Alacoque was born on July 22, 1647. The accounts of her life are recorded in Life and Works of Margaret Mary Alacoque (a publication of the monastery of Paray le Monial).

Esteem Each Other

According to the Roman Church, the wise men who came from the East to pay tribute to the infant Jesus were King Melchior of Arabia, King Balthazar of Saba and King Gaspar of Tar shish and the Isles. All three died in the same month in the year A.D. 54. Melchior was first, on January 1st, at the age of 116 years; then Balthazar on January 6th, at 112 years; and last, Gaspar at 109 years. They were all buried in the same vault.

We are told that when the body of Balthazar was lowered into the grave, the dead body of Melchior miraculously shifted to one side leaving the place of honor to his companion. Likewise, when Gaspar died, the two kings' bodies miraculously shifted right and left, respectfully awarding the place of honor to the King of Tarshish.

If there is a moral to this story, it would certainly have to be the apostolic precept, "Let each esteem the other better than himself."

This account is given in Les Petits Bolfandistes, 7th edition, Volume I. The Three Wise Men are celebrated on July 23rd.

Christina the Astonishing

Christina died at the early age of twenty-two. Or at least everybody thought so.

She was a plain but attractive young girl born into the peasant class in Brusthem. Orphaned at age fifteen, she was taken in by her two older sisters who cared for her very much. However, at twenty-two she suffered a seizure and was declared dead.

At her funeral she was carried in an open coffin to the church, where a requiem was begun, but at some point near the end, Christina suddenly sat perfectly upright and soared to the beams of the roof "like a bird." Thoroughly frightened, the crowd fled from the church, with the exception of one of Christina's sisters who could not believe their eyes. Together with a priest, she coaxed Christina down from the rafters and the following tale was narrated.

Christina had indeed died. She was escorted by angels to Hell where she recognized many of her friends, then to Purgatory where still more friends were seen. She was at last taken to Heaven and told she could either remain there or return to earth, where through the agency of her prayers and humiliations, she could liberate the friends she had seen in Purgatory. She elected to return, and when she discovered herself reunited to her body, she also discovered she was unable to tolerate the smell of sinful human bodies and so leapt to the rafters to escape the stench.

Her life after that experience was equally remarkable. Unable to bear the smells of humans she would flee to remote areas, climbing trees, mountains or high towers. She was often seen climbing into roaring ovens or submersing herself in freezing waters in winter or praying while rolling herself into a ball or balancing on a beam. She was naturally thought to be both mad and dangerous and was captured and confined to cells and chains. However, she always escaped by unknown means.

Her life was a simple one. She dressed in rags, begged for food and spent the remainder of her days in prayer. Because most people were utterly terrified of her, she had only a few friends, but they were good and true friends. Saint Lutgardis often sought Christina's advice, and Beatified Mary of Oignies and the prioress of St. Catherine's convent praised her. Louis, Count of Looz, regarded her his personal friend and invited her to his castle, accepting her rebukes with sincere humility.

All in all, her story is a remarkable one and stands unique in the canon of saints.

This account is given by the firsthand evidence of Cardinal James de Vitry and Christina's biographer, Thomas de Cantimpre, also a contemporary. Christina lived from 1150-1224 and is celebrated on July 24th. She died and was buried at the convent of St. Catherine in Saint-Trond.

An Open Mind

Miracles were common for those who lived in proximity to Saint Hermenland. However, the Count of Nantes and Rennes, a logical man, did not think so. To him Hermenland was little more than a talented illusionist. Resolved to put him to the test, he journeyed to Hermenland's monastery and asked if he might freshen himself with a glass of his wine.

Hermenland obliged and immediately the count engaged him in a debate. As they spoke, the count assumed his skeptical disposition having become Weary of Hermenland's apparent simplicity. But Hermenland encouraged him to develop a more open-minded view of the world, suggesting that miracles were everyone's birthright, and confirmed the existence of an all-merciful creator. So saying, he multiplied to overflowing, the small sip of wine remaining in the count's goblet.

The count conceded his position, opened his mind, and followed after the mastership of Saint Hermenland.

Hermenland lived until A.D. 720. His many miracles concerning the multiplication of food or drink are recorded in the Analecta Bollandiana, Volume XXIX.

A Miracle to Come

Supernatural phenomena which occurred in Garabanal, Spain have been the topic of controversy. Four children were the recipients of heavenly apparitions which began in 1961 and concluded four years later. They received communion from the hands of angels, in which ecstasies involving deformation of the neck were witnessed.

Messages were received which are similar to other modern apparitions, and a promise of a great miracle at Garabanal was given. The visionaries swear they were told that all present would be cured of their infirmities.

Thirty years later, the citizens of Garabanal are faithfully awaiting the promise and a permanent sign. However, as one of the visionaries has retracted her original testimony, judgment of the matter has become complicated.

Some photographic evidence is available. Information may be obtained through The Pittsburgh Center For Peace.

July 27 — Duel of Strength

Saint Pantaleon, meaning all-compassionate, lived during the third century. His teaching was well established in both East and West and continues to this day. He was a successful physician in Nicomedia, who served both kings and paupers 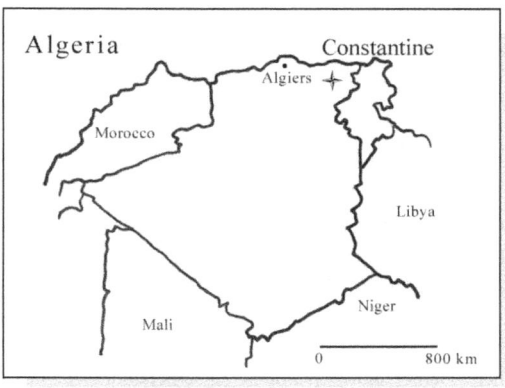 alike. With the flourishing of Christianity, after much sober skepticism, he wholeheartedly embraced it though realizing the dangers. Consequently, he was arrested, and having enraged Maximian, Emperor of Nicomedia, he was tortured with the intent of purging his obstinate resolve. Ultimately, the emperor sought to make a spectacle of the young physician, and he was condemned to be cast to the wild beasts.

The theater was full, as Pantaleon had won many admirers. When the emperor gave the command for the beasts to be released, everyone shuddered at the expected result. There was no sign of fear in Pantaleon's face. His very posture spoke of firm resolution. The beasts approached in a rush but stopped dead in front of him. Sniffing at Pantaleon for a moment, they lay peaceably at his feet, each of them refusing to budge until he lay his hands upon them in blessing. The theater was unrestrained. Shouts of, "The Lord, He is God! The Lord, He is God!" rang up in unison like a battle chant. But the cries pierced the emperor like a sword, and his anger was enkindled a hundredfold.

Now a duel of strength between the emperor of Rome and the young doctor of Nicomedia commenced. According to legend, Pantaleon was subject to five further attempts to execute him: by fire, liquid lead, drowning, the wheel, and the sword. He frustrated every attempt, until at length, he permitted himself to be beheaded. From his veins poured milk, instead of blood, and the olive tree, to which he was bound, sprang into fruit.

Saint Pantaleon is honored as one of the greatest wonderworkers of the East. Relics of his blood are preserved at Constantinople and are said to liquefy yearly on July 27th, the feast day of Saint Pantaleon. The following story is taken from the Acta Sanctorum, Bollandists, July 27.

Fiery Personality

While offering the sacrifice of the mass, following his consecration as Bishop of Dol, all the assistants of Saint Samson watched as his face seemed to be, literally, on fire. Flames burst from his mouth, ears and nostrils. A burning orb encircled his head with rays like those of the sun. His biographers add, it was not unusual to see crowds of angels at his side or a luminous dove settled on his head.

Saint Samson of Dol died in A.D. 565 and was canonized shortly afterward. The accounts of his life are given in Lives of the Saints of Brittany by Dom Lobineau. He is celebrated on July 28th. Dol is located near St. Malo, Brittany.

Hostess

Saint Martha was the sister of Lazarus (resurrected) and Mary Magdalene (with Christ). She lived in a small town named Bethania and was friends with the disciples of Jesus, as she had hosted them many times during their stay in Judea.

Following Jesus' crucifixion, many of his disciples gathered at Martha's home, which they unanimously decided to convert into a basilica. At this gathering, the number of guests in the house was large and the wine supply soon was exhausted. Martha, however, not neglectful of her duties as hostess, knelt in silent prayer and miraculously transformed water in the pots, into wine—a precise imitation of Jesus at the marriage feast at Cana, in Galilee.

This story is found in Monuments inedits de l'Apostolat de Sainte Madeleine. Saint Martha is celebrated on July 29th, as Patron of housewives.

Angelo's Flood

At age twenty-six, Saint Angelus was dispatched to Jerusalem to be ordained a priest. When he arrived at the Jordan River he found it impassable, as its banks had overflowed with the seasonal flood. Being gifted with miracles, he prayed that the river not prevent him from his duty and the keeping of his vow. He commanded the waters, in the name of the Almighty and by the merits of Elijah and Elisha and in consideration of his vow, to give him passage, and the river obeyed. The current arrested, and the remaining waters continued to the sea. In this manner, a passage was formed and Angelus and his retinue crossed.

Saint Angelus (Angelo) lived during the thirteenth century. His miracles were witnessed by many and are recorded in the Ecclesiastical Annals, by Baronius.

Defending Heaven

Ignatius of Loyola was raised to be a commander in the Spanish army. He was a chivalrous man, easily amused by romantic tales of the knights of old. His military career, however, was cut short when a cannon ball shattered his right leg. For months he remained bedridden with fever and coma. No one expected him to survive, however, he did, and the remainder of his life was filled with miracles.

He frequently received visits from angels, and enormous volumes of knowledge were ascertained from his visions. On one occasion he was subsumed in an ecstatic state, whereby all the mysteries of the Christian faith were explained to him. His insights into the nature of spiritual regions seemed new and unorthodox and were not readily accepted by the order of the day. But his visions were so clearly manifest and received with such justification, he declared he would lay down his life in defense of any of them. In 1540, his revelations were officially recognized by Pope Paul III, and he was chosen the first superior general of the new order he had founded. His book Spiritual Exercises was published in 1548.

Saint Ignatius, founder of the Jesuit order, lived from 1491-1556. Although unorthodox in his day, the Jesuits are now a world order. The visions of Ignatius led to his canonization in 1622, where he was declared Patron Saint of schools, churches and colleges. He is celebrated on July 31st, the day he died.

August

1 Saint Bear's Fountain
2 Ruins
3 The Dignity of Simplicity
4 Fit for a King
5 New Habits
6 Tears of Hiroshima
7 Medallion
8 Relocation
9 Conservation of Energy
10 For the Good of the World
11 Saintly Satisfaction
12 A Visit to Heaven
13 A Single Word
14 Fine Wine
15 Golden Rosaries
16 Rock of France
17 Hotbox
18 Never Thirsty
19 Black Elk
20 Athlone
21 Knock
22 It's All Greek
23 Roman Valor
24 Earth to Infinity
25 Time of Birth
26 The Flying Mason of Cordova
27 The Family Profession
28 Child's Play
29 Miracles of Hrushiv
30 Divine Tutor
31 Volunteers Needed

Saint Bear's Fountain

Aside from his gift for miracles, Saint Ursus, Archdeacon of Aosta, was a man of personality and charm, who carried a distinct air of authority. He was an emotional man, who liked to get involved with causes for change, and took his missions very personally.

One of his miracles occurred during an especially hot summer season when he overheard his fellow towns people lamenting over the need for water in the community. He recalled the biblical text *all things are given to those who believeth,* and so inspired, he struck his pastoral staff to the rock beneath his feet. Immediately water issued forth in a stream.

This miraculous spring, where waters are renowned for their delicious taste, continues to flow today and is locally referred to as *Saint Bear's Fountain.*

Saint Ursus lived during the sixth century. He left his native land, Ireland, and was afterward appointed Archdeacon of Aosta. This story is found in The Life of St. Ursus, Archdeacon of Aosta.

Ruins

Francis of Assisi was a passionate man. While he appeared to be reserved, gentle and forgiving, inside he was a bright burning flame of uncompromising discipline.

One morning he wandered into St. Damian's Church, a veritable ruin. Sick with pain from lack of spiritual direction, he fell before the battered crucifix and in tears cried out:

"Great God, and you my Saviour Jesus Christ, dispel the darkness of my soul; give me pure faith, lasting hope, and perfect charity. Let thy will O God, be my will. Make me and keep me Thine, now and forever."

No sooner had he finished his prayer when the miracle for which he is famous occurred. The Crucifix spoke, repeating to him three times, "Go Francis, and repair My church that is falling into ruins. Go Francis. . ."

Francis believed he was to repair St. Damian's church, the ruin where he was kneeling, so he did. But with time he understood it was the universal church which was in need of repair. He undertook this task, armed only with the weapon of humility, and succeeded.

Saint Francis, founder of the Franciscan Order, lived from 1181-1226. The cross from which this miracle occurred, along with his other relics, may be viewed in Assisi, Italy. Life of Saint Francis of Assisi.

The Dignity of Simplicity

Saint Peter Celestine brought his own special sparkle into the lives of those who knew him. He is affectionately remembered for his big-hearted innocence and elementary blunders in the practical affairs of daily life. He preferred a simple life, and it was no surprise when he retired to Mount Majella with a few of his disciples.

During the three years he spent on the mountain, his life was filled with miracles. The mysterious sound of celestial bells seemed to ring all day, and frequently heavenly voices were heard singing in the air. A mysterious dove, whiter than snow, often sat on Peter's oratory, and when his new church reached completion angels appeared, clothed in gowns of white, and were overheard to say, "Let us attend the dedication."

While celebrating the office, a beautiful seamless garment, like that worn by the angels, fell upon the shoulders of Saint Peter, apparently a sign of Heaven's approval of his sanctity. Forty-three years later at age eighty, Peter Celestine, though reluctant to accept, was elected Pope and brought the dignity of simplicity to his station. A few months later he voluntarily abdicated because a simple life was all he ever wanted.

Saint Peter Celestine lived from 1215-1296. He was canonized seventeen years after his death.

Fit For a King

Oswald, King of Northumbria, is celebrated among England's national heroes. His bravery, military skills, generosity and piety, a sacrificial death in battle for country and faith, and a miracle or two, (including the incorruptibility of his bodily relics) have earned him a position in the heart of England and the Roman Catholic calendar. The following account, though lacking miracles per se, best describes the true nature of Saint Oswald and is worthy of mention.

While dining one evening, King Oswald was served an extra-special dish of regal delicacies on a superb solid silver platter of exquisite craftsmanship. But just before he was about to begin his meal, someone whispered in his ear that a crowd of mendicants was at the gate clamoring for food. The saintly king bade his steward take the food from his own table and distribute it to them. He then divided the royal feast among them, giving each an equal amount. That night the king fasted. It is believed that fasting on this day, August 4th, in honor of King Oswald, brings foreknowledge of one's own death.

Saint Oswald lived during the seventh century. He is celebrated on August 4th. This story is found in Bede's Ecclesiastical History, Book III.

New Habits

One of the most colorful and amusing apparitions of the Virgin Mary was recorded on August 5, 1109, in a Cistercian monastery, under the direction of Saint Alberic. The traditional uniform for Cistercian monks was the grey or black habit, but on this particular day, the tradition was changed. While the monks were chanting their matins in the chapel, "in plain sight of them all," an apparition of the Virgin Mary, accompanied by innumerable saints and angels, descended from a heavenly region to join their assembly. The Virgin Mother walked gracefully among them, then approached the abbot, Saint Alberic, and covered his shoulders with a pure white robe. As she did, the vestments of all the monks were instantly transformed to white. This done, the Virgin vanished, together with her escort of saints and angels.

From that day forward, this miracle has been commemorated by the Cistercian order under the title, *The Descent of The Blessed Virgin Mary at Citeaux, and the Miraculous Change of the Black Habits for White Ones, while Alberic was Abbot.* The traditional uniform for the Cistercian monk is now a white habit.

Recorded in the Acta Sanctorum and The Annals of the Cistercians, Volume I.

Tears for Hiroshima

A very different kind of miracle took place in the home of Allen Demetrius of Pittsburgh, Pennsylvania. On August 6, 1945, the day the United States dropped an atomic bomb on Hiroshima, Demetrius noticed that a bronze statue of a young Japanese maiden began to weep tears. Excited by the inexplicable nature of the event, he contacted the local press. "It was like she was weeping about the bombing. The tears were running down her face." Numerous witnesses have testified to this episode and photographic evidence documents the occurrence.

A second incident occurred on March 18, 1979, ten days before the nuclear reactor accident at Three Mile Island near Harrisburg, Pennsylvania. Again the maiden began to cry.

"It was as though the statue wanted to warn us something was going to happen," Demetrius reported.

It is primarily the somewhat unreligous nature of this supernatural phenomenon that makes it worthy of mention. No messages, visions or healings of any kind have ever been reported. The Japanese maiden seems only to be moved with compassion for the injury and death of innocent human beings.

This miraculous statue remains at Allen Demetrius' home in Pennsylvania where it has currently gained public attention again.

Medallion

Many miracles have occurred through the relics of saints, and noteworthy among them is the story of Lucy de Villanzan who lived to exceed one hundred and twenty years.

Lucy de Villanzan was baptized by Saint Francis Xavier, whom she loved dearly, and to whom she remained forever devoted. In reverence to her master, she designed a medal of Saint Francis, which was fashioned for her at Coccinum. For twelve years she employed this medal as if it were a magic wand, touching the sick and diseased alike, and "as many as she touched were instantly made whole." Ulcers and cancers, boils and wounds of every description were cured by merely washing them in the water in which the medal had been immersed.

The marvels of this medal are too numerous to mention, but the details are given in full in Cardinal de Monte's speech to Pope Gregory XV, at the Act of the Canonization of Francis Xavier, 1622.

Relocation

Saint Peter the hermit was a simple man, ever aglow with happiness, and always eager to please. Although he never formally trained as an architect, he learned the principles of the trade by perseverance, trial and error and listening to birds. Many miracles regarding birds occurred in his life, and his biographers recount the following tale which suggests that his education came slowly but surely.

On one occasion, the lords of the Apennines awarded Peter the necessary supplies for building a monastery of his own design. Accordingly, he laid the foundation and raised the walls about six feet high. However, one night his efforts were inexplicably reduced to little more than rubble and dust. The hermit was stupefied by this mystery and immediately instituted a religious procession to pay honor to the saints of old who had endeavored to build monasteries of their own. As the procession marched forward, it eventually reached Vallombrosa, where a flock of doves was waiting for Saint Peter. By picking up mouthfuls of wheat in their beaks and dropping them on the ground in advance of the procession, the doves formed a perfect series of letters which read, AVE MARIA. The message was plain enough for Saint Peter. He relocated his monastery to the new site and construction began without delay.

Saint Peter is respectfully celebrated for his efforts. The accounts of his life are recorded in the Acta Sanctorum, Volume II.

Conservation of Energy

Saint Hermann loved to meditate. He would gladly have done so all day if allowed, but it often upset the routine of the monastery. His biographers tell us that during the performance of mass, he was generally in an ecstasy and would remain motionless in meditation for three or four hours afterwards. He never appeared to be disturbed by the activities around him and was apparently unaware that there were disturbances. It was often awkward to work near him, but it was noted that certain minor miracles occurred around him during these times. It had been proven time and again, without a doubt, that while Hermann remained in meditation, the candles, though burning, ceased to consume any wax.

Saint Hermann lived until 1230. The accounts of his life are found in Life of Saint Hermann, Bollandists.

For the Good of the World

Saint Catherine of Siena ranks among the greatest mystics and spiritual writers of Europe. She was a woman of simple, stately dignity, devoid of false pretense and very much an introvert, but often her visions and ecstasies moved her to behave in alarming and unorthodox ways. Frequently she was seen tumbling into bodies of water or pits of fire where she remained for long periods without injury. Once, during her stay in Pisa, she was so deeply transfixed in an ecstacy that she appeared lifeless and was pronounced dead. However, after lying in this state for 24 hours, she returned to life uttering the words, "Oh my soul, unhappy thou!"

She told her fellow sisters that the mysteries of heaven had been revealed to her. She had seen the glories of the heavenly beings and the confusion of those souls who cared only for their earthly needs. She saw the "Almighty Deity," who proclaimed that her hour had not yet come and, for the good of the world, she must return to earth and teach the children to abandon their evil ways.

This experience significantly changed her life and afterward she devoted herself wholeheartedly to caring for the sick and distributing alms to the needy. In the years that followed many miraculous healings were credited to her touch, and on occasion she was discovered levitating above the ground while in prayer. Long before her death she was regarded a saint.

The extraordinary nature of her visions, which she carefully recorded, won her the official recognition of the Apostolic See, who raised her to the dignity of Doctor of the Church, only the second woman to bear this illustrious title. In 1939 she was declared Chief Patron of Italy.

Catherine lived from 1317-1380 and was canonized in 1461. Her earthly belongings are preserved at her house in Siena where a surviving portrait reveals her remarkable beauty. Her visions were recorded by Raymond of Capuain, her confessor, in Life of Saint Catherine of Siena. Many of her written works including Dialogue of Saint Catherine have survived. Her body remains miraculously incorrupt and may be seen at her shrine in Siena, Italy.

Saintly Satisfaction

Saint Tiburtius was not the sort of man to waste time with anyone who lacked resolve or spirit. He had a way of focusing on the details of any matter and was at times domineering—usually for a person's own good, as he might have put it. He was, however, a highly respected holy man of his day, and the following account is but one of many taken from the records of his life.

Saint Tiburtius once came across the scene of an accident. A young man had fallen from a very great height, and it seemed apparent to all that nothing could be done, so a burial was being prepared. Tiburtius went to the parents and said, "Give me leave to speak a word or two to your son. It seems to me that all hope of his recovery should not be abandoned." Then saying the Pater Noster and the Credo over the young man, he had the satisfaction of seeing him revive, stand on his feet and go to his parents in perfect health.

Saint Tiburtius lived during the third century. The accounts of his life are recorded in The Life of Saint Sebastian taken from the public registers. He is celebrated on August 11th.

A Visit to Heaven

Some people may call Betty Eadie crazy, but she learned long ago to handle the abuses of others. At age four her white father and Sioux Indian mother separated leaving her to be raised in a religious boarding school where the words heathen, half-breed and sinner were synonymous with her name. She is not a well-educated woman, but what happened in 1973 has kept her on *The New York Times* best-seller list since the summer of 1993.

She was a thirty-one year old mother of seven at the time, and following a hysterectomy, her heart suddenly stopped. She felt her soul lift out of her body, weightless and glowing as she proceeded down a dark tunnel leading to an effulgent brilliant light which seemed to fill every atom of her being with unconditional love. There she met Jesus, angels and other beings of light, many of whom were preparing for lifetimes on earth.

She was shown many regions of heaven and allowed to review her own life. Her questions were answered telepathically. She was told that she had died before her time and must return to Earth with a mission. This mission is not yet clear to Betty, but she believes her book, *Embraced by the Light*, has something to do with it.

Betty is neither surprised nor concerned about her multi-million dollar publishing success. She plans to use her royalties to help Native Americans regain their pride and respect. Currently, she gives public lectures and seminars to sell-out audiences throughout the United States.

Embraced by the Light, by Betty Eadie, Gold Leaf Press. This interview was given in the national newspaper USA Today, August 12, 1993.

A Single Word

Miracles were little more than a means to an end for Saint Francis of Paola. Although often accused of ostentatious acts, he felt he had little time for false modesty. He acted simply according to his instincts. For example, once, during the construction of his monastery at Calabria, a huge boulder broke free from a neighboring mountain. It threatened to destroy both the building and the workmen within. The danger was imminent, and a cry of fright rose from the men. Without the slightest hesitation, Saint Francis, not in the least alarmed, arrested the rock in mid motion, with a single word. Approaching the boulder, he struck his staff in the ground before it and bid the rock to roll no further. There it remained until it was split up and used in the construction of the monastery.

At another time, he suspended a huge rock on a promontory. This rock was suspended in a manner which seemed to be a natural impossibility. It appeared to all observers that it must fall, but it remained for literally hundreds of years.

Saint Francis of Paola lived from 1416-1507 and was canonized twelve years after his death. He is respectfully honored as the Patron of seafarers, because many of his miracles are connected with the sea. The accounts of his life are given in the Acts of Canonization, compiled by Father Giry.

Fine Wine

Saint Hermenland was more of an observer than a philosopher. He did things in a simple, methodical, calm and unhurried way. He was also a worker of miracles and once, while visiting the city of Coutances, in Normandy, he was assisted in a miracle by a wealthy inhabitant named Laune. Laune offered the holy man a glass of fine wine from the only pint in the house and Hermenland accepted but insisted that it first be given to quench the thirst of all huge crowd that had come to hear him speak. Many hundreds had gathered, and it seemed an impossible task, but Laune did as the saint suggested.

To his surprise, after everyone received an ample portion, more remained in the vessel than when he had filled it.

Saint Hermenland lived until A.D. 720. The accounts of his life are recorded in the Analecta Bollandiana, Volume XXIX.

Golden Rosaries

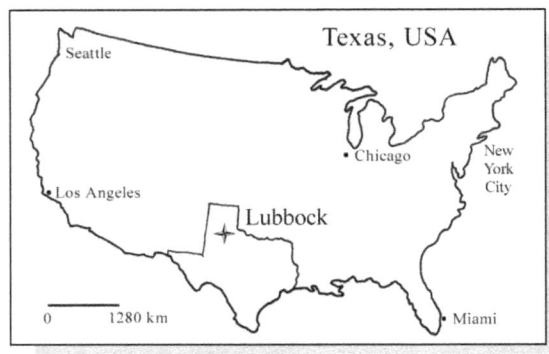

1988 was a good year for the citizens of Lubbock, Texas. Three local visionaries, Mary Constancio, Michael Slate (a retired Air Corps Officer) and Theresa Werner (a cosmetologist) announced that the Virgin Mary had told them a miraculous sign would occur at St. John Neumann's Church, on August 15, 1988. Their credibility was doubted, but an estimated twenty thousand people came to prove them either right or wrong.

According to Father Rene Laurentin, a majority of the spectators testified that at 6:10 p.m. certain supernatural occurrences transpired in the sun. Numerous healings were reported, rosaries were miraculously transformed to a golden color and an apparition of Mary and Jesus appeared in the sky. Many people said the sun danced, and some witnesses with cameras produced photographs (apparently of the apparitions). The images are not scientifically explainable.

As might be expected, the visionaries' credibility soared. The messages being conveyed were similar to those of other modern apparitions of the Virgin Mary—an urgent invitation to prayer, fasting and peace for the world.

Currently, Michael Slate and Theresa Werner are no longer receiving messages, but Mary Constancio has continued to have visions. As recently as 1991, healings and supernatural phenomena have been reported at St. John Neumann's Church.

Further information may be obtained from The Apparition of the Blessed Virgin Mary Today by Father Rene Laurentin.

Rock of France

For Rock it was easier to help others than it was to help himself. He was attracted to worthy causes like a magnet and seldom considered any personal benefit. Little is known about Rock, but it is believed he was born in Montpellier, France, apparently the governor's son. At the age of twenty he was left both orphaned and rich. Finding Italy plague-stricken, he dedicated himself and his new wealth to its cure.

He visited the major areas of epidemic and worked tirelessly to care for the sick, embracing his formidable task with undaunted optimism. At Piacenza, however, he became infected and, not wanting to be a burden to others, dragged himself into the woods to die. As fate would have it, he was discovered by a dog who remained with him and fed him for a time. Soon afterwards, the dog's master discovered Rock and attended him as Rock had attended others. When he recovered he seemed to glow with a new and mysterious vitality. He returned to Piacenza and renewed his original devotions to the sick, but now he attended them with miracles.

He cured hundreds of families as well as their cattle by merely making the sign of the cross over them. However, when he returned to his hometown, for reasons not known, he was imprisoned by his surviving uncle, who failed to recognize him. For five years, he was imprisoned and died in captivity. When his body was examined, his identity was determined and as the son of the former governor, a public funeral was performed.

Rock's accomplishments after death, in 1378, were even more impressive than while he lived. The number of miracles accredited to his tomb are too numerous to mention and continue today.

Veneration of Saint Rock remains popular today. He is particularly invoked for battles against pestilence. His celebration is held on August 16th.

Hotbox

Among the great martyrs of Greece, Saint Mamas is perhaps the best celebrated. His death is attributed to Aurelian and Alexander, the Governor of Cappadocia. Having refused to sacrifice to Apollo, Mamas was sentenced to death in the furnace.

Making the sign of the cross, Mamas was hurled into the furnace, and there he lived for three days and nights untouched by the flames. Growing weary of the flames, on the third day he departed from the furnace more radiant and lively than before. Accordingly the president declared him to be an evil magician and commanded that he be cast to the wild beasts. A bear and a leopard, hungry from deprivation, were set loose against him, but the bear laid affectionately at his feet and the leopard placed its forepaws on the shoulders of the holy man and licked his face lovingly.

Saint Mamas lived until A. D. 315. He is celebrated on August 11th. The accounts of his life are found in Vie de St. Mammes, L'Abbe Tincelin.

Never Thirsty

Saint Florus was an uncomplicated man of great will and equal patience. He was a contemporary of Jesus and a disciple of Saint Peter. His inner voice was strong and it especially guided him in detecting the slightest fallacy in the actions of others. The account which follows is one of the many miracles of his life.

In his travels to Aquitaine Saint Florus and his companions camped on the flats of a hill to rest for a night before resuming their journey. Parched with thirst, the company searched for water, but found none anywhere. In this emergency, Saint Florus struck the ground with his staff and a spring of water immediately burst through. To this day the spring continues to flow and the record shows it has never been exhausted.

This account is given in Pro pre de St. Flour et de Clermont.

Blake Elk

Born on the Little Powder River in Wyoming, Black Elk is currently venerated as one of the greatest holy men of North America, not only by his own tribe, the Lakotas, but by other tribal groups as well. He was blessed with many visions and powers from childhood, but not until a great vision at the age of eighteen did he begin to understand the depth of his earlier experiences.

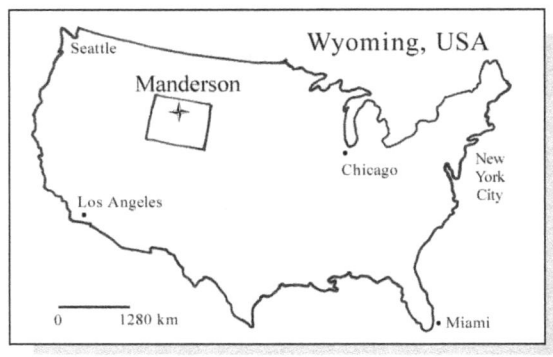

In 1881 he began his career as a medicine man, practicing the traditional native ways and introducing understandings that were revealed to him in visions. However, Black Elk was a true man of the times. The Indian way of life was changing with the European settlers, and Black Elk wanted to better understand what the white ways had to offer. In 1886 he elected to travel with the white man and joined Buffalo Bill's Wild West Show which journeyed to New York and Europe.

He returned four years later to witness the slaughter of his people, the Lakotas, at Wounded Knee. For fourteen years afterwards he practiced traditional healing ceremonies, at the end of which time he converted to Roman Catholicism. Baptized Nicholas Black Elk on December 6, 1904, he pursued a career as a Catholic catechist.

During the 1930s and 40s, he was discovered by the poet John G. Neihardt. To John he gave his trust and narrated his visions and the sacred 10 teachings of the Lakota ways, hoping to preserve them for further generations. This information, still in print, was first published in 1932, and the book, *Black Elk Speaks*, has been translated into at least eight languages. Black Elk has left, in his passing, detailed and insightful descriptions of the Indian traditions that have yet to be paralleled. He died on August 19, 1950.

Black Elk made his home at Manderson, Wyoming on the Pine Ridge Sioux Indian Reservation. His photographs are preserved in the National Anthropological Archives, Smithsonian Institute.

Athlone

Sunday evening, August 20, 1882. A large congregation was gathered for the usual Sunday ceremony at the Franciscan Church in Athlone, Ireland. As the priest, Rev. Father McDermott, concluded his sermon, a brilliant light lit the congregation. Afterward it resumed its former appearance.

Those who saw it rose from their seats in different parts of the church and pushed to the altar. A scene of frenzied excitement followed. All religious services were suspended, but the congregation refused to leave the church. It remained crowded until late into the night and even then, took great effort to clear. By morning, the thoroughfares near the church were crowded with people. The numerous accounts of this miracle, given by witnesses, are in accord in every detail. The religious implications of this vision are not clear.

This account was taken from a newspaper, August 22, 1882, Athlone, Ireland.

Knock

Knock, a remote village in the west hills of Ireland, marks the scene of a remarkable apparition of the Virgin Mary on August 21, 1879. In all, about eighteen people saw the apparition. Nothing whatsoever was spoken and no massage was given. Those are few who witnessed it were 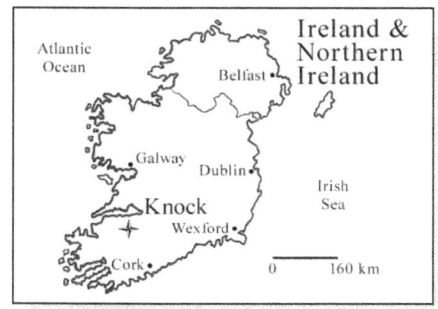 in no way lifted in spirit or elevated to any inspirational heights. They were simply passing by the church one rainy August evening.

Where did they see? They saw the south gable of Knock suffused and covered in brilliant golden light. The light itself sparkled and the scene was as bright as noon. It was a pulsating light, sometimes reaching out to the sky, then collapsing onto itself and growing ever more brilliant and white. In the middle stood three figures clothed in dazzling white gowns that shone like silver. Prominent among them was a lady—a queen, for she wore a brilliant crown a white cloak that fastened at the throat and fell in ample folds to her ankles. Her hands were extended upward in prayer, and her gaze was fixed on the heavens.

The Group gathered closer. One of the boys saw angels "hovering for the whole time, for an hour and a half or longer." He "saw their wings fluttering but not their heads or faces which were not turned to me." Another boy saw "two angels flying back and forth."

One woman spontaneously knelt at the feet of the radiant queen. But when she closed her arms to embrace them, only empty air remained. "I felt nothing in the embrace but the wall. Yet the figures appeared so lifelike. I could not understand it and wondered why my hands could not feel what was so plain and distinct to my sight."

When the apparition vanished, the spectators returned to their homes. By morning the news had spread, and crowds gathered at the gable wall. Soon cures began to be reported, and before long, fanatic pilgrims had all but collapsed the wall, for want of a souvenir. (A common feature of miracle sites.) The wall, however, was preserved and restored and is intact for all those who wish to see where the queen of heaven appeared, one rainy August evening in Knock.

It's All Greek

Bernardino of Siena was among the many saints who possessed a miraculous gift of speech. His biographers tell us that he was frequently asked to speak at public assemblies. On one occasion he was asked to speak to a gathering of Greeks. Not knowing Greek, he delivered his speech in his native tongue, Italian. Speaking in Italian at a Grecian assembly made little sense to Bernardino's disciples, but by the completion of his talk, they were astonished to find the gathering was flattered by his eloquence and mastery of their native tongue. Not once, but many times he spoke with equal eloquence in a myriad European languages.

Saint Bernardino lived from 1380-1444 and was canonized in 1450. His body remained miraculously incorrupt for decades after his death and is currently enshrined in the Basilica of Saint Bernardino, L'Aquila, Italy. The accounts of his life are documented in Life of Saint Bernardino, written by his contemporary, Barnaby Siena.

Roman Valor

We are told from Roman history that in the year 362 B.C. a vast chasm, from some unknown cause, appeared in the Roman forum. The Roman wise men who were learned in the science of omens declared it would never be filled unless Rome deposited its most valued treasure into it.

"Rome's best treasure is a self-sacrificing, devoted patriot," declared Mettius Curtius.

So saying, he mounted his charger and leaped into the gulf, which immediately trembled and closed over him.

Recorded in De Factis Dictisque Memorabilibus, by Valerius Maximlls.

Earth to Infinity

Underneath an apparent air of skepticism, Saint Owen, Bishop of Rouen, harbored an innate love of mankind with a rare blend of exalted morality. He was a man who liked to deal with the visible world, rather than unseen metaphysics. His deep and honest intellect led him to mull things over for extended periods of time, to avoid any chance of erroneous conclusions. Thus, the many miracles which happened in his life seem all the more enriching.

His biography tells of an event which occurred on his return journey from Spain. While passing near Louviers, his mule suddenly stopped and refused to budge. Surprised at this behavior, Owen looked for the cause. Lifting his eyes to the sky, he saw a luminous cross, "very brilliant, the light of which shone everywhere." Owen understood this to mean that the spot was a holy place, so he traced a cross on the ground and buried some relics there. Mounting his mule, he encountered no further resistance on his way.

The following evening a pillar of fire was seen "reaching from earth to infinity and more brilliant than the blazing sun." The column stationed itself on the sacred spot where it was clearly witnessed by all the inhabitants. A century later in honor of the miracle, a monastery was erected on the site by Saint Leufroi.

Saint Owen lived from 600-684. He is celebrated on August 24th. The account of his life are recorded in the Acta Sanctorum, Volume IV.

Time of Birth

The study of the stars has often been woven into the Christian story. The attendance of three wise men at the birth of Christ and Christ's discussions with the elders in the temple of Jerusalem, bear credence to the validity of this ancient science.

Saint Bernard, Abbot of Tiron, likewise had a passion for the study of the stars and was gripped with a burning desire to know the precise hour of Christ's nativity. Being present at a church on Christmas Eve, he prayed earnestly that the Holy Ghost would inform him of these unknown facts. To his delight, his prayers were more than adequately answered when the child, Jesus, appeared and informed him minutely of the day and hour of his birth in Bethlehem.

Saint Bernard of Tiron lived until A.D. 1117. This account was recorded by Godfrey, Saint Bernard's secretary, in The Life of St. Bernard.

The Flying Mason of Cordon

Saint John Baptist de la Conception lived a quiet life, seldom seen and seldom heard. But it can not be said that he lacked authority or power. He was both leader and recluse. The following record provides an insight into his character.

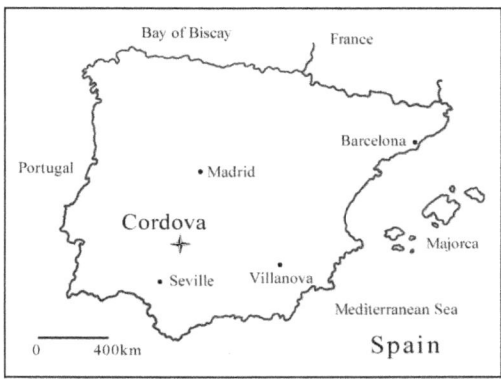

During the period when the convent of Cordova was under construction, a mason carrying a huge stone atop a ladder lost his balance and tumbled to the ground. John Baptist happened to be present during the calamity and extending his arm upwards, he cried aloud, "In the name of the holy Trinity, stop!"

Instantly, the stone and the workman ceased falling. The mason adjusted himself to an upright position and both he and the boulder descended slowly to the ground.

"A miracle! A miracle!" shouted the workmen. Wishing to avoid attention, John quietly returned to his cell.

Saint John Baptist de la Conception lived from 1562-1613. This story is recorded in Vies des Saints, by Godscard.

The Family Profession

Domenico was one of eight children born to a shaman family at the Rincon Reservation in California. As a youngster his enthusiasm for his father's profession was deep, and in preparation for his own career as a shaman, he spent much of his time in solitude and meditation. Stories began to spread about the spiritual sanctity of the child, but most members of the tribe, including some family members, doubted that he possessed any gifts. His mother was the first to recognize his spiritual powers, and by the time he was eighteen years of age, his power were active.

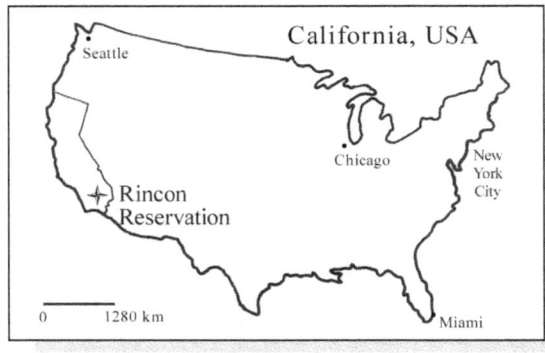

He was an astonishing clairvoyant and clairaudiant. Having been tested as a healer, he began taking patients and sharing in their sufferings to bring about their cure. It is said that he spoke to the patient's guardian spirit who would appear to him. Domenico would not heal the patient's body unless he could also heal their heart.

His fame soon spread well beyond the Native American community and Europeans, Americans, Blacks, Orientals and people of every faith were cured through his intercession. He took particular care to deal with those whose difficulties were purely emotional. Although his techniques were primarily Native American, he would recommend hospital surgery, if required.

No patient was ever formally charged a fee. All services were administered freely, or on a contribution basis. It was also said that through his intercession, the weather was cooperative.

Domenico died in 1963 when he suddenly became ill. No apprentice had been trained, and thus no successor continues his mission.

The Encyclopedia of Native American Religions, by Arlene Hirschfelder and Paulette Molin.

Child's Play

August 28, 1464, marks the day John of Sahagun was professed a monk. Whether his mastery of miracles came before or after he chose a religious life is not known, but his talents were never exploited for personal glory, and the miracles he performed were always in service to others.

The following incident took place during the time Saint John was living with the Augustinian friars of Salamanca. It happened that a small child fell into a well, and even though the citizens of the community made every effort, they were unable to secure its rescue. Arriving at the scene of the accident, Saint John assisted with a miracle. He simply laid his waistband on stones forming the walls of the well and requested the waters to restore the child. To the delight and disbelief of everyone present, the waters rose to the level of the coping and buoyed up the child, who was then lifted to safety by its parents.

Saint John of Sahagun lived from 1430-1479. He was favored with many miracles, both before and after his death, and was canonized in 1690. This account is given in the Acta Sanctorum, Bollandists, Volume II.

Miracles of Hrushiv

On the first anniversary of the Chernobyl nuclear accident in 1987, an apparition of the Virgin Mary visited the village of Hrushiv, in the Ukraine. She, together with the infant Jesus,  appeared to a twelve-year-old girl named Marina, above a small church in the area. Her mother who was nearby also witnessed the apparition.

Thousands of people flocked to the site and reported to have seen the blessed Virgin. The *Moscow Literary Gazette* reported that forty-five thousand people a day were visiting the little village of Hrushiv. On one occasion eighty thousand people arrived. Within four months of the first appearance of the Virgin Mary, it was estimated that over half a million people witnessed the apparition. More than ten thousand reported to have heard her speak.

Before the apparition appears, an iridescent, pulsating light bathes the small church and the surrounding area. The Virgin emerges from this celestial light and remains visible above the roof of the church. She urges forgiveness and asks that the rosary be taught to the children as a weapon against evil.

"I have come on purpose to thank the Ukrainian people because you have suffered most for the church of Christ in the last seventy years. I have come to comfort you and tell you that your suffering will soon come to an end. Ukraine will become an independent state."

After August 1987, no further apparitions occurred until April of the following year. During the period of the Virgin's absence from Hrushiv she was reported to have been seen in eleven other shrines in the Ukraine. It is believed that appearances are continuing at more remote shrines in the country to the present day.

Additional information may be obtained through the Pittsburgh Center For Peace.

Divine Tutor

Speaking to angels was not uncommon for Benedicta, a simple shepherdess. She was sensitive with a stately charm and dignity that made one feel surrounded by the finer things of life. She never understood why it happened to her, but on one occasion in May, while tending her sheep, an angel appeared and instructed her to drive her flock to Saint Steven's Valley. There she was told the Virgin Mary would be waiting for her. The following morning Benedicta's flock went, of its own accord, to Saint Stephen's Valley, instead of Saint Maurice's Downs as was the usual routine. When the shepherdess arrived shortly after the flock, she saw a lady, "unsurpassed in beauty," holding an infant in her arms, more radiant still. At first Benedicta could not persuade herself that the vision was Mary, the Madonna. Rather, she thought it was some saintly woman and generously offered her what little she had, a piece of bread. The lady smiled lovingly and said nothing at all.

For months, Benedicta would go to Saint Steven's Valley every day and gaze upon the heavenly lady who was always waiting in the exact same spot when she arrived. With the passing months, the countenance of the young shepherdess appeared spiritualized. Her skin shone with a subtle, ethereal light and speech was like that of an angel. Her familiarity with the vision became so natural and comfortable, it seemed almost commonplace. Then suddenly one day, quite by surprise, the Virgin broke silence and spoke. She prayed together with Benedicta and taught her certain litanies entirely in those parts. She instructed her in divine practices, meant for her alone and spoke to her of things which she was not to reveal to anyone.

Rumours of Benedicta's visions soon caught the wind and naturally skepticism bred ridicule. To end these adolescent persecutions, the Virgin Mother spoke thus to Benedicta: "I am Mary, the mother of Jesus, and my son wishes to be honored in this valley. Bring to this hollow the girls of Saint Stephen, in procession." Benedicta did as she was asked.

On August 30th, the girls of St. Stephen, led by Mons. Fraisse, pastor of the parish, journeyed to the designated cove in procession. All were asked to note attentively everything that transpired. When the children arrived, the Virgin Mother was waiting, just as she had waited every day for Benedicta. She was visible to all and not one among them doubted that the Virgin Mary had bestowed a blessing on their valley, second-to-none ever granted in this world.

In 1640 a chapel was erected where the vision had occurred. It was dedicated under the title Notre Dame de Bon-Rencontre.

This account is recorded in Vies des Saints, Volume V, by Mgr. Guerin, Chamberlain to Pope Leo XIII.

Volunteers Needed

Spanish and Portuguese sailors have a great veneration for Peter Gonzalez, whom they invoke as the Patron of mariners. He was born into a noble Castilian family and spent much of his life improving the spiritual ecology of his country, especially the coastal regions. During his life he constructed many houses for the practice and study of religion, and having a conscientious love for mankind, he took the greatest of care to see that his numerous workmen were well cared for. He made it his personal responsibility to see them properly nourished. From time to time, however, food was short and on such occasions he would set out in search of the nearest river. Kneeling at the river bank, he would politely explain his dilemma to the resident fishes. Having heard his supplication, they would immediately respond by throwing themselves on the bank of the river in great numbers, voluntarily offering themselves to his service.

Through these and other such miracles Peter Gonzalez was venerated in Portugal and Spain long before he died.

Beatified Peter Gonzalez lived from 1190-1248. He is venerated in Portugal as Patron of mariners, his cultus being officially confirmed in 1741. The accounts of his life are recorded in the Acta Sanctorum, Volume II.

September

1 Royal Mishaps
2 From Pillar to Post
3 Thy Will, Not My Will
4 Never Thirsty
5 Miracle of Turzovka
6 Provided For
7 Earnest Kiss
8 Test Every Theory
9 Dazzling Personality
10 Horse Thief
11 Deserts of Egypt
12 Luminescent Extravagance
13 Ignorant of the World
14 Mount Etzel
15 The Good Mother
16 The Holy Drought
17 Mystic Revelation
18 Flyboy
19 Our Lady of La Salette
20 Triumph
21 Queen of Plants
22 The Apostle of Hungary
23 Holy Macaroni
24 Slave Labor
25 Champion of Angels
26 Belle of Valentia
27 Rescued
28 Meditation: A Spectator Sport
29 Great Noise
30 The Mascot

Royal Mishap

Athenian by birth, Giles the Miracle Worker was renowned throughout Greece for the abundance of his supernatural charities. He possessed a vitality and sustaining energy that made him seem almost invincible at times, but he soon realized that miraculous cures drained his energy and caused others to become dependent on him. This dependence limited their spiritual progress. Thus, he resolved to retire from the world and sought a solitary retreat, which he found in a forest near the mouth of the Rhone River.

There was a cave at the spot, and, as it happened, a young mother deer and fawn were living there. They seemed willing to share the shelter with the Saint and daily the hind offered herself to be milked by Giles. Giles enjoyed his new roommates, but daily food was not always an urgent necessity for him. Frequently he remained fixed in meditation, often for days or weeks at a time. Thus, the recluse and his forest family lived harmoniously together in the cave.

As fate would have it, King Flavius came upon the deer during a hunting expedition. Together with his dogs, a chase ensued whereupon the deer retreated, into the mouth of the cave. Surprised by the dogs' refusal to enter the cave, a huntsman discharged an arrow into the opening. Dismounting, the king proceeded to enter the cave and discovered Giles kneeling in silent meditation with an arrow thrust within his body. Desperate with concern, he offered Giles the services of the royal physician and promised to give him money.

Giles replied, "I need no physician but God. And as for money, give it not to me, but spend it in founding a monastery to the glory of God."

This the king did, and with full pomp and ceremony, Giles was appointed its first abbot.

Saint Giles lived during the seventh century. He is celebrated on September 1st. The accounts of his life are given in The Life of Saint Giles, by Gilbert, Bishop of Carnotum.

From Pillar to Post

In all the biographies of saints, it seems doubtful that there ever lived a character more awesome than Saint Simeon Stylites. His way of life provided a spectacle which was at once challenging, repulsive and divine. At an early age, his search for solitude led him to develop a hermetic life, which due to its severity is surely meant for only a few in this world. He was the first and most famous of the pillar-hermits—hermits who spend their lives in almost continual prayer, living atop sixty-foot pillars in the remotest deserts or abandoned regions.

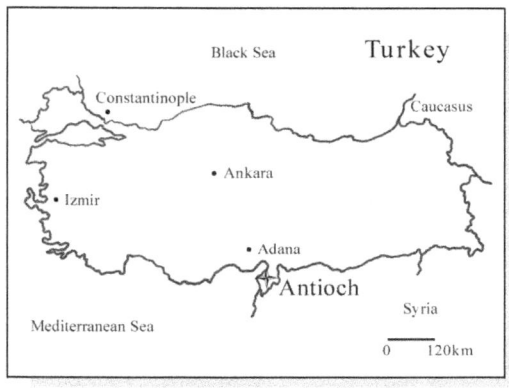

Simeon lived the ideal of human hermeticism and his sanctity was well know. He was the object of pilgrimage and veneration from people of all countries and faiths. Emperors, kings, princes and social leaders of every background swarmed to him for council on matters of social administration. Paupers and prostitutes, Jews, Christians, Muslims, Hindus, all races, all religions, all creeds found the common ground of understanding and freedom in Simeon's words of wisdom.

His way of life suited his true nature. When he started his reclusion, he chose to live on a nine-foot pillar, which he never left for four years. His second home was an eighteen-foot pillar, where he remained for three years, and later, a thirty-three foot pillar, for ten years. His final home, built by his admirers, rose six stories from the ground, with a platform only six feet wide—barely enough room to lie down. There he remained, satisfied with a life of continual prayer for twenty years. So holy was this man that not a single person who saw him thought otherwise.

When he gave up his pure soul to God, he was fixed in meditative prayer. A maggot, from a sore on his body, fell from his pillar to the ground, landing near the foot of Basilicus, King of the Saracens. With reverence, the king lifted the maggot in his hand and placed it on his eye. A moment later it was transformed into a magnificent pearl, "so large, so beautiful and of such fine water, that Basilicus valued it more than his entire empire."

Saint Simeon died on September 2, A.D. 495. The tradition of pillar hermits was continued by Saint Daniel of Constantinople and another Saint Simeon of Antioch. The undisputed authenticity of the acts of Saint Simeon are recorded in Church History *by the historian Theodoret.*

Thy Will, Not My Will

Gregory the Great was one of the most important popes and influential writers of the middle ages. He was a brilliant man, driven by both enthusiasm and creativity, yet left to his own devices, he would gladly have chosen the contemplative life of a monk.

His biographers tell us that when he heard he was likely to be appointed pope, he fled to a distant mountain to hide. A search party was dispatched to discover his whereabouts, but it seemed an impossible task. In the course of their search, however, a mysterious column of fire appeared in the sky. It descended to the ground, and the party agreed it was an intercession from heaven showing them the whereabouts of Saint Gregory. They were correct, for the fiery column led them directly to the cave on the mountain where Gregory had hidden.

The party implored the saint, time and time again, to return with them to Rome, but Gregory had no such intentions. He flatly refused their supplication. Finally, Gregory's refusals went unheeded and the party forcibly transported him to Rome. Once in Rome, Gregory accepted his appointment and reigned for fourteen years until March 12, A.D. 604, when he died.

His accomplishments as an administrator are too numerous to mention, but may be found in his biographical records. It is during his reign as pope that he gained the title, Gregory the Great. He is celebrated on September 3rd.

Never Thirsty

Catherine of Racconeigi was a uniquely gifted child. She was the recipient of many heavenly favors even from infancy, but by age five she had established a considerable friendship with the denizens of heaven. It was apparent she was fated for the life of a spiritual mystic when, on one occasion, an angelic dove flew into her chamber and lighted on her shoulder. She was taken by surprise and cried out in fear, but a ray of light emanating from the dove's beak entered her mouth and comforted her with the words:

"Take, my little daughter, and drink this wine, by virtue of which you will never thirst again and will grow daily stronger in your soul."

She tasted the wine and found it to be of heavenly sweetness. In time, the dove's words proved true. She grew strong and mature beyond her years and wise in the ways of the soul.

Catherine's childhood was filled with numerous playmates from both earth and heaven, yet while still in her tender years she chose to enter a convent, which brought her happiness for the remainder of her life.

Beatified Catherine of Racconeigi lived from 1486-1547. She is celebrated on September 4th. The accounts of her life are recorded in Les Petits Bollandistes, Volume X.

Miracle of Turzovka

Matous Losuta was a simple forester in the village of Turzovka, Czechoslovakia. The last thing he ever expected to find in the forest was an apparition from heaven. But during the summer of 1958 a heavenly lady appeared to him. She identified herself as the Blessed Virgin Mary and showed him a vision, first of heaven, then of the world on fire. The vision lasted three hours, at the end of which Matous was instructed, "Make it known to the world."

On six other occasions during that year, apparitions appeared to Matous. He was told that certain chastisements would befall the world due to its ignorance or insensitivity to God, but that these reprimands could be avoided or lessened through the agency of fasting and prayer.

As instructed, Matous began to tell the villagers of his apparitions and the massages he received at that time. A spring bubbled up on the mountain where the apparitions had first appeared and numerous healings were accredited to it. But despite miraculous cures and the support of many other witnesses Matous suffered personal persecution and humiliation. He was eventually arrested by communist authorities and confined to a mental institution for ten months. Following his release, he was discharged from his job and deprived of all his rights.

Devotions at the apparition site had carried on in Matous' absence and were flourishing again upon his return. He was arrested a second time and imprisoned for three years, but devotions continued. Communist authorities discredited the new institution and started propaganda programs, through radio and print media, hoping to frighten the people. But their efforts failed. Automotive transportation to the area was forbidden, and on sixteen occasions, altars, statues and devotional objects which covered the mountain were forcibly shattered in the hope of disbanding the new organization.

Thirty-five years later, pilgrims from many counties continue to journey to the miracle site of Turzovka, Czechoslovakia.

The church has not rendered an official judgement of this occurrence.

Provided For

Simon Stock lived in the trunk of an enormous tree in the vast forest of Toubersville in Kent.

His food consisted of raw herbs, bitter roots and wild fruits, and he drank only water. It seems that the pure of heart are always happy and well provided for, and so is this true in the case of Simon stock. For every day a wild dog would bring him a small portion of heavenly bread, "beautifully white and delicate." In this way he lived to exceed a hundred years.

Saint Simon Stock lived until 1265. His relics are preserved at Aylesford in Kent. The accounts of his life are recorded in the Monumenta Historica Carmelitana.

Earnest Kiss

While on a journey to Rome, one of the disciples of Saint Mayeul confessed that he was guilty of a heinous offense and demanded absolution with penance from his master.

"Are you in earnest?" asked Saint Mayeul. "Is it penance you desire?"

"Doubtless," replied the erring disciple.

"Then look to the leper there, who is seeking alms. Go to him and give him the kiss of peace."

Instantly the disciple went to the leper and kissed him. No sooner had he done so then the leper was healed.

Saint Mayeul lived during the tenth century and was known to be an advisor to almost all the great men of his period. Emperor Otto granted him sovereignty over all monasteries of Germany and his empire. Likewise, the Empress and her son, Otto II, supported his wishes. He was revered by all the saints of his time and Capet, the King of France, declared himself to be his principal devotee.

The accounts of his life are recorded in Les Petits Bollandistes, Volume V.

Test Every Theory

Bent with the intention of putting the text to the test, a certain Jew resolved to prove, once and for all, whether the Almighty would really reimburse any charities given to the poor. He distributed in alms all that he possessed, except two pieces of silver. Then he waited to see the results of his experiment. Nothing whatsoever occurred for many days. In utter disappointment and despair, he journeyed to Jerusalem to see the high priest and lodge a complaint against Solomon for falsehood in his teaching. On his way, he encountered two men who stood quarreling over a highly polished stone which they had found near the road. He offered them his two remaining silver coins in exchange for the stone. The two men, delighted, accepted the offer, and the quarrel was resolved.

Arriving in Jerusalem, he presented the stone to a jeweller. Here he was told it was one of the precious stones dropped from the ephor of the high priest. Immediately he returned it to the pontiff and, much to his surprise, recieved in reward many times the sum of money he had distributed in alms.

Experiment concluded—Solomon and the Almighty were promise keepers.

This story was recorded by Cedrenus.

Dazzling Personality

The face of Saint Francis of Hieronimus was too dazzling to be looked upon.

Cardinal Wiseman wrote that Francis was the recipient of unusual ecstasies, which caused his face to shine so brightly, it hurt the eyes of onlookers. On one occasion, while Francis was engaged with his regular duties, "his face actually burned with celestial light, the flames radiating a magnificent purifying influence."

His biographers wrote that during his ecstasies spontaneous miracles and cures occurred to those who witnessed the spectacle. Throughout his life these ecstasies occurred, increasing as he grew older.

Saint Francis of Hieronimus lived from 1642-1716. He was canonized in 1839.

Horse Thief

Saint Eman had a way with horses. On one occasion he was invited to visit with Bladiste, a Grand Seigneur of Chartres, and since the journey was too great for a single day, he spent the night in an inn at the side of the road. Late that night, a man named Abbon, who had watched the saint arrive, waited patiently for an opportunity to steal his horse. When he was sure the saint was sleeping, he mounted the horse and galloped away. However, the next morning the horse and rider were found standing motionless and transfixed at the door of the inn where the saint had spent the night.

Eman thanked the man for bringing the horse to the door and placed a little money in his hand saying, "Should the temptation to steal ever arise again, perhaps these few coins will take it away."

Saint Eman lived until A.D. 560. The accounts of his life are recorded in the Acta Sanctorum, Bollandists, Volume II.

Desert of Egypt

The deserts of Egypt have long been sacred to hermits of both ancient and modern times. Tens of thousands of men and women have lived there unnoticed, absorbed in silent devotions, while the rest of the world pressed on. Saint Paphnutius, an early Egyptian abbot, was curious to visit the desert dwellers and study. Their lives to see if it was a life suited for himself.

He met with many adventures, but the following was his most memorable.

On his seventeenth day of travel, he was startled at the sight of what appeared to be to be an aged man with hair and beard so long that it dragged on the ground. He wore a loin cloth made from the leaves of a tree, and his limbs were so heavily covered with hair, they appeared like the fur of an animal. So alarming was this sight that Paphnutius ran in fear for his life, but the figure called to him, assuring him that he also was a servant of God.

For hours the two men spoke and Paphnutius learned that the hermit was Onuphrius who had lived alone in the desert for seventy years. Onuphrius conducted Paphnutius to his cave, and when the sun began to set, bread and water suddenly appeared before them. Both men ate heartily, then prayed together until morning.

As the sun rose, Paphnutius was distressed, but Onuphrius spoke, "Fear not, brother Paphnutius, God has not willed this life for you. In His infinite mercy, he has sent you here to bury me."

At these words Onuphrius knelt on the ground and died. The

following illuming occurred after Paphnutius had completed the burial, the cave collapsed over Onuphrius' body, and the date palm which grew outside his cave withered and died, indicating to Paphnutius to leave that place.

This story was committed to writing by one of the monks who later studied under the mastership of Saint Paphnutius.

Saint Paphnutius lived until A.D. 350. He was appointed Bishop of Upper Thebaid by Saint Antony, the father of monasticism. He is celebrated on September 11th. The accounts of his life are recorded in the Acta Sanctorum.

Luminescent Extravagance

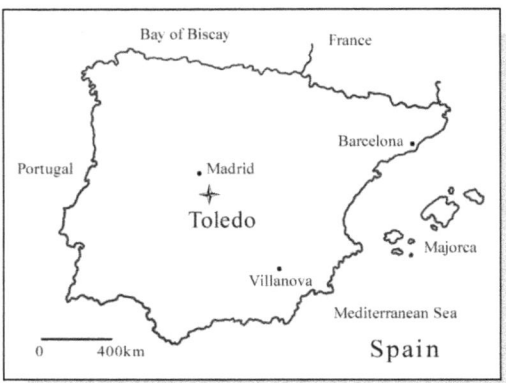

Alfonso was an extremist, at times stubborn, explosive and tyrannical, and at other times the epitome of balance and gentility. He had a way of making dreams come true and made life seem luminescent with possibility. His literary works possessed a remarkable glow of enthusiasm, almost bordering upon extravagance, but the testimonies of his contemporaries give ample reason to believe that it was Alfonso's ardent devotion to the Holy Mother that favored him with miracles.

One night, in his station as Archbishop of Toledo, he, together with his clerks and several others, set out for their church to chant songs of honor to the Virgin Mary. It was a cool December evening and the party moved quickly, but on nearing the chapel, they found it shining with a light so dazzling, they were frightened. Everyone fled except Alfonso and his two deacons. They entered the church together and approached the altar. Before them they witnessed the Virgin Mary seated on the bishop's throne, surrounded by a troop of virgins singing songs of paradise.

Mary beckoned Alfonso to draw near. When he did so, she fixed her eye on him and said, "You are my chaplain and faithful notary. Receive from me this chasuble which my son sends you from his treasury." So saying, the Virgin herself invested him with it, instructing him to wear it only on the feast days held in her honor.

This apparition together with the acquired celestial chasuble were so unquestionable that the council of Toledo ordained a special feast day to perpetuate its memory. The event is documented in the Acta Sanctorum as The Descent of The Holy Virgin and her Apparition.

Saint Alfonso (Ildephonos) was born in Toledo, Spain where he lived from A.D. 606-669.

Ignorant of the World

Benezet surprised everyone, including himself. He was a poor shepherd boy born at Hermillon in Savoy, uneducated and ignorant of the world. On September 13, 1177, he was sent to the pasture to attend to the sheep, but when he arrived a solar eclipse held him fixed in suspense. Suddenly in the darkness he heard a voice calling three times, "Benezet, My son, harken to my words."

On the third calling, the boy, who was only twelve years old, replied, "Who are you? I hear your voice, but I see no one."

The voice resounded, "I am the Lord, who by a single word created the heavens and the earth, the sea and all that ever was."

Unafraid but puzzled, the boy responded, "What would you have with me?"

"Leave these few sheep and erect a bridge across the River Rhone," came the answer.

"But I have never heard of the Rhone and know nothing of how to find it. And what of these sheep, they belong to my mother. . . . how can I leave them?"

"Trust in me," said the voice. "I will gather the sheep in their fold and one I will send, to show you the way."

The boy continued with reasons why he could not go, but soon his concerns were resolved, and he journeyed on his way following the sheep God had chosen. After some time he was joined by an angel who led him to to the River Rhone. Seeing the river, he was aghast at its size and cried in terror, "It's not possible to build a bridge across such a river!"

"Fear not," said the angel, "go to the ferryman and ask him to row you to the opposite shore. Then go to the bishop of Avignon and tell him why you have come."

So saying the angel left him. Benezet made his way to the ferryman, and being set on the other side, he went at once to the cathedral where the bishop was preaching to an assembly. "Listen to me!" cried the boy. "I have a message from our Lord! He wants me to build a bridge across the River Rhone!"

The bishop was indignant at the unwarranted interruption from an evidently rustic young boy. He dispatched the church marshall to chide the child for his insolence, but the boy insisted that the Lord had sent him to build a bridge across the Rhone.

"Nonsense!" cried the marshall. "How is a boy like you to build a bridge across this river, which even Charlemagne would not undertake to do?"

Still the boy insisted he was sent to build the bridge. Finally the marshall said laughingly, "Why don't you start with that stone over there," pointing to a huge boulder, thirty feet long and seventeen feet across.

Benezet walked to the stone, made the sign of the cross, lifted it onto his shoulders and carried it to the spot where the bridge was to start. The entire assembly was momentarily breathless. No longer doubting the boy's story, money poured in from every reserve. Everyone wanted to be a worker on the bridge that was commissioned by God. And it was indeed built. The details are recorded in the public documents drawn up at the time, which are still preserved at Avignon.

Benezet died at the early age of nineteen and was buried on the bridge. His body has since been disinterred twice. In 1669 when a section of the bridge collapsed, the body was found to be entirely without decay, "Even the bowels being sound." Again, five years later, in

1674, his body, still unspoiled, was transported with royal pomp into the church of the Celestines.

A full description of the life of this remarkable boy may be found in the Acta Sanctorum, Bollandists, Volume II.

Mount Etzel

"Consecrate the new church!" was the order of the day.

It was September 13, A.D. 948 when Conrad, Bishop of Constance, accompanied by the Bishop of Augsburg and a number of pilgrims, arrived on Mount Etzel to consecrate a newly erected church. At midnight preceding the 14th, Conrad, the monks and pilgrims were in silent prayer when a sweet melody suddenly burst forth. On raising their eyes they beheld a choir of angels. The heavenly visitants were chanting the very psalms and hymns set down for the morning ceremony. Then Jesus appeared arrayed in violet and celebrated the Dedicatory office. At his side were Saint Peter, Saint Gregory, Saint Augustine, Saint Stephen and Saint Laurentius. At the front of the altar sat "Mary, the Queen of Heaven, on a throne of light."

When the ceremony concluded, the visitors from heaven simply vanished. Since this apparition was seen by all equally, there was little doubt that the chapel had indeed been consecrated by Christ and his angels.

This event, known as The Miraculous Consecration, is among the most authoritative and thoroughly documented events in the ecclesiastical records.

The Good Mother

Miracles are increasing in number as we approach the twenty-first century. Visions of the Virgin Mary have increased all over the world. In San Nicholos, Argentina, a series of apparitions and messages began on October 13, 1983. Since then over eighteen hundred messages have been received by Gladys Quiroga de Motta, and the response has been overwhelming.

Every month tens of thousands of pilgrims travel to San Nicholos to hear messages of the Virgin Mary. Medical cures associated with the gatherings have become so numerous that a medical bureau has been established to document the cases. The movement has gained support from both church and state. Every year on September 25th over one hundred thousand people gather to celebrate the anniversary of the apparitions. The following narration is one of the messages received during the winter of 1989.

Mary to Gladys: "My child, yesterday it was Lourdes; today it is here, but it is always good for the mother to be in search for her children. I expect of them prayer, fasting, conversion. They will find salvation if they do not flee from the Lord; if they accept the Lord. Many souls lack peace. If the soul looks for peace, it will find God."

An Appeal From Mary in Argentina, by Fr. Rene Laurentin.

The Holy Drought

Abraham of Smolensk was a man of courage and powerful intelligence. Everything about him was profound, including his passion for understanding the deepest significance of human spirituality.

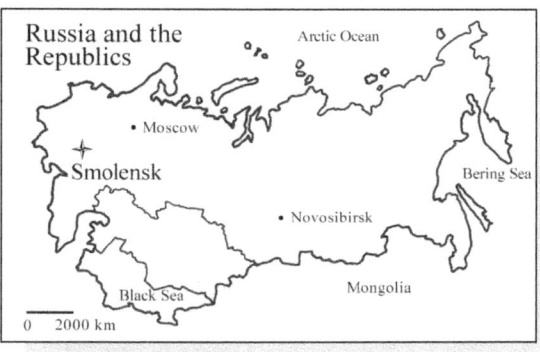

His attention to detail was astonishing, and he seemed to possess an instinct for pioneering the more practical elements of religious doctrines.

Having lost his parents, he was professed a monk at an early age, and his natural genius, together with his cheerful and energetic personality, allowed him to exert considerable influence over the Russian lay folk. However, the more ignorant clergy were jealous of his learning and popularity as a spiritual director and conspired to turn others against him.

He was charged with cohabiting with women, heresy, claiming to be a prophet and reading secular philosophies. Eventually he was arrested, dragged through a jeering crowd, and tried by two separate tribunals, neither of which found him guilty of any offenses. Nevertheless he was banished from Smolensk and restricted from the ceremonies of a priest.

Abraham hadn't even left the city when petitions from its citizens flooded the bishop's office forewarning of disasters should mistreatment of an innocent holy man be allowed to continue. They proved right. For the next five years Smolensk was devastated by drought. Bishop Ignatius decided to re-examine the case of Abraham and reinstated him to his rightful office. He begged Abraham's forgiveness and asked him to return to Smolensk to pray for the city.

"He hadn't even reached his cell before God sent rain," wrote Ephrem, his biographer.

Such were the miracles of Abraham of Smolensk.

Saint Abraham of Smolensk was born during the later part of the twelfth century and lived until A. D. 1221. He copied manuscripts and became a learned and industrious scholar who was blessed "not only to read, but to interpret, so that nothing in the sacred writing could be hidden from him." The accounts of his life are recorded in Russian Religious Mind by Fedotov.

Mystic Revelation

Hildegard, daughter of the Count of Spanheim was called, even in her own time, one of the greatest figures of the twelfth century. First among the great German mystics, she was a physician, a poet, a prophet and a political moralist who rebuked popes, princes, bishops and layfolk with complete fearlessness and unerring justice.

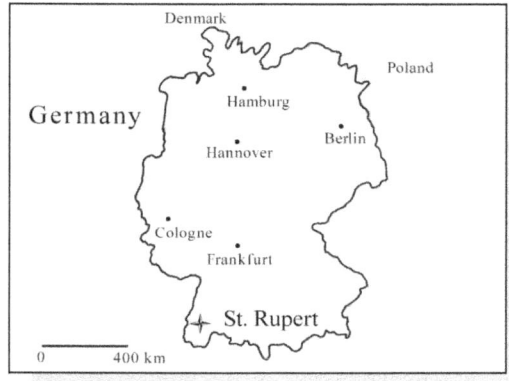

As a child she received numerous divine revelations and was instructed by heavenly messengers to record them in a journal. These revelations, Scivias, fill three volumes and received the express sanction of Pope Eugenius III. Saint Bernard, Abbot of Clairvaux, was commissioned to examine the contents which he pronounced undoubtedly genuine. The following is a brief introduction in Hildegard's own words.

"From infancy to the present day, now being seventy years old, I have received without cessation visions and divine revelations. In these divine communications I seem to be carried through the air to regions far, far away, and I see in my mind's eye the marvels shown to me. I do not see them with my bodily eye, or hear what is being said by my bodily ears, nor do I discover them with the agency of any of my bodily senses, nor do they come into my I thoughts, nor are they dreams, or trances, or ecstasies, but I see them with my eyes open while I am wide-awake, sometimes in the night, and sometimes by day. What I see, I see in my soul, and what I hear, I hear in my inner self." It is impossible to give even a summary of Hildegard's revelations. But one hundred forty-five of her letters and numerous volumes of other works may be seen in Migne's *Patrologie Latine*, Volume CLXVII.

Saint Hildegard lived from 1098-1179. She is celebrated on September 17th. Her letters and original works are preserved in the monastery of Saint Rupert.

Flyboy

The acts of canonization of Joseph of Cuppertino refer to his levitations and ecstasies. He was forever floating or transfixed in ecstasies which varied in intensity depending on the company he kept. Some seventy public instances of levitation

were recorded. The occurrence was so commonplace to him that he thought it strange for someone to marvel when a man passed from earth to heaven and back again. In his ecstasies, he was catatonic, remaining like a statue, whether sitting, kneeling, standing or walking. No physical force would affect him at these times. He was often pricked or branded with needles, and sometimes a torch or candle was held to his sides, but he felt nothing.

On one occasion he commented to the Cardinal of Lauria, "Sir, my brother mock me for my ecstasies. They burn my hands, they break my fingers," and he showed him the blisters and broken fingers.

But the cardinal only asked what his ecstasies were like.

"They seem like transportations into a gallery of the new and the beautiful, where as in a glass, one sees the wonders which it may please God to show."

Saint Joseph of Cuppertino lived from 1603-1663. He was canonized in 1767, not for his levitations, but for his extreme patience and humility. His tomb in Osimo, Italy, is the object of great veneration and pilgrimage. He is celebrated on September 18th.

Our Lady of La Salette

Near midafternoon on Saturday, September 19, 1946, Melanie Mathieu, age fourteen and Maximin Giraud, age eleven, drove their cows from the grazing fields to a nearby ravine for water. Melanie glanced over the lip of the ravine and stopped thunderstruck in her tracks. Below her she saw a large circle of brilliant light, easily outshining the sun. She cried out, "Maximin! Come quickly! See the light down there!"

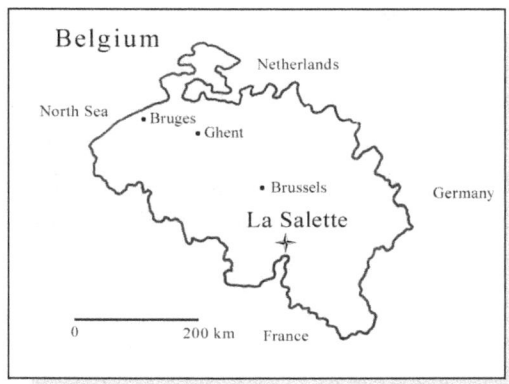

He dashed to her side. "Where?" he wanted to know. She pointed, and he saw it too. At first they were frightened, but then suddenly the circle began to open up, and their fear disappeared. Gazing inside they discerned the figure of a woman. She was seated with her face in her hands and appeared to be weeping. Slowly she rose. The beauty of her grieving face was magnetic. She wore a crown on her head. Her dress was netted with bursts of light. Her slippers were edged with roses and she wore a crucifix from a chain, a hammer on one side and a pair of pincers on the other. Everything was suffused with light.

As they gazed, the woman spoke, "Come to me, my children. Do not be afraid. I am here to tell you something of the greatest importance." She spoke in French, then later in their own dialect. She told them her tears were the tears of a mother who had been forgotten by her children. Having forgotten her, they had gone astray and doubted her existence. She told them a great famine would soon be coming, but added, "If the people are converted, then the rocks themselves will become piles of wheat, and it will be found that the potatoes have sown themselves."

She paused, then looked to the children, "Do you say your prayers well, my children?"

"No," they murmured shamefully. "We say them hardly at all."

"My children, it is very important to say them at night and in the morning. When you don't have time, at least say an *Our Father* and a *Hail Mary*. And when you can, say more."

Then she looked earnestly at them and repeated, "My children, you will make this known to all my people, to all my people."

Walking to higher ground, she paused for a moment, then rose into the air. Her figure and the circle of light grew more resplendent and then vanished.

In the days that followed, the children did their best to convince the elders that the vision was real and its message must be heeded, but they were laughed at. Twice they were conducted back to the scene of the miracle and interrogated by clergy and police. They were threatened with jail and punished with sleeplessness, but never was a single detail of their story inconsistent.

Again at the ravine, the children were made to reconstruct the event. One of the men moved a rock from the location of the vision and found that a spring was gushing forth. This was unheard of at that time of year, so some water was bottled and returned to the town for examination. Later, it was given to a lady who had long been seriously ill. When she was restored to perfect health, the children's story was no longer doubted.

Soon citizens from the surrounding villages were toiling up the mountain to secure some of the marvelous water for themselves. The catalog of cures grew steadily as did the numbers of daily visitors. The message of prayer was heeded and famine was avoided. Five years later, this miracle was sanctioned *Our Lady of La Salette*.

Triumph

Francis of Posadas believed he was unworthy of his God and would weep without ceasing during the celebration of mass. At the elevation of the host his whole body would tremble, and he was unable to control his joyous sighs. Often he would fall into an ecstasy and be lifted from the ground. When his ecstasies diminished, and he was no longer transfixed, he would say, "I cannot tell whether I left the earth or the earth withdrew from me."

On one occasion while pronouncing the words of consecration, his spirit left his body, and his body rose into the air and remained suspended. When he returned to the ground again, the entire congregation saw that he was encompassed with a great light, and his natural wrinkles had completely disappeared from his face. His skin was as transparent as crystal, and his cheeks were red as fire.

He was often misunderstood by his fellow monks, who made him the brunt of their ridicule and petty persecutions. But he triumphed over their jealousy through perseverance and humility, and having won their hearts was hailed a saint among them.

Francis of Posadas was born in Cordova, Spain and lived from 1644-1713. He wrote several books which revealed his remarkable insight into the lives of other saints. After forty years of uninterrupted spiritual exercise he died, triumphant. He was beatified in 1818 and is celebrated on September 20th.

Queen of Plants

From youth, Catherine Emmerich possessed an intuitive ability which allowed her to discern the medicinal qualities of plants. She spoke frequently to the plant kingdom and could hear their thoughts as easily as if they were spoken words.

She was equally clairvoyant with people and sought to help them in whatever way she could. She was a recipient of ecstasies and like Christian saints before her, bore the wounds of the stigmata, which, we are told, were visible for all to see and would bleed every Friday at the same hour.

Catherine was poor and uneducated and made her living by tending cows, but despite her simple character, while absorbed in ecstasies, she spoke with such illumined presence, it seemed she was the voice of God Itself.

Along with her many miraculous endowments, she could also see in the dark as if it were day. And while others slept, without the aid of a candle or lamp, she kept herself busy sewing clothes for the poor.

Saint Catherine Emmerich lived from 1114-1824. The accounts of her life are recorded in Ecstaticas of the Tyrol.

The Apostle of Hungary

Stephen was born to be king. In the year A.D. 995, at age twenty, he married Gisela, sister of Emperor Henry II of Bavaria, and two years later, he succeeded his father to the throne of Hungary. His methods of administration differed greatly from modern-day socioeconomic plans. Rather, he was far more interested in the spiritual development of his people. He believed that the prosperity and fulfillment of Heaven far exceeded that of earth, and he sought to create an ideal society, rich in wisdom, piety and charity.

He instituted harsh punishments for murder, theft, adultery and other public crimes and made himself easily accessible to people of all ranks to listen to their complaints. He was particularly fond of the poor, knowing them to be most easily oppressed, and often in disguise he would sneak from the palace to distribute alms to beggars. On one occasion a troop of beggars knocked him down, hustled him, and carried away his purse. He laughed at the indignity, especially when they pulled at his beard, but it wasn't enough to stop him from his charities.

Stephen eventually died at age sixty-three, at which time the miracles that accompanied his life became public. His biographer revealed that his spirit was often lifted out of his body into the air, in what he called "communion with God," and many times his body followed as well, being buoyed into the air where it remained suspended for a considerable time. Once, while rapt in prayer and floating, he reported that he had been cradled in the arms of angels.

Following his death, miracles continued to occur at the site of his tomb. It became a popular place of pilgrimage and veneration, and Stephen was hereafter referred to as *The Apostle of Hungary*.

Saint Stephen (Istvan) lived from 915-1038. His relics are currently enshrined in a chapel within the great church of Our Lady of Buda, Budapest, Hungary. The accounts of his life are recorded in The Life of St. Stephen, King of Hungary, by Chartruiz, Bishop of Hungary.

Holy Macaroni

"I no sooner begin to pray than my heart becomes consumed with the fire of love; this fire does not resemble any fire of this lowly earth. It is a sweet and delicate flame that consumes yet causes no pain. It is so sweet and delicate that it satisfies and satiates my spirit to the point of insatiability. Dear God! The most marvelous part for me is the fact that perhaps I will never comprehend it until I get to Heaven…"

Padre Pio's experiences of heaven began at an early age, but did not mature until 1916 when he was drafted into the army. His service hardly lasted a few weeks when he was stricken ill with a condition the doctors were unable to diagnose. Ordinary thermometers broke from the heat of his fever and the special ones indicated temperatures of 120° to 125°F. However, he never lost consciousness or became delirious, and this made his condition seem all the more mysterious. Finally, he was discharged from the military with a prognosis to live only a few months.

Shortly after his discharge, his temperature returned to normal and it was at this time that his experiences of the stigmata began. We are told that the wounds on his hands and feet were so severe one could see from one side through to the other.

Padre possessed many other gifts, including clairvoyance, a heavenly body odor, miraculous cures, prophetic insight and bilocation, but he had little concern for transitory miracles. He was far more concerned with the souls of his brothers and sisters. He wrote, "If I know someone who is afflicted in soul and body what would I not do with the Lord to see him delivered from these evils? I would freely take upon myself all his pains to free him, leaving him the reward of his sufferings if the Lord would allow me to do so."

Padre, however, was not an overly serious monk. Despite his austere lifestyle, he had a witty style, often using puns or amusing vernacular to make people laugh. Even before his death, people spoke about his probable canonization, at which he replied, "If they make me a saint, anyone who comes to me seeking a favor will have to bring me first of all a crate of macaroni; for each crate of macaroni, I'll grant a favor!"

Padre Pio died on September 23, 1968, at the age of eighty-one. His cause for beatification is currently active. His tomb in San Giovanni is an object of great veneration and pilgrimage.

Slave Labor

Peter Nolesco founded *Our Lady of Ransom* based on the following miracle.

While deep in meditation, Nolesco was visited by an apparition of a glorious woman. She informed him that it was God's pleasure that he should establish an institution called *Our Lady of Ransom*.

"Who am I," said Peter, "that God should honor me thus? And who art thou, who knowest so well the secrets of the Most High?"

"I am Mary," was the answer, "the mother of Jesus. My son, who came to give liberty to the world, is distressed by the many people bound in captivity. He wishes the order to be established."

When Nolesco heard this, he was transported with joy and hurried to inform the King of Aragon. When he arrived at the palace, he learned that the vision had also appeared to the king. And further, Saint Raymond of Pennafort had also had the same vision. Without delay, the bishop and chief ministers of Barcelona helped Nolesco lay the first stone of the new monastic edifice. The king authorized the order to bear the royal arms, quartered with those of the Bishop of Barcelona. Nolesco was invested Grand Master of the order; the order's accomplishments in ransoming slaves from the Moors of Spain are recorded in history.

This story is given in The Life of Peter Nolesco, by R.P.F. Zumel.

Champion of Angels

Nicholas von Flue was a natural-born fighting man—a champion in everything he did. He fought in two wars, leading his troops to victory and retired as a judge in Flueli, Switzerland. On one occasion, while engaged in his normal household affairs with his wife Dorothy and ten children, three men of exceeding nobility appeared before him and addressed him:

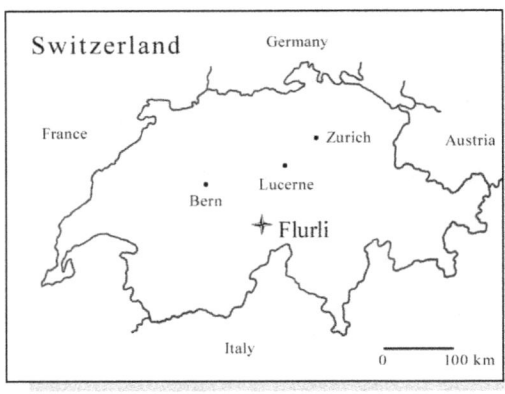

"Tell us Nicholas," one of them said, "will you place both your body and your soul under our charge?"

"I can place them," he replied, "only under the charge of Him who is the source of my being. I have long wished to be one with Him."

"If this is so," said the first speaker, "I promise you, when you are seventy years old, you shall be lifted from the troubles of this world, and as you have been patient and generous to all, you will be a leader in the army of angels." Then the three men vanished from sight.

Twenty-five years later, in 1487, at age seventy, Nicholas, already regarded a saint by the citizens of Switzerland, died peacefully. We presume he is presently a leader in the army of angels.

Nicholas von Flue lived from 1417-1481 and was canonized in 1947. He is celebrated on September 25th in Switzerland.

Belle of Valentia

Much has already been said about the miraculous life of Saint Vincent Ferrier. But as this minor miracle is so original and the events of his life so well documented, the charm of the following anecdote must be mentioned.

While passing through one of the principal streets of Valentia, Saint Vincent and his suite heard a thunderous voice, tremulous with anger and rich with profanity. Immediately he set a course for its origin and entered a house. Once inside, he was passed by a man towering with passion, who rudely dismissed himself by bullishly marching through the door. He found the lady of the house no less excited and still uttering blasphemies. He soothed her a moment and asked the reason for such imprecations. Still sobbing, the lady replied, "Father, this is not the first time my husband and I have argued. Every day he taunts me, merely because I am unattractive. It is not life, my father, but a daily death, a damnation on earth. My home is a hell."

"My daughter," said Vincent, "moderate your speech. It is not right to talk thus. And if, as you say, want of beauty is your only fault, we can soon remedy the situation."

Raising his right hand to the woman's face he continued, "My daughter, you are no longer without beauty, but remember there is no beauty like that of holiness."

This woman was thereafter the Belle of Valentia. So much so, that when any women was deemed unattractive, it was customary to say, "She wants the hand of Saint Vincent."

This story later developed into a well known proverb.

Rescued

"Placidus, fetch water from the river!" was the command given by Saint Benedict to his disciple.

Placidus immediately obeyed, but when he leaned over to dip the bucket, his foot slipped on the wet ground and he plunged head first into the rushing rapids. Benedict saw the accident by divine revelation and quickly dispatched Maurus to save his fellow disciple. Maurus went, but when he reached the river, the current had already carried Placidus downstream. Without hesitation, he darted onto the water, solely concerned for the well-being of his companion. Overtaking the current, he clutched hold of his friend and pulled him safely to the shore. Apparently Maurus had run above the water, rather than on it, for no part of him, not even the soles of his shoes, were damp.

The rescued Placidus remarked, "As I was lifted out of the water, I saw distinctly the hood of Master Benedict held over the head of my rescuer."

This story is taken from Dialogues, by Saint Gregory.

Meditation: A Spectator Sport

When Francis of Paola sat in silence in his usual place of meditation, all the monks from the abbey and the visiting priests and brothers from an adjoining monastery would gather together to watch him being surrounded by a heavenly light. On one occasion, three crowns of golden light, resembling those of the pope's tiara, appeared above his head. On another occasion an archangel of enormous proportions brought a shield from heaven and presented it to the saint. The shield contained a coat of arms with the word CHARITY written in letters of gold on an azure field. Francis was instructed, "Adopt this device for the purpose of teaching simplicity and giving."

Among the great wonderworkers recorded in history, no one was more simple or charitable with cures than Saint Francis of Paola.

Saint Francis of Paola lived from 1416-1507. He was canonized in 1519.

Great Noise

Wovoka had a particular fondness for hard work. He was the son of Tovibo, a visionary and leader among the Paiute Indians of Nevada, but he had never experienced any visions himself. He was a

simple man, who was employed cutting wood and doing farm chores for a neighboring white farmer, David Wilson, whom he loved and respected greatly. However, on January 1, 1889, something extraordinary happened.

During an eclipse of the sun, he heard a *great noise*; then losing outer consciousness, he was irresistibly absorbed into the regions of heaven. When he was revived, he told of his experience. His soul had been taken into heaven, where he spoke with the creator who charged him with many responsibilities. He gave him many supernatural powers, including the ability to read the thoughts of others, healing, the gift of prophecy and five songs for influencing weather conditions. He was instructed to teach his people to live in peace with the white man and to abandon warfare, lying and stealing. If they did these things they would be reunited with their loved ones in heaven where sickness, old age or death did not exist.

Wovoka followed his instructions and had success as a teacher. Emissaries representing over thirty tribes learned his teaching and returned home with hope for their people. As the new Indian revival took root, its practices were opposed by government officials and missionaries who succeeded in their efforts to suppress it. On December 29, 1890, federal troops opened fire on men, women and children at

Wounded Knee in South Dakota.

Wovoka's new teachings, however, were not silenced. With the aid of certain white settlers, he continued his teachings to other tribes by correspondence. He traveled great distances to other reservations and served as a shaman and healer, but the last fifteen years of his life were spent at the Yerington Indian Colony in Nevada, where he died peacefully in his own home on September 29, 1932.

Wovoka (Woodcutter) was born in 1856 near Walker Lake in present-day Esmeralda County, Nevada.

The Mascot

Visiting guests would often join in the lectures of Saint Jerome, the learned scholar and doctor of the church, but never before had the class been so abruptly dismissed with the arrival of a new guest. Students and scholars quickly departed through the rear exit when a mature, four-hundred pound lion entered the classroom. Though lame and limping on three paws , the creature's sheer size frightened the class members half to death. But not their learned teacher.

Saint Jerome waited quietly until the lion came near. Lifting its afflicted forepaw, he found it swollen and bleedin from an imbedded thorn. He extracted the thorn, washed the paw and dressed it. In the minutes that followed the lion regained the use of its paw, yet despite open doors and appropriate lures and entreaties, it refused to leave the classroom. The lion stayed, the new monastery mascot and personal escort to Saint Jerome.

Saint Jerome lived from A.D. 345-420. His feast day is celebrated on September 30th. In Christian art he is often depicted with a lion at his side. The accounts of his life are documented in Lives of The Saints, by Edward Kinesman.

October

1 Growing Up
2 A Tidy Flight
3 Rise Up
4 Patron of Ecology
5 Vengeance Belongs to God
6 Obtaining a Son
7 Naval Victory
8 What to Leave Behind
9 Patron of France
10 Pass on the Message
11 You're Under Arrest
12 Visions in the East
13 Fatima
14 Answered Prayer
15 The Interior Castle
16 A Warm Campfire
17 Study the Details
18 A Secret Discovery
19 Vexed
20 A Mustard Seed
21 In Demand
22 Mended Holes for Mended Souls
23 Captivating Captive
24 Tour of Egypt
25 Patron of Farmers
26 Love in Action
27 Form of Victory
28 Innocent Defense
29 Tears of Neglect
30 No Pain, No Gain
31 Flight Records

Growing Up

Remi was a wanderer. He was young and restless, and not the sort to look for responsibility. He loved his freedom and if it was threatened, the urge to wander usually overcame him. The citizens of Rheims, however, were wholly impressed with the natural sanctity of the boy and tried repeatedly to elect him their bishop. He declined of course, on the grounds that he was only twenty-two years of age, but the people refused to compromise their choice.

The assembly raised its collective voice in shouts of "R-e-m-i ! R-e-m-i !" and suddenly, from a mass of clouds overhead, a brilliant beam of light burst forth and rested on Remi's head. In the moments that followed, a holy dew descended and bathed him with divine baptism. An odor sweeter than any earthly fragrance filled the air and the assembly swooned with delight. It seemed that heaven itself had confirmed their choice of Remi for bishop and even Remi agreed. He dismissed his irresponsible wanderings, accepted the office of bishop and devoted himself to the citizens of Rheims, like a father to his children.

Saint Remi lived from A. D. 438-533. He is respectfully celebrated on October 1st. Recorded by Hincmar in The Life of Saint Remi.

A Tidy Flight

The following statement is quoted by Father K. G. Schomoger in his book, *Life of Anne Catherine Emmerich*, published soon after her death in 1824.

"When I was doing my work as a vestry nun, I was often lifted up suddenly into the air, and I climbed up and stood on the higher parts of the church, such as the windows, sculptured ornaments, jutting stones; I would clean and arrange everything in places where it was humanly possible. I felt myself lifted and supported in the air, and I was not afraid in the least, for I had been accustomed from the time I was a child to being assisted by my guardian angel."

Anne Catherine Emmerich was a German stigmatic, visionary and mystic who lived from 1774-1824.

Rise Up

"Will he survive the night?"

This was the thought on everyone's mind during the evening of October 3, 1396, when Vincent Ferrier fell gravely ill. At the moment when all were sure that his time had come, suddenly the room filled with mysterious light. The intensity of the light increased to a celestial splendor, and a multitude of angels crowded into the room, together with the patriarchs Saint Dominic and Saint Francis.

They presented themselves to the sick man and spoke: "Vincent, rise up safe and sound. Go forth and teach the wisdom of life. For this end have you been chosen."

Then touching his face, they spoke together, "Rise up. O my Vincent, rise up."

With these words the angels vanished. And where once lay the infirm body of a man near death, now was a saint, fully restored to a healthy life.

Saint Vincent Ferrier lived from 1350-1419. He was canonized in 1455. The accounts of his life are recorded in the Acta Sanctorum (See April 5th).

Patron of Ecology

The twentieth century has witnessed a widespread revival of interest in the life of Saint Francis of Assisi, one of the most attractive and best loved saints of our time. He was a nature lover and a sentimentalist, yet beneath his gentility and kindness was a character of immovable discipline. Although he is often best remembered for his flying miracles, his biographer, Chavin de Malan, tells us he also possessed a miraculous gift of speech:

"He often preached to the cattle of the field, and birds of the air, to the fishes of the sea, and even to the beasts of the forest, showing to them their obligations to God and calling upon them to praise His holy name. These simple creatures, without human reason, would listen attentively and testify by their movements the joy they felt in his discourse, and after the sermon was over they would praise the Lord, each in his several way."

On another occasion, while Saint Francis delivered his sermon in Alviano, the twittering of swallows became so loud, the assembly could not perceive his words. Considerably annoyed, Saint Francis suddenly broke off his sermon and addressed his feathered congregation, "My sisters, the swallows, please keep peace while I am preaching."

It need scarcely be mentioned that not a twitter was heard for the remainder of the sermon.

Saint Francis lived from 1182-1226. He was canonized in 1228, his celebration set on October 4th. His tomb is among the most popular pilgrim sites in Italy today. The account of his life are recorded in The Life of Saint Francis of Assisi.

Vengeance Belongs To God

Many miracles have occurred during the course of battles, but none so dramatic and decisive as that of the tale of Galla and the Lombards.

During the middle of the sixth century, an army of Lombards invaded Dauphine and besieged Valence. The attacking soldiers secretly scaled the walls and threw open the city gates. In minutes the inner streets were filled with looting invaders. In the midst of this madness, Saint Galla was silently praying in the basilica when a panicking mob of citizens burst in and implored her for protection, crying in fear, "Save us, please save us, dear servant of God! Save us, or we all will perish!"

"Fear not," said Galla, "Saint Peter will defend you." As she spoke, the skies were suddenly filled with shadows. It was the flight of many hundreds of eagles, soaring in the open sky above the city. In utter astonishment the Valencians watched as the eagles dropped stones on the besiegers. The invaders were struck down by the thousands and in fear, fled for shelter.

"Pursue them!" cried Galla to the crowd, "Pursue and stop not! Let each take back his spoils! Drive them from the city! Close the gates! But take care to spare the fugitives! For vengeance belongs to God alone!"

The city was cleared, and the gates were shut. The Valencians were safe and a feeling of awe overcame them. Even the Lombards were moved to piety. Thanks to Galla, God had entered their lives.

This story is recorded in Les Petits Bollandistes, Volume II. Saint Galla lived until A.D. 550 and is respectfully honored on October 5th.

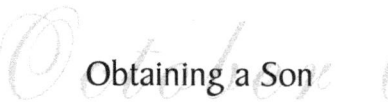

Obtaining a Son

Arsinda was barren. She deeply desired to be a mother, but her physicians diagnosed that she would never be able to bear children. She was the wife of William Taillefer, Count of Toulouse, and although they wanted a child for many years, it appeared the physicians were right. It was the year A.D. 975, a period in history when being barren was often less preferable than death. Overcome with despair, she organized a religious pilgrimage to the church of Saint Foi d'Agen. That night, a vision occurred. The spirit of Saint Foi appeared before her and commanded her to offer the rich bracelets she was wearing to the church.

"I will," said Arsinda, "but obtain for me a son."

"I will intercede on your behalf," said Saint Foi, who then vanished from sight.

The following morning the countess journeyed to the monastery of Conques. There she presented her offering to the monks, as she had agreed. The bracelets were exquisitely made of gold tissue, artistically designed and enriched with exceptionally well cut precious stones. Her sacrifice did not go unrewarded. In the same year, she brought forth her first child and named him Raymond. Not long after, she had a second son, Henry.

This account is recorded in History of The Church of Toulouse, by Salvan.

Naval Victory

On October 7, 1571, Selim II, Sultan of the Turks, was utterly destroyed in a disastrous naval defeat near the harbor of Lepanto. This great victory is always ascribed to Pope Pius V and is mentioned in his canonization in 1712.

At the hour of battle, a procession of the Rosary began its march to the church of Minerva. The pope was present, and quite unexpectedly he walked to a window, threw open its doors and stood in a trance for a considerable time. Returning to the cardinals, he remarked, "It is now time to give thanks for the great victory which has been granted us."

Officials later compared the time of the pope's words with the records of the battle and found them in precise accord. But the real reason for crediting the pope with the victory came from the mouths of the prisoners taken in battle. They attested, with unquestionable conviction, that they had seen Jesus Christ, Saint Peter, Saint Paul and a multitude of angels, sword in hand, fighting against Selim and the Turks, blinding them with smoke.

This account is given in the Acta Sanctorum, Volume I.

What to Leave Behind

Briocus was in popular demand. According to his biography, before his birth an angel appeared to both his parents while they slept and instructed them to send their child to France to be reared by Saint Germanus. They did, and by the time the child was sixteen he was known as a master of miracles. Like his parents, Briocus received visions during dreams. On one occasion an angel appeared to him in his sleep and bade him to return to "Latium," which he did in the company of over one hundred sixty-eight disciples.

On their journey the ship suddenly stopped and appeared to be slightly lifted from the water. We are told that a great sea monster obstructed their course, but yielding to the prayers of Briocus the primitive serpent vanished into thin air. Continuing their journey, they sailed to an estuary on the coast of Brittany near Treguier where Briocus and his company settled and built a monastery.

As the community flourished under Briocus' guidance, many new saints were produced. Before long, Briocus heard news of a pestilence that was devastating his native home, Cardiganshire. He returned to his homeland, and under the influence of his prayers, the pestilence was quickly arrested. Briocus returned to Brittany where he established a second monastery. Shortly after its completion he died, having reached the age of one hundred. He left dozens of saints to carry on his work and guide others as he had guided them.

All of these events are said to have occurred on the site of present day Saint-Brieuc in France.

A portion of his relics are preserved in the cathedral at Saint-Brieuc. Briocus lived during the sixth century. He is celebrated on October 8th.

Patron of France

Dionysius, patron of Paris, was a man of mystery and few words. He was known for many miracles during his life, but none more remarkable than that which occurred at the time of his death, October 9, A.D. 258.

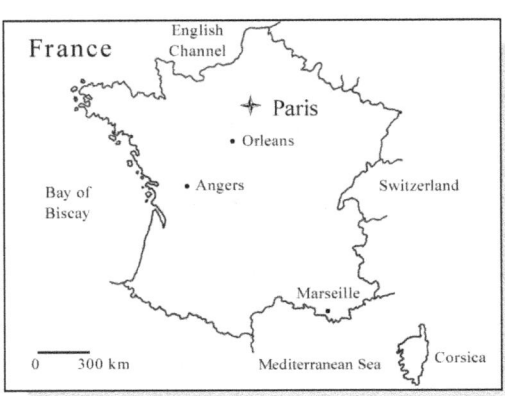

Having refused to renounce his faith, Dionysius was condemned to death by Fescinnius, Governor of Gaul. He was taken to an execution site (Montmartre) where an enormous crowd had gathered to watch. He was successfully beheaded, but the moment his head touched the ground, his dead body rose on its feet, picked up its head and walked, "in triumph," through the midst of the crowd.

In this manner the body, led by an angel, carried the head from Montmartre (near Paris) a distance of two miles, where the abbey church of Saint Denis now stands. Here, Dionysius' body, now surrounded by singing angels, gave its head to a pious woman named Catulla, then fell flat to the earth at her feet. Catulla received the head with unspeakable joy and hid it carefully away in her house.

This event was recorded by numerous witnesses and is found in Vies des Saints, Manager Guerin. Saint Dionysius is Patron of headaches.

Pass On This Message

Bernardo Martinez was fifty years old, out of work, out of money, out of luck, out of patience and he wanted to die. He was born into a Nicaraguan peasant family and his future looked bleak. However, his experiences from May to October of 1980 changed everything. One afternoon at three o'clock, he was transfixed in a vision of a woman who told him she was Mary from heaven. She told him to recite the rosary every day and said, "Nicaragua has suffered terribly since the earthquake, and there is more suffering in store. You will continue to suffer unless you change. The Lord has chosen you to pass on this Message."

Bernardo, however, did not know whether or not he had gone crazy. Perhaps he had hallucinated the entire event. Besides, what could a simple peasant accomplish. It was too risky to pass on the message.

A week later, a second apparition occurred to Bernardo, "Why did you not pass on what I asked you to say? Do not be afraid. I will help you. Go and speak to the priests."

Bernardo found the priests more receptive than he had anticipated. They listened to him with respect and did not discourage him in any way. In the weeks that followed Bernardo received four more visits from Mary, with messages for the people of Nicaragua. In October, she visited Bernardo for the last time with the following message.

"I am asked for things which are unimportant. Ask for faith, so that each of you may have the strength to carry your cross. The sufferings of this world cannot be taken from you. The sufferings are the crosses which you must bear. . . . Do not turn to violence; ask for faith so that you may be patient.

From now on you will not see me in this place. Do not worry, I am with you though you do not see me. I am your mother, the mother of all sinners. Love each other. Pardon each other. . . . Make peace, if you do not make peace then there will be no peace. Do not turn to violence. If you do not change your ways you will provoke the third world war. Pray, pray my children for the entire world."

Bernardo then watched as Mary rose to the top of a tree and disappeared.

The aforementioned apparitions occurred in Cuapa, Nicaragua and have been given an informal approval by the local bishop.

You're Under Arrest

Saint Francis of Paola was often in trouble with the authorities. On one occasion Ferdinand I, King of Naples, dispatched a captain with forty soldiers to arrest him. But when the officer came into the presence of the saint, he was so awe-struck by his radiance, he fell at his feet and craved to be pardoned. Francis did so and ordered food prepared for the captain and his men. Only two small loaves and a single pint of wine were at hand, but Francis blessed the food and asked God that it might be multiplied. And it was. All forty-one soldiers ate and drank liberally. No one attempted to arrest Saint Francis, and he journeyed peacefully on his way.

Saint Francis of Paola lived from 1436-1507. This account is recorded in the Acts of his canonization.

Vision in the East

Stephen Ho Ngoc Ahn fought for the South Vietnamese army during the Vietnam War. His service in war rendered him both paralyzed and without the ability to speak. However, on October 12, 1975, he was caught up in an apparition of the Divine Mother who said to him, "I will cure you so you can walk and talk again."

Although the cure was not immediate, other apparitions followed. Two and a hair months later, in the presence of four hundred witnesses, Stephen was totally cured by way of a miracle. He walked a distance of two hundred yards and spoke his first words which were choked with emotion.

The accounts of Stephen's cure reached the ears of the communist authorities, who arrested and interrogated him. Without a trial, he was convicted of being a revolutionary against the state and as he would not admit that his cure was other than miraculous, his back and legs were broken and his tongue made to be speechless again.

Stephen, however, had been forewarned of these events in an earlier apparition and was willing to accept what came to him. In subsequent apparitions he has been told that he will once again be cured and has written certain parties to inform them when and where the cure will transpire, so they may bear witness to it.

Communication with Stephen Ho Ngoc Ahn is nearly impossible as it is subject to the controls of the communist police.

Fatima

On the night of October 12, 1917, in the pouring rain, tens of thousands of pilgrims from every part of Portugal converged on the tiny town of Fatima. By then news of the visions seen by the children of Fatima had reached everyone. Over forty thousand people had gathered to watch the miracle which was promised for the morning of October 13th.

When the morning sun rose, the weather was no less severe, yet no one was disappointed. For true to her promise, the lady of light appeared. The faces of the visionary children assumed an ecstatic expression, and the air was charged with excitement. The vision of the heavenly lady appeared and announced, "I am the Lady of the Rosary."

She extended her hands outward, and beams of light were emitted, which traveled in the direction of the sun. Suddenly the sun grew pale and appeared a silver disc. Spectrums of brilliant light emanated in every direction: red, blue, yellow, green. The sky itself appeared to be revolving, and the sun spun wildly like a gigantic wheel of fire. Everyone and everything was surrounded a brilliant light, "such as the human eye has never seen before," which allowed no shadow to occur. The sun continued to spin and dance, then stopped, and continued again. Three times this pattern occurred, until suddenly the sun appeared ripped from its place in the heavens and hurled downward to the earth, "wildly, without direction." The crowd fell to the ground in abject terror. Each believed it was the moment of death.

Then suddenly their fears disappeared. The raging sun remained poised for a moment, then as quickly as it had descended, it resumed its usual place in the sky.

A cry of astonishment resounded on every side from a still trembling crowd, not sure that some greater disaster was yet imminent. Then another marvel was discovered. The ground was dry. Their rain-drenched garments were also dry. Only minutes before the torrents had inundated them.

Only a few on this earth have witnessed a miracle such as this. The miracle of Fatima is, undoubtedly, the most remarkable of this century.

Answered Prayers

Necessity is the mother of invention, and Angadrisma was in dire need. She was young, flawlessly beautiful, well-educated and born in a noble family. Throughout her life miracles occurred from her prayers. She had hoped to pursue a godly career in a convent; however, when she reached the age of marriage, she was promised to a young gentleman named Ansbert. Not wanting to disobey the good intentions of her father, she prayed that the Almighty would render her so unsightly that the marriage would be abandoned. But nothing happened. Believing it was God's will, she prepared herself for marriage.

After all the arrangements and contracts had been fulfilled, on the evening before the wedding, she was struck with leprosy. Naturally, in consideration of this tragedy, the marriage was broken off. Angadrisma was overjoyed, and she revealed her prayers to her father. When he learned of her love for the convent, he gave his consent and she received the Veil of Virginity that evening.

Saint Ouen, Archbishop of Rouen conducted the rites and at the moment she received the veil, the affliction dissolved completely. Angadrisma was later sent to a monastery and in due time was appointed abbess.

Angadrisma lived during the seventh century. This account is given in Vie des Saints de Beauvais. She is celebrated on October 14th.

The Interior Castle

At age seven Teresa wanted to be a saint. Or at least she wanted to live in heaven. It seemed to her that the martyrs of old had bought heaven very cheaply by their torments. So, in hope of dying for her faith, she convinced her brother Rodrigo to accompany her to the country of the Moors, where they were sure to be martyred. Afterwards, they would certainly go to heaven. Rodrigo agreed, and the mission began.

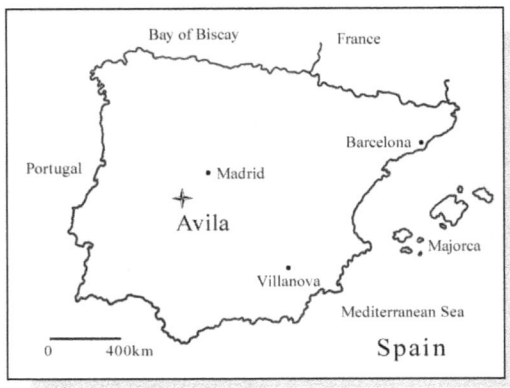

Secretly, they set our on their journey, made an admirable attempt, but fortunately went only as far as Adaja. There they met an uncle who returned them to their frightened mother. Rodrigo blamed it all on Teresa.

The experience seemed to temper Teresa's astonishing urge to live in heaven and before long she returned to the predictable preoccupations of a girl her age—romance, fashion and perfume. It didn't last, however. Soon she had determined that the quickest path to heaven was through the convent, which she immediately joined after her twentieth birthday. There her dreams became a reality. For during her prayers she was seized with raptures and ecstasies, filled with conversations and visions from the denizens of heaven. She was often seen elevated from the ground and lifted into the air, "suspended on nothing, until she desired of her Lord the cessation of this miraculous favor."

On one occasion, the Bishop of Avila, Dom Alvares de Mondosa, came to see her to investigate the nature of her strange experiences. When he arrived, he found her floating above the window where the sisters usually received their holy bread.

For the remaining fifty-seven years of her life, miracles accompanied her. After an illustrious career as founder of the Discalced Carmelites, she died peacefully in the arms of Beatified Anne-of-Saint Bartholomew with the words, "At last, my daughter, the hour of death has come."

Saint Teresa of Avila lived from 1515-1582 and was canonized in 1622. She is celebrated as Patron of the Spanish army on October 15th. Her body, which has remained miraculously incorrupt for over four hundred years, is exposed for veneration in silver and crystal reliquaries at Alba de Tormes, Spain.

The accounts of her life are recorded in her autobiography, The Interior Castle.

A Warm Campfire

The lives of saints are often filled with feats of heroism and splendor. In some cases the elements, animals and all of nature, rise to obey their command. We are told that it is not extraordinary to be endowed with miraculous gifts; it is natural. Having acquired miraculous abilities, many saints prefer to keep them concealed, but sometimes they just happen. The tale which follows captures this naturalness.

Gall was a solid and self-controlled man with a well defined set of principles. He was born to a family of Irish aristocrats and reared in the monastery of Bangor. Growing tired of narrow-minded monks, he sought a simpler life, so together with two companions he retired to a hermitage in the mountains of Switzerland. One evening while his fellow brothers slept, he elected to spend the night in prayer. Soon afterwards a bear appeared at the camp and proceeded to carefully gather the remains of their evening meal.

Saint Gall remarked to the bear, "I beg you friend, in the name of Christ, put a few logs of wood on the fire, would you?"

This the bear did and Gall gave him a loaf of bread from his pouch. "Now go back to the mountain," instructed the saint, "and be sure to hurt neither man nor beast."

The bear departed, as he was instructed.

Saint Gall lived during the seventh century. He is celebrated on October 16th. This story is given in Vies des Saints, Volume XII, by Manager Guerin.

Study The Details

Although he possessed a brilliant intellect, Saint Ignatius preferred to rely on his creative insights. He was not the type to be found mulling over mundane manuscripts, but rather his genius sprang from swift, spontaneous realizations.

Eusebius of Caesarea, Socrates, and Baronius all attest that it was Ignatius who established the custom of singing the Psalms antiphonally. Furthermore, the idea was originally suggested to him by two choirs of angels that appeared to him while he was Bishop of Antioch. Ignatius listened carefully and studied the details of the celestial choir as they sang.

"The sounds of earth ought to imitate the sounds of heaven," he would say.

Accordingly, he introduced singing, in alternate choirs, to his followers. The majesty of modern day choirs owes much to Ignatius and this miracle.

Historic art shows Ignatius represented with a harp, listening to angels on each side of him, singing antiphonally. Saint Ignatius lived until A.D. 107.

A Secret Discovery

Customarily those who experience miracles keep them secret. But it is seldom easy and accidental discovery occurs frequently. The following narrative is an eyewitness account of the well-documented levitations of Francis Suarez, a Spanish priest, theologian and teacher who became professor of divinity at the University of Coimbra by the direct appointment of King Philip II.

Suarez was late for a class he was teaching and a fellow priest, Jerome de Silva, had been sent to fetch him. This is what he saw:

"Across the door of his room I found the stick which the Father usually placed there when he did not wish to be interrupted. Owing, however, to the order I had received I removed the stick and entered. The outer room was in darkness. I called the Father, but he made no answer. As the curtain which shut off his working room was drawn, I saw through the space left between the curtain and the jambs of the door a very great brightness. I pushed aside the curtain and entered from the inner apartment. Then I noticed that a blinding light was coming from the crucifix, so intense that it was like the reflection of the sun from glass windows, and I felt that I could not remain looking at it without being completely dazzled. The light streamed from the crucifix upon the face and breast of Father Suarez and in this brightness I saw him in a kneeling position in front of the crucifix, his head uncovered, his hands joined and his body in the air lifted three feet above the floor on a level with the table on which the crucifix stood. On seeing this I withdrew, but before quitting the room I stopped bewildered, and as it were beside myself, leaning against the door post for a space of three Credos."

It is due to humility and perhaps the fear that public recognition might hinder spiritual growth that supernatural gifts are kept secret. Francis Suarez lived from 1548-1617.

Vexed

It's unlikely that Saint Paul of the Cross could be accused of chauvinism, but certainly he was an excitable, emotional man. The following anecdote gives insight into his character.

It happened that Paul of the Cross reproved a woman for deliberately distracting the congregation with her scanty and immodest dress. But another woman, a certain French lady, was vexed by Paul's remarks. Determined to express her displeasure, she planted herself just under the missionary's eyes, in a greatly exaggerated low-cut costume. Paul, thoroughly annoyed, fixed his stare on the lady and gradually her face, hands, arms, neck, shoulders and whole body became as black as charcoal. The congregation exploded with excitement and the lady fell at Paul's feet imploring his forgiveness. He graciously consented, but it took two or three days before she recovered her former appearance.

Paul was renowned for the many miracles and healings that occurred during his sermons.

Saint Paul of the Cross lived from 1694-1715. He was canonized in 1861 and is celebrated on October 19th. The accounts of his life are recorded in The Life of St. Paul of the Cross, Founder of the Passionists, *by Father Pius.*

A Mustard Seed

For Thoretta, success came easily in quiet, unseen ways. She was a simple shepherdess by occupation, but was regarded a saint by all who knew her. It seemed even the sheep recognized her sanctity, for when she occupied herself in meditation, they would group around her, nibbling the grass close by. If she ever left the flock, she had only to plant her staff in the ground and they would remain in close proximity. Her flocks were never endangered by wolves or other natural predators and the elements presented no threat to their safety.

Once, while Thoretta was searching for better pasture, an ominous storm gathered on the horizon and her guardian angel spoke to her in assurance, "Fear not virtuous maiden. Though the rain falls in torrents and will flood the whole country, the sky over thy head shall be calm, and the pasture of thy sheep shall be ever fresh. As Gideon's fleece was dry when all around was wet, so shall it be with thee."

On another occasion a river overflowed blocking the passageway home. Thoretta called to mind the scriptural promise, "If ye had faith, even as much as a grain of a mustard seed, ye should be able to move mountains." Making the sign of the cross, she touched the water with her staff and immediately a dry path was made for her sheep and herself to pass over.

Thoretta lived during the twelfth century. Her story is found in Legende de Sainte Thorette.

In Demand

Hilarion was an extrovert of the highest order. His kindly disposition made it nearly impossible for him to refuse the genuine supplications of others. He had an irrepressible spontaneity and dynamism which made him irresistible. This, together with his liberal application of miracles, made him the most sought after saint of his time.

Hilarion tried many ways to avoid the company of others by retiring to the deserts of Egypt or to deserted islands. Sooner or later he was discovered and flocks of would-be disciples, unwilling to surrender the treasure they had found, demanded that he be their master. "I have returned to the world!" he would say. "All Palestine regards me, and I even possess a farm and household goods, under pretext of the brethren's needs."

In time he founded many monasteries and ceased his search for solitude, at least for a while. On one occasion, while touring his monasteries, he passed a vineyard that greatly impressed him. Entering it, he requested the enormous crowd that followed him to do the same. He blessed the vineyard and its owners and asked everyone to "enjoy to their heart's content, the fine fruits of the garden."

Generally, this vineyard yielded a hundred measures of wine annually, but this year, twenty days after three thousand people had enjoyed its fruits, it yielded more than three hundred measures of wine.

Innumerable miracles, from healings to wealth-giving, are credited to Hilarion and were recorded by Saint Epiphanius and other contemporaries.

Saint Hilarion lived from A. D. 291-371. He is celebrated on October 21st. The accounts of his life are recorded in Ecclesiastical History, by Nicephorus Callistus.

Mended Holes For Mended Souls

"May I mend your clothes for you?" asked a woman of Marlhes, upon seeing the garments of Saint Regis torn in holes.

"You may," consented the saint, and he readily changed into fresh attire.

At the time, the woman had two sick children, one of whom was near death with scarlet fever. She believed that her service to the saint would bring God's grace to her children and restore them to health. And she was right, for as soon as she laid a piece of the saint's garment on each child, sickness left them and each was restored to perfect health.

Long before John entered into a religious profession, he was regarded a saint. His greatest hope had been that he might be sent to the Canadian frontier to share wisdom with the native American Indian, but it never came to be.

Saint John Francis Regis lived from 1597-1640. He was canonized in 1737. The accounts of his life are recorded in The Life of Saint John Francis Regis, *by Father Daubenton.*

Captivating Captive

Even though he was warned, Servatius elected to undertake his travels from Liege to Rome at all costs. It was a matter of religious security, but as expected, he was captured and made a prisoner by the Huns who were ravaging Italy. They bound him and threw him into a deep pit while waiting to decide what should be done with him.

At midnight, however, they were astonished to see a brilliant light shining from within the pit where they had imprisoned him. Their surprise was even greater when they discovered that the light shone from the face of their captive. Furthermore, there was an eagle hovering over him, covering his body with one wing and fanning him with the other.

The Huns were terrified and threw themselves at their captive's feet, imploring his pardon. Servatius did so and was released. He later arrived safely in Rome, where the pope awarded him his key, *Claves Confessions S. Petri*, as a bestowal of honor.

His relics, a staff, drinking cup and key are preserved in a beautiful reliquary in Maastricht. The drinking cup is popularly supposed to be a gift from angels and is said to possess the ability to heal fevers.

Saint Servatius lived until A. D. 384. The accounts of his life are recorded in the Acta Sanctorum.

Tour of Egypt

An apparition of a heavenly lady, bearing all the familiar signs of the Madonna, appeared above the Coptic Orthodox Church of Saint Mary in Zeitoun, near Cairo, Egypt. As many as a quarter of a million people of every conceivable background—Moslem, Christian, Jew and atheist—witnessed the phenomenon which was too spell binding to ignore.

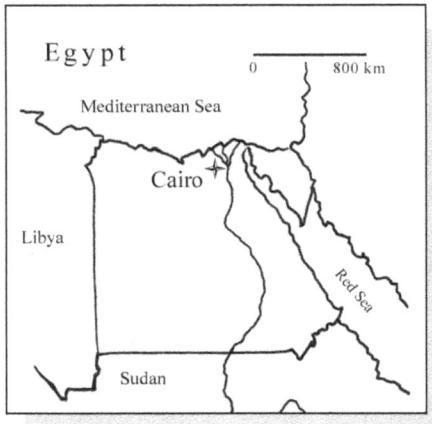

The apparitions first began on the evening of April 2, 1968. Since then, until May 29, 1971, apparitions, lasting an average of two hours, have occurred throughout Egypt, at Bitakh, Edfu, Maddi and Shoubra. During a number of the apparitions, the Madonna was accompanied by the boy Jesus and a vast number of angels. It is estimated that many millions of people have witnessed the phenomenon, perhaps the largest public manifestation of a miracle in recorded history.

Because photographic evidence has also been collected by witnesses, it is difficult to refute the reality of this supernatural occurrence.

The description that follows was given by Mr. Wadie Tadros Shumbo, a Protestant who was working with the Mobil Oil Company in Egypt at the time.

"We picked what we thought was the best place from which to watch and then sat there. At about 9:50 we saw lighting over the church, much stronger than one could make with a flashlight. I had a feeling something was about to happen. A thin line or edge of light appeared like the light you see when you open the door to a lighted room. Within seconds it formed itself into the shape of the Virgin. I could not speak. All who were with me said, 'It is Impossible!'

The Moslems all started to cry. This sight lasted for five minutes, when the figure rose and vanished. I could distinguish only a difference in color between the skin in the face and hands and the veil. There was some color in the face and the hands. It was evident when St. Mary walked back and forth. When she disappeared from our side of the church, the people from the other side claimed they were seeing her. Then she returned to our side for five minutes.

When I returned to the car for something I found it impossible to get back to the church because of the crowd. I could hear the people shouting. Above the center dome I saw Mary in full body, standing before the cross. I cannot describe what I felt."

Additional information may be easily acquired through the Pittsburgh Center For Peace.

Patron of Farmers

According to his biographers, Saint Isidore was the model of perfection. The whole of his life he worked diligently as a farmer in Madrid, a disguise which successfully concealed his sanctity. On one occasion, having returned home after a day's work he found a poor pilgrim at his cottage door asking for food. He requested his wife to give the man something to eat and she replied, "I wish I could fulfill this request of yours, dear husband, but we have nothing in the house."

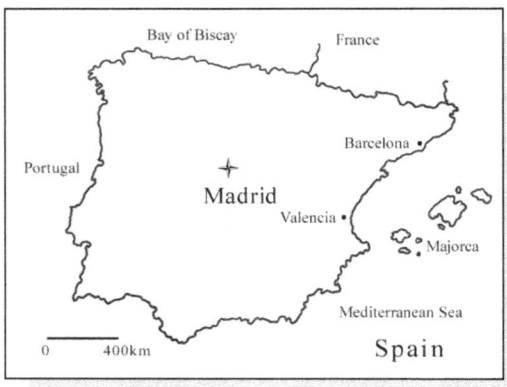

Isidore bade his wife, "Look into the pot where you usually cook."

But she replied, "It is quite empty, my husband. I have just rinsed it and set it by."

"Go, wife, and fetch the pot and see what God will give to the hungry," said Isidore.

On returning to the pot, she found it was very heavy. When she lifted the lid, she was delighted to find it full to the top with excellent meat, cooked and ready to eat. A table was set and each enjoyed liberal portions. Later, when they checked the pot again, not a single spoonful had been consumed.

Saint Isidore lived from 1070-1130 and was canonized in 1622, by Pope Gregory the XV. His body, perfectly intact, has remained miraculously incorrupt for over eight hundred years and may be seen in the Cathedral of Madrid, Spain.

Love In Action

The most compassionate woman in the world today is, without a doubt, Mother Teresa.

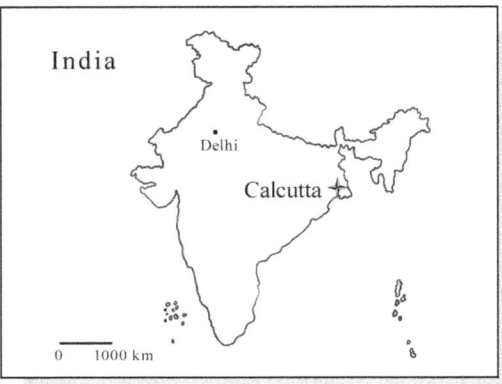

Born in Skopje, Yugoslavia, to a peasant class family, she enjoyed an exceptionally happy childhood, one she still loves to speak about. However, in 1922, at age twelve she heard the inner voice of God summon her to duty. Though she loved her family dearly, she realized that her mission required that her love be expanded to universal proportions.

In 1929, she joined a convent school which took her to Calcutta where she enjoyed teaching eager school girls in the pleasant courtyard gardens of Loreto convent. During a visit to the poorest streets of Calcutta, she discovered countless refugees from neighboring countries wasting away in the parks and alleys. She then realized that this is where she was meant to be. She felt a calling from the thousands of homeless children who were abandoned, orphaned and starving. Her mission seemed impossible and the obstacles to be surmounted overwhelming, but she was called and would not refuse.

She encountered objections from family and friends, but finally, after patiently waiting for two years, she was released from her vows and returned to the world to follow stricter vows of her own devising. With only five rupees in her pocket, she made her way to an almost forgotten sector of Calcutta, found lodging there, gathered a few abandoned children and began her mission of love-giving. This choice, to live in the slums amidst the deepest dirt, disease and misery of our world, reveals a spirit so indomitable and a love so abounding that it clearly redefines our measure of human compassion.

"What the poor need most," Mother Teresa tells us, "more than food or clothing and shelter (though they need these too), is to be wanted." It is the outcast state which their poverty imposes upon them, that is most agonizing.

By God's grace, Mother Teresa has a place in her heart for everyone. She loves them all, young and old, as though they were the children of her own womb. She has achieved a standard of human love reminiscent of the life of Christ. Like Christ, she lives among the needy, eats the same food, wears the same clothes and shares in their lives.

She maintains a very practical view about money. Even though she needs every penny, she makes no public appeals. Much of the money she receives supports her leper colonies. She has refused government grants and has set up numerous medical and social work institutions based strictly on voluntary donations. This, she says, requires no book keeping, which remains consistent with the message she is giving us.

At times her institutions report that all monies are exhausted. "Then you must beg," she might say, having joyously undertaken this task to fulfill the ends of her mission.

Mother Teresa has made it clear that she is not fond of the mention of miracles concerning her life. With respect for her wishes, no mention will be made. It is sufficient to say that she has proven herself to be the embodiment of love in action and this is her message to all.

Mother Teresa died on September 5, 1997 in Calcutta, India. Information regarding her missions may be obtained from Mother Teresa Missionaries of Charity, 335 East 145th Street, Bronx, New York 10451.

Form of Victory

Emperor Constantine began his march against Maxentius who declared war against him in A.D. 312. While Maxentius was stationed in Rome with a vastly superior army, Constantine marched from the Rhine, through Gaul, traveling towards Rome by way of Verona. By the light of midday, having passed through the Alps, he and his legions witnessed the sight of a bright, shining, heavenly cross in the clouds above them. Believing it was the sign of victory from heaven, Constantine's troops were greatly elated.

The following night, an angel appeared to Constantine while he was sleeping. The angel carried a cross in his hands that resembled the vision in the clouds. He commanded Constantine to have a standard made resembling the form of the cross. When morning came, the emperor gave orders for such a standard to be fashioned and named it the *Labarum*. He selected fifty of his best men to carry and guard this banner.

The battle was fought in Quintian fields, near the Milvian bridge. There, on October 27, A.D. 312, Maxentius was utterly destroyed. Constantine entered Rome in triumph and ascribed his victory to this miracle.

Innocent Defense

After the death and resurrection of Jesus of Nazareth, two of his disciples, Simon and Jude, decided to join forces to carryon his teaching and proliferate the new religious movement. While they were in Babylon consecrating a new bishop, Abdias, and ordaining priests and deacons, slanderous accusations were made against them. It happened that the unwed daughter of a Babylonian nobleman had recently given birth to a baby boy. To protect the identity of her real lover, she charged one of the deacons with the crime.

Intent on discovering the truth, Simon and Jude requested of the king that the deacon, mother and infant be brought before the judge for trial.

This being done, both Jude and Simon fixed their eyes on the new born child entreating, "We adjure thee, by the living God, tell us truly if this deacon is thy father or not?"

The infant answered, "This man is not my father. He is good and chaste and has never in his life committed any carnal sin."

The assembly was awe-struck at this display, and the infant was further petitioned to give the name of his real father.

"It is for me to defend the innocent, not so, to disclose the guilty," came his just response.

Saint Simon and Jude are celebrated together on October 28th. This story is told in The Lives of Saints, by Edward Kinesman.

Tears of Neglect

The summer of 1985 saw the beginning of a new unexplainable phenomenon in Naju, Korea. A statue of the Virgin Mary, owned by a forty-year-old mother of four children, Julia Kim, began to weep tears. Other than her immediate family, the phenomenon, which continued for about three months, was revealed to no one. Outing this time, Julia reported that she was receiving messages from the Holy Virgin which were intended to be given to priests.

In October, 1986, the statue, which had previously wept tears, now wept blood for a period of seven hours. This phenomenon of weeping tears and blood has continued repeatedly until the present day, and as many as three hundred people have crowded into Julia's apartment to witness the affair. Often the Virgin's tears continue for many hours.

Why is the statue crying?

Julia says the Virgin cries because her children's spiritual pursuits and practices have become casual, mediocre or forgotten entirely.

The events relating to this miracle are under the watchful eye of the Archbishop of Kwanju.

Further information may be obtained from the Pittsburgh Center For Peace.

No Pain, No Gain

Alphonsus Rodriguez is celebrated among the great mystics of Europe. He was a husband, father and businessman, but clearly different from the numerous commercial men in his hometown, who lived exemplary but unheroic lives. He was taught the rudiments of mental meditation from his two sisters, and despite the unimaginable discomfort he experienced whenever he formally set himself to meditate, he faithfully dedicated himself for two hours every morning and evening to its practice.

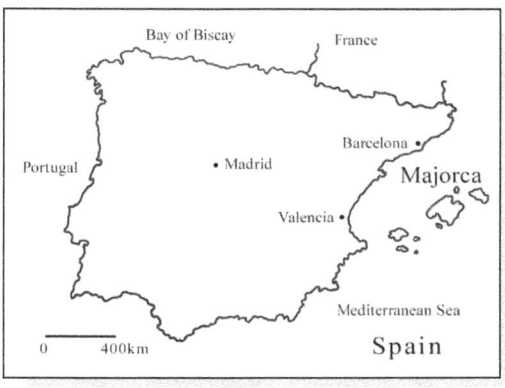

Before long his spiritual genius was recognized, and the number of eyewitness reports of miracles produced by Alphonsus filled volumes. He had merely to pray, and his prayers were answered. "He could not raise his eyes in spirit to Jesus and Mary without their being at once before him."

Knowing the power of his prayers, he took great care to pray for the enlightenment of all humanity. Never would he miss this personal dedication. During these moments of prayer, he was so elevated in spirit he would breathe life into the soul of every man or woman—indeed all the souls of the world. On occasion he was assured by God that his spiritual practice merited as much as if he had actually liberated the entire human race. Yet all that time he bore a constant, intolerable physical agony.

At age eighty-four, on the evening of October 30th, Alphonsus lay, as it were, in an unbroken ecstasy which ended with his death. His funeral was attended by the Spanish Viceroy and nobility of Majorca and by endless crowds of poor, sick and afflicted whose love and faith were rewarded by miracles. For generations after his death, miracles were recorded at the site of his tomb.

Saint Alphonsus Rodriguez lived from 1533-1611 and was canonized in 1888. He is celebrated on October 30th. The accounts of his life are recorded in The Life of Alphonsus Rodriguez.

Flight Records

A typical account of spontaneous levitation was recorded by Sister Maria Villani who lived in a small Italian convent during the seventeenth century.

"On one occasion when I was in my cell I was conscious of a new experience. I felt myself seized and ravished out of my senses, and that so powerfully that I found myself lifted up completely by the very soles of my feet, just as a magnet draws up the fragment of iron, but with a gentleness that was marvelous and most delightful. At first I felt much fear, but afterwards I remained in the greatest possible contentment and joy of spirit. Though I was quite beside myself, still, in spite of that, I knew that I was raised some distance above the earth, my whole body being suspended for some considerable space of time. Down to last Christmas eve (1626) this happened to me on five different occasions."

This narration is extracted from a statement made by Sister Maria Villani to her spiritual director and was originally published in 1717.

November

1 Honeycomb
2 Thumbs Up
3 Our Lady of Kibeho
4 Two-in-One
5 Aggression
6 John VI
7 Riches Beyond Imagination
8 Greatness
9 Miracles in Ireland
10 A Pair of Shoes
11 The Almsgiver of Alexandria
12 Bilocation
13 Real Mother
14 Six Ounces of Bread
15 The Wedding Gift
16 Patron of Scotland
17 Another Moses
18 Happy Saints
19 Queen of Hungary
20 Blessed
21 A Special Gift
22 Miracles of Damascus
23 Who Can Stop the Sea
24 Open Door
25 Great Balls of Fire
26 Thousands of Monks
27 Miraculous Medal
28 Recluse of Siope
29 Somewhere to Gather
30 No Peace in the Hermit's House

Honeycomb

Marinus was originally a monk from Moriana, Italy. He loved his monastery friends but felt a yearning for a deeper solitude which he never found in the bustling routine of monastic life. Thus resolved, he left the monastery and retired to a cave on the edge of a nearby mountainside. There he celebrated his new home with a three-day fast and would have continued longer, but unexpected guests arrived. To his surprise, two bears, each with a honeycomb full of honey, slowly approached him and laid their food offerings at his feet. Crouching low, one of the bears licked his feet, while the other made unmistakable signs, inviting Marinus to taste the food they had brought him. This he did and in return graciously invited the bears to visit again another day. Almost every day the bears returned, and with each visit they brought with them a gift of two delicate loaves of bread. For four years these wild beasts assumed the nature of lambs, showing Marinus every mark of genuine reverence, while delivering his daily bread. There he remained until his dying day, joyfully hidden and guarded, while pursuing his mystic career.

Saint Marinus lived until A.D. 131. He is celebrated on November 1st. The accounts of his life are recorded in Vies des Saints de Diocese de Poitiers.

Thumbs Up

Working in the fields, two miles from the monastery of Bobbio, a resident monk fell victim to a terrible accident which severed the thumb of his left hand in two parts. Panic stricken, he hurried to the monastery and implored his abbot, Attalus, to restore him to wholeness. Attalus dispatched a man to retrieve the missing thumb and having done so, he anointed it with spittle and replaced it on the monk's hand. The thumb was repaired instantly, and the monk resumed his activities as if nothing whatsoever had happened.

Saint Attalus lived until A.D. 627. This story is recorded in The Life of Saint Attalus, *by Jonas, an eyewitness and disciple of Saint Attalus.*

Our Lady of Kibeho

"The world has teeth. . . . sins are more numerous than drops of water in the sea."

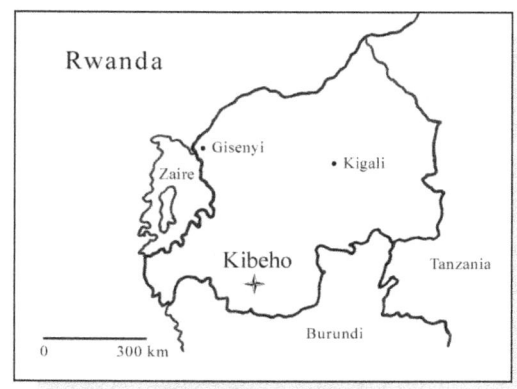

These words were spoken to one of seven young African visionaries during an apparition of the Virgin Mary who appeared in Kibeho, Rwanda, in 1983. Three of the visionaries were living in a college run by nuns in a poor section of the country. Three others were living in the bush. The last, Sagatasha, a young pagan boy from Kibeho was instructed in certain religious practices through an apparition of Jesus Christ.

Though the apparitions began in November of 1981, only one visionary, Alphonsine, continues to receive messages. The messages emphasize the importance of loving ourselves and others, and not underestimating the power of prayer, especially the rosary. The messages particularly encourage young people to set a good example for the world. As in other modern-day apparitions of the Virgin Mary, the messages emphasize fasting and spiritual growth.

After seven years of investigation of the apparitions in Kibeho, Rwanda, first stage approval was awarded by Bishop Msgr. Gehanany.

Contact the Pittsburgh Center For Peace for further information.

Two-in-One

Suor Maria was blessed with three supernatural gifts. She could read the thoughts of others, she was known to levitate, and, perhaps most unusual, she possessed the talent of bilocation—being in two places at one time.

Suor Maria was the Abbess of the Franciscan convent of the Immaculate Conception at Agreda. As a child she enjoyed many visions and ecstasies and took quite naturally to perpetual fasting, an austerity that even an accomplished ascetic might find challenging. Her many visions inspired her to write *The Mystical City of God* (1643) which is still considered a classic of mystical literature.

Over five hundred experiences of her bilocations were thoroughly documented by Father Ximenes Samaniego who wrote a biography of her life. Her bilocations followed a common pattern. While praying in her convent cell she was suddenly transported to Mexico. Thereupon, she instructed the native people in the teachings of Christ and sent them to local missionaries for formal baptism. Even though the missionaries collected reports of the appearance of this mysterious woman, none had ever seen her before.

Years later they received corroborative evidence from Suor Maria herself. She described areas of Mexico with detailed familiarity and confirmed that the rosaries distributed among the natives were taken from her personal stock. Father Alonzo de Benavides was in charge of the missionary activities in Mexico at the time, and he recounts this story himself in his *Revised Memorial of 1634*.

Aggression

Stephen Harding was the third abbot of Citreaux. He was an active man with noticeable vitality and a never ending compulsion to find the truth at any cost. This tendency often grew to an overaggressive obsession which would invariably lead him to his sickbed. On one such occasion, being particularly ill, he was revived by way of a miracle.

Due to weakness he was unable to leave his bed or feed himself. When fed by his fellow brothers, he was seized by severe convulsions making it impossible for him to retain any food. The residents were sure he would die, but one afternoon a bird entered the room through an open window and landed on Stephen's chest. The bird carried a cooked fish in its beak and proceeded to feed the sick man by forcing open his mouth and depositing food, as if Stephen was one of its own brood. In this way Stephen's life was restored. He assumed again his position as abbot, watching and waiting patiently for God's will, rather than his own.

Saint Stephen Harding lived until 1134 and was canonized in 1623. The, (counts of his life are recorded in the Acta Sanctorum, Bollandists, Volume II.

Passover

After this Jesus went to the other side of the sea of Galilee, which is the sea of the Tiberias. And a multitude followed him because they saw the signs he did on those who were diseased. Jesus went up into the hills and there sat down with his disciples. Now the Passover, the feast of the Jews was at hand. Lifting up his eyes, then, and seeing that a multitude was coming to him, Jesus said to Philip, "How are we to buy bread, so that these people may eat?" This he did to test him, for he himself knew what he would do. Philip answered him, "Two hundred denarii would not buy enough bread for each of them to get a little." One of the disciples, Andrew, Simon Peter's brother, said to him, "There is a lad here who has five barley loaves and two fish, but what are they among so many?" Jesus said, "Make the people sit down." Now there was much grass in the place, so the men sat down, in number about five thousand. Jesus then took the loaves, and when he had given thanks, he distributed them to those that were seated, so also the fish as much as they wanted. And when they had eaten their fill, he told his disciples, "Gather up the fragments left over, that nothing may be lost." So they gathered them up and filled twelve baskets with fragments from the five barely loaves, left by those who had eaten. When the people saw the sign he had done, they said, "This is indeed the prophet who is come into the world."

The Holy Bible, John VI.

Riches Beyond Imagination

Francis of Paola was particularly popular among the wonderworkers of Christian history. His supernatural powers were apparently inexhaustible and the sheer number of miracles credited to him seems endless. Wherever he traveled, miracle seekers followed, and in time, many became miracle workers themselves.

On one occasion Francis passed through Naples on his way to a meeting with King Louis XI in Tours. While in Naples, he was entertained at the palace of Ferdinand I. His highness invited the saint to breakfast at the royal table, but Francis refused saying it would not be suitable. The king, who was astonished and concerned that Francis was in some way not pleased with his hospitality, sent him a royal platter of fresh, fried fish. When the platter arrived, Francis blessed the fish and at the same moment they returned to their former state, fully restored to life. Francis then asked the page to return the fish to the king, who, on seeing the platter declared, "God has blessed this man with riches beyond our wildest imagination."

Saint Francis of Paola lived from 1416-1507. He was canonized in 1519. His portrait was depicted by many famous contemporaries including Goya, Murillo and Velazquez. The accounts of his life are recorded in the Acta Sanctorum.

Greatness

Martin was a humble man who had a calming effect on people, like a medicine that both soothes and relaxes the mind. He was very affectionate and for this reason was greatly honored and loved by Emperor Maximus and his wife. It wasn't at all uncommon to see the empress waiting on Martin, bringing him water to wash his hands or humbly bowing when he entered the room. He was regarded a saint in his own time and was treated accordingly.

However, when Valentinian II, an Arian, succeeded Emperor Maximus, no such relationship continued. Martin's reputation and powerful influence over the people threatened Valentinian who hated and despised him.

On one occasion, when Martin entered the royal court the courtiers rose from their seats, as was the custom, but the emperor refused to rise from his seat, as a deliberate show of disrespect. When Martin approached the throne, Valentinian continued to remain seated. Then suddenly, without warning, Valentinian's throne burst into flames. Valentinian jumped from his seat in alarm while the guards extinguished the flames. Then approaching Martin, he knelt before him.

"True greatness requires true humility," was Martin's assurance.

Saint Martin of Tours lived during the fourth century. He died on November 8, A.D. 397. The accounts of his life are recorded in The Life of Saint Martin, *by Sulpicius Severus.*

Miracles in Ireland

Heavenly apparitions have recently been reported in Ireland, starting as early as 1985. Near Inchigeela, three children, Rosemary O'Sullivan, Marie Vaughan and Kelley Noonan, and a mother of nine, Mrs. Mary Casey, have reported to have seen the Blessed Madonna and received messages from her.

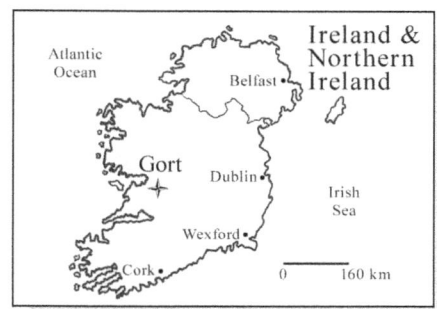

The apparitions occurred in two distinct locations, both in grottos near the village of Inchigeela. The messages received were the messages of peace.

"Peace. Prayer is the best weapon you have. It is the key that opens God's heart. Let your prayer be genuine gratitude to the Father."

At another grotto, that of St. Peter and Paul's Church in Bessbrook, Ireland, a series of apparitions occurred to Beulah Lynch and Mark Treanor.

During the spring of 1987, Mark reported that he felt an involuntary urge to go to the grotto. There he saw a beautiful lady dressed in white looking directly at him. Her hair was golden and wavy and adorned with a golden crown. Her face was very beautiful, with blue eyes and red lips that smiled lovingly. Her skin was shining and pale yellow.

Three days later the apparition appeared again, this time to Beulah Lynch. She describes the lady as young and unspeakably beautiful. She was surrounded by light and assumed a motherly demeanor. In her hand she carried a rosary.

"I am your Mother," she said. "I love you. The world must behave. The world must change. A great catastrophe will happen to the world. Tell them to hurry. This is a command from God. The messages here are the messages in Medjugorje. The children in Medjugorje are the children here. . . . My child, the messages are not to be taken foolishly. They are serious. . . . You have been given a gift from God. Tell the people to come and pray. Pray and fast and do penance."

Similar apparitions have occurred in Melleray Grotto, in 1985, and, during the winter of 1988, in Gortnadreha, Ireland.

Currently these apparitions are under investigation.

No official judgment has been rendered to these apparitions.

A Pair of Shoes

Endowed with a crusader's sense of social justice, Saint Bernardino loved to launch attacks bent on changing what he viewed to be misguided or wrongheaded directions. His biographers tell us he was renowned for his ability to heal the sick. The most memorable of his miracles is as follows.

On one occasion, Saint Bernardino, being moved with compassion, offered a pair of his shoes to a poor leper who had none. The delighted leper immediately put them on his feet, and as he stood admiring them, his leprosy dissolved as though it had been washed away like mud in a rain storm. When the transformation was complete, his health was restored as though he had never been afflicted. Such was the sanctity of this saint.

Saint Bernardino lived from 1380-1444 and was canonized in 1450. He is celebrated as the Patron Saint of advertisers. The accounts of his life are recorded in the Life of Saint Bernardino, by Barnaby of Siena, his contemporary.

The Almsgiver of Alexandria

John the Almsgiver was both a thinker and a doer and had little time for established ways of order. He was a natural success and could easily compute a hundred things at one time. He was nobly descended, exceptionally rich, blessed with a good family, and admired by the people of Cyprus where he lived. He was a brilliant organizer, an impressive balance of prudence and productivity.

When he arrived in the city of Alexandria, his new residence, he sought to eliminate its poverty entirely. First, he requested an exact list of all his masters. Questioned as to who these masters were, he answered, "The Poor, of course." The total number of "masters" was tallied and amounted to seventy-five hundred. These John personally protected and furnished with necessities. His second action in Alexandria was to distribute eighty thousand pieces of gold from the treasury of the church to hospitals and monasteries.

John believed that all charities given would be returned a hundredfold, and he proved it many times. All his financial dealings were subject to this axiom. One day he gave a written order to his treasurer to confer fifteen pounds of gold on a nobleman who was reduced to utter poverty. The treasurer, believing the sum to be too generous, secretly erased the 'one' from John's order and gave the man only five pounds. On the same day, a donation of five hundred pounds of gold was received from a wealthy lady. John heard of the incident and thought it odd that on this occasion his axiom had faltered. He invited the lady for tea and inquired about her donation. During their conversation, she remarked, "Originally, I wrote my order for fifteen hundred pounds, but this morning I noticed that the 'one' on your order had been erased, so I erased the 'one' from my own."

Saint John of Alexandria lived until A.D. 620. Life of The Patriarch John of Alexandria.

Bilocation

Teresa Higginson is unique among mystics. She led an active secular life as a school teacher at Saint Catherine's Convent in Edinburgh, Scotland during the 1800s. She was commonly regarded by her students and coworkers as "a sweet little schoolmistress," but behind the scenes, in her private life, she concealed an intensely spiritual personality that was blessed with miracles. She experienced many ecstasies and visions and suffered the stigmata. When she began to experience bilocation (being in two places at the same time) "she felt bound by her obedience to relate them to her director."

The following letter was written in Teresa's own hand and describes what she believes to be a bilocation to Africa.

"Well for some length of time I have from time to time found myself among the negroes, but how I am transported thither I really cannot say—I mean that I do not see myself going (just as a person might close their eyes and when they open them again they find themselves in a different place) not in spirit but personally present. I find myself with them whom it pleases our dear Divine Lord I shall assist, and yet I am able to continue where I was and go on with the duties I was performing here. I have all along tried to persuade myself that I was deceived and yet I feel so positive of what I did. It is not always the same place that I visit or the same people, though I have (been) most of all with a tribe whose chief is lately deceased, and whose name is Jaampooda. He and his people were savages and lived by hunting I should imagine, by the fur and ivory which they possess in great abundance. It is now over four years since I have visited these people and they were stricken down by a sickness which turned their bodies purple and black, and of which many or them died; then I did all I could to relieve their bodily suffering, and I was instructed to gather some bark off a tree which grew commonly there and make a beverage for them and which I understand they call bitter waters and waters of life."

Teresa Higginson was born in Lincolnshire, England, and attended a convent school at Nottingham. Her correspondence was collected by Cecil Kerr who used it to construct a biography, Teresa Helena Higginson— Servant of God *(1926).*

Real Mother

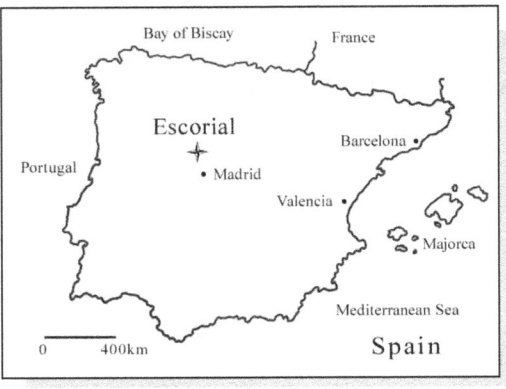

Since childhood Amparo Cuevos worked hard to get by. Her mother died when she was six months old, and her stepmother showed no kindness toward her. As a child she earned money by selling objects on the streets of Spain and given strict instructions not to return until everything was sold. Often that meant sleeping outside in the snow without food. Her home life was also uncomfortable and often, while lying in her cupboard bed, she prayed she would die in the hopes that she might be reunited with her real mother in heaven.

However, on November 13, 1980, her life began to change dramatically when a series of apparitions of the Virgin Mary occurred to her in Escorial, Spain. Similar to other modern-day apparitions, the Madonna requested a return to daily repetition of the rosary, and she warned of global chastisement should mankind not seek the path of peace.

Since the time of her first vision Amparo has become a stigmatist. She was told her suffering would alleviate the suffering of the world, and she has graciously accepted what heaven has deemed fit for her.

A new book from the Riehle Foundation has been compiled to tell the story of the Madonna's extensive messages to Amparo.

Six Ounces of Bread

Antony of Egypt was an immensely popular saint. He was born in a village south of Memphis in upper Egypt. Having lost his family at an early age, he found himself heir to a considerable estate. However, his destiny was clear to him. Without the slightest reservation, he abandoned the properties left to him and endeavored to imitate a reclusive life while still a young and ignorant boy. Before long he was blessed with visions. However, frequently the Devil appeared to him in the form of an amorous woman and sought to seduce him. To oppose these assaults, he observed the strictest fasts. His daily sustenance was six ounces of bread soaked in water, to which he sometimes added a few dates. It was a diet he maintained for the remainder of his life, one hundred and five years.

In search of more remote solitude, Antony withdrew to an old burial place. Again he was assaulted by the Devil and beaten until almost dead. When he regained consciousness, the voice of God echoed from the sky, "Antony, I was here the whole time. I stood by thee and beheld thy combat, and because thou hast manfully withstood thy enemies, I will always protect thee, and will render thy name famous throughout the earth."

In time, numerous disciples sought Antony's mastership and he was obliged to build a monastery. Soon many more monasteries were needed, and Antony traveled from one to the other imparting instructions to each monk individually based on their inner experience. He advised them to reflect every morning that perhaps they might not live until night, and every evening that perhaps they might not see the morning. "In this manner do every action as if I were the last of your life."

His life was filled with miracles of every description, but he gave them little importance. When the crowds of miracle seekers became too large he would say, "As fish die if they are taken from the water, so does a monk wither away if he forsakes his solitude."

To the blind he would say: "Do not regret the loss of eyes, which is common even to insects, but rejoice in the treasure of that inner light which the apostles enjoyed, by which we see God and kindle the fires of his love in our souls."

On other occasions when learned scholars tried to mock him for his ignorance, he would ask, "Which is best, good sense or book learning, and which produced the other?" "Good sense," replied the philosophers. "This then, is sufficient of itself," said Antony.

Once again during Antony's life, the Devil appeared before him, but this time Antony disposed of his enemy with the words, "Ask what you please. I am the power of God," and the Devil vanished.

In the year A.D. 356, Antony knew his time to die had come, and distributing his few possessions, he said, "Farewell, my children, Antony is departing and will no longer be with you."

At these words, his disciples embraced him, and without any outward sign, he stretched out his feet and calmly ceased to breathe.

Antony the Great lived from A.D, 251-356. He is regarded the patriarch of monks and is celebrated on various dates throughout the world. The maxim of his teaching, which he frequently repeated is: knowledge of ourselves is a necessary step and the only step by which we can ascend to the knowledge and love of God. The accounts of his life were recorded by Saint Athanasius, his contemporary.

The Wedding Gift

The following newspaper article appeared in La Sicilia in 1953.

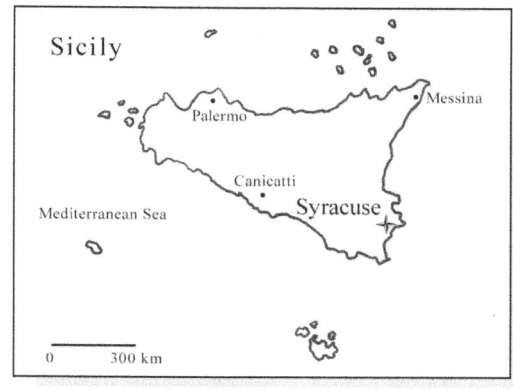

"All Syracuse has seen the Madonna cry. The entire city is reeling under the impact of this startling event. People everywhere are talking about it—on the streets, in their homes; there is the constant clash of contradictory theories and comments in an effort to find an explanation for, his incredible phenomenon. One thing is beyond dispute—tears are flowing from the eyes of the Madonna of the Via degli Orti, and the miracle, if this astounding and baffling phenomenon can be so styled, has been confirmed by thousands and thousands of people who have incessantly funneled into the home of Antonietta Giusto to gaze with amazement at the tears of the Madonna.

Skepticism, for all its inherent obstinacy and prejudice, must bow to reality. The little bust of the Madonna, mounted on a black plate glass, has kept up a steady flow of tears all day long except for a few brief intervals. The skeptics themselves, profoundly agitated and trembling pathetically as they pressed their pads of cloth to the face of the Madonna, have yielded to the compelling force of truth. The news which was spread across our early morning edition has been drawing huge crowds; they stand throughout the day hoping to witness the phenomenon and to kneel near the statue that is regarded as miraculous. A great number have had their desires fulfilled and the impression they have carried away baffles description."

This event occurred in the home of Angelo and Antonietta Giusto, a poor Sicilian couple living in Syracuse, Sicily. They had only recently been married when this incident occurred. The statue, which was a wedding gift given to them by Angelo's brother, was an eighteen-inch common plaster casting that was purchased at a local gift shop. Numerous miracles have been credited to it.

Patron of Scotland

Margaret was a queen. She was the grand-daughter of Edmund Ironside and the daughter of Edward the Atheling. Having married Malcolm III, King of Scotland, she was crowned queen. Their union was an extremely happy one, for both Margaret and Malcolm as well as the Scottish court and nation. Margaret was greatly loved by the Scottish people, and she took great care, without regard for expense, to secure the highest standard of education for her fellow countrymen.

She held considerable influence over her husband, and although initially rough in character, he was utterly transformed by her love. His biographers wrote, "What she loved, he, for love of her, loved too."

Margaret was a shy women with refined sensibilities and a subdued dignity. She was the mother of eight children, two of whom became kings. When she found the time to be alone, it was spent quietly reading scriptures or in prayer.

The king, however, could not read, but for love of her, he would cherish her hooks and see to it that they were embellished with artwork and gold. Margaret's life was a festival of miracles and the anecdote which follows is but one, given in connection with her books.

One of the queen's books was accidentally dropped into a river during a picnic outing, and there it remained for a great length of time before its absence was noticed. A search party was dispatched to recover the book and in time it was sighted, pages open, at the bottom of the river where the accident occurred. It was believed to be entirely washed out, but a rescue ensued just the same. To everyone's surprise, when the book was drawn to the surface of the river, no injury could be detected. Not a spot or discoloration on a single page. The delighted queen acknowledged the miracle and the book. Apparently the same book is preserved in the Bodleian Library at Oxford.

Queen Margaret of Scotland lived from 1046-1093. The document of her canonization did not survive, but she is regarded as Patron of Scotland and is currently celebrated on November 16th. This story is given by Durham, the queen's confession.

Another Moses

Matthew 17: 20. "If ye have faith, ye shall say to this mountain, Remove hence to yonder place; and it shall remove; and nothing shall be impossible unto you."

This was certainly the case for Gregory the Wonderworker. "The mysteries of Christ's teaching," he would say, "being past human understanding, are confirmed in the manifestation of miracles."

Gregory was an energetic man, a natural extrovert with an enormous capacity to organize anything to the finest microscopic detail. Together with his brother, he studied under the mastership of Origen, who instilled in them the understanding, "that in all things, the most valuable knowledge is that of the first cause." He opened their minds to all that the philosophers and poets had written concerning God. He showed them what was true and what was erroneous in the doctrines of each and demonstrated the incompetence of human reason alone for attaining to certain knowledge.

After several happy years with Origen, Gregory's studies were complete, and he returned to Neocaesarea. However, no miracles were produced by him until after he had received a letter from his master which encouraged him "to employ, for the service of religion, all the talents he had received from God."

"Show us a miracle that we may believe!" were the indignant cries of sincere but doubtful priests from Neocaesarea. Being put to the test, Gregory pointed to a rock of mountainous proportions and replied, "I will command is rock to move hence to yonder place, that you may believe."

He gave the command and the rock obeyed. The priests were convinced and requested immediate baptism for themselves, their wives, children, servants and all who followed them.

Saint Basil tells us that "through the co-operation of the Spirit, Gregory had a formidable power over evil spirits; he altered the course of rivers; dried up a lake that was a cause of dissension between two brothers; and his foretelling of the future made him equal with the other prophets. . . . Such were his signs and wonders that both friends and enemies of the truth looked on him as another Moses."

Saint Gregory lived from A.D. 213-270. He is celebrated on November 17th and is particularly popular in Italy and Sicily where he is invoked in times of earthquake and flood. The accounts of his life are recorded in The Life of Saint Gregory the Thaumaturgist.

Happy Saints

"Enjoy yourself as much as you like—if only you keep from sin."

This was the maxim of Saint John Bosco who as a child loved to entertain crowds with juggling and acrobatic feats. He had an excellent sense of humor which he carried with him in his life as a priest.

He received his first vision of Our Lady at the age of nine and throughout his life he witnessed prophetic and instructional dreams which became the pillar of his spiritual growth. So many miracles occurred in his life that Pope Pius XI commented on him, that, "The supernatural almost became natural, and the extraordinary, ordinary."

Although there are thousands of miracles credited to John Bosco, the most colorful involves a mysterious, large greyhound dog who would suddenly appear every time danger threatened the life of the saint. After the emergency, the dog disappeared as silently and mysteriously as it had appeared.

John's work primarily involved the building of schools and churches for the homeless and the poor, a mission he received by instruction in his dreams. He wanted his students to be saints—happy saints, not "long faced saints."

"First tell the devil to rest, and then I'll rest too. While I have time, I must work." This was the final maxim of John's life, when at age seventy-two, he entered heaven, from which he was just a step away. Happily, he lived to see the spread of his new congregation which is currently the largest in the world.

John Melchior Bosco was born on a small farm at the foot of the Italian Alps. He lived from 1815-1888 and was canonized in 1934.

Queen of Hungary

Elizabeth was an intriguing woman with a distinct outward majesty. She was the daughter of King Andrew II and married King Louis IV, whom she kept very happy. She was the mother of three children, and their family life together was the envy of the kingdom.

Elizabeth was known to everyone, for she kept no airs about her. She devoted herself to the service of her people and is particularly remembered for a hospital she had constructed adjoining the family castle. With a hospital so close to her quarters, she could attend to the sick and poor herself. Occasionally she had patients placed in her own bed when the hospital beds were filled.

Her husband King Louis was not entirely supportive of her behavior. He thought her generosity too lavish and excessive even for a woman of her station. Although he had heard she was blessed with miracles, he found it hard to believe. They became apparent to him for the first time when he caught her and her favorite domestic, filling the skirts of their gowns with eggs, bread and other foods to be distributed to the poor. He reveled at the thought of catching them red handed and when he sprang upon them, he called out, "Heyday, Elizabeth, what have we got here?"

"Only roses," replied Elizabeth, and opening her lap he saw it was filled with the most exquisite red and white roses. It was winter when no roses grew.

Astonished, he saluted his wife, but stopped short when he noticed a luminous cross directly above her head. From then on he granted her liberty to give as she pleased. Taking one of the roses, he traveled to Wartenburg to execute the duties of the day.

Elizabeth lived from 1207-1231. She was canonized in 1235 by Pope Gregory IV, her celebration being ascribed to November 19th. Her relics, kept in the church of Saint Elizabeth at Marburg, were the object of popular pilgrimage, until 1539 when they were removed to an unknown place. This story was recorded by the Count of Montalembert in The History of Saint Elizabeth of Hungary.

Blessed

"If it pleases the lady mother to show herself, I shall rejoice with exceeding great joy."

These were the final words spoken by Saint Clare at a point near her death. She spoke them in response to her attending nurse who asked to be blessed with a vision of the Holy Mother. With these words the room was filled with heavenly virgins dressed in gowns of white, with golden crowns adorning their heads. The Queen of Heaven herself appeared, "From whose face proceeded such ineffable splendor, the midday sun was easily eclipsed." The Queen bowed courteously to Saint Clare and bade the virgins of her suite to give her the mantle brought from heaven. Saint Clare knew well that her hour had come and as she breathed out her soul, the virgin train carried it with them from whence they came. This was the vision which occurred to the attending nurse.

Saint Clare lived from 1194-1253. She was canonized two years after her death, her celebration being set for the month of August. The accounts of her life are found in The Life of Saint Clare, *written at the express command of Pope Alexander V.*

A Special Gift

Cadoc of Wales had a passion for the Latin poet, Vergil. He was an incurable romantic, and everyone knew it. At times he was the subject of much friendly fun-making. However, one afternoon, while out walking with Gildas, the historian he put his valued book of poems under his arm and began to weep with compassion for the beloved poet. At the same instant, an enormous gust of wind lifted his arm and the book was blown forcibly into the sea. The loss was an unspeakable grief to Cadoc, but he bore it well. The following morning a fisherman arrived at his kitchen with a delivery of fine fresh salmon. In preparation, the cook discovered that in the belly of the fish was the very book which had been lost on the previous day. Cadoc's joy was far beyond the common joy. Not only had his treasure been returned to him, but it was entirely uninjured.

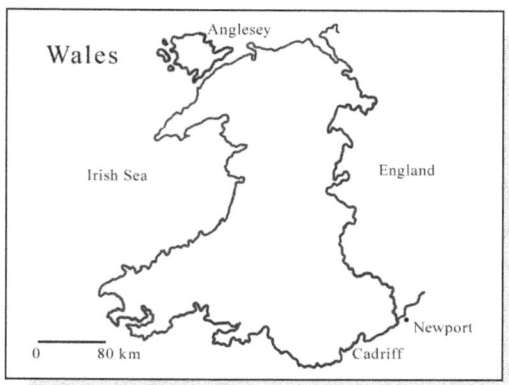

Cadoc of Wales lived during the sixth century. His life is documented in Lives of The Cambo-British Saints, *by Rees.*

Miracles of Damascus

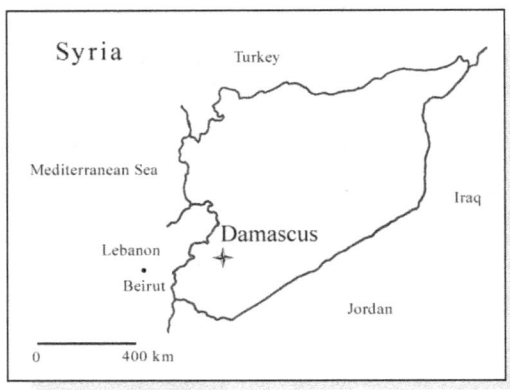

The first miracle that ever occurred to Mirna Nazour took place on November 22, 1982 in the old city of Damascus, Syria. She was kneeling next to her sister-in-law, praying for her recovery, when oil suddenly began to flow from her hands. She spontaneously placed her hands on her sister-in-law, who recovered instantly. This event occurred a second time when she was praying next to the bed of her sick mother. Again the oil began to flow and again the cure was instantaneous. Two days later, Mirna's icon of the Virgin and Child began to exude oil. This miracle continues to the present day and numerous healings are ascribed to the oil.

This oil which exudes from both Mirna's hands and the icon has undergone exhaustive investigation. No trickery has been discovered and a chemical analysis of the oil reveals an unusually pure, one hundred percent olive oil of unknown origin.

The healings and miraculous events surrounding the mysterious oils have received approval by the local bishops of Damascus. The details of these ecstasies, healings, and miracles have been documented on video recordings and may be obtained for private collections.

For further information contact the Pittsburgh Center For Peace.

Who Can Stop The Sea?

Pope Clement was banished from Rome and exiled to the Crimea by Aufidianus, in the reign of Trajan, A.D. 102. There he was forced to work in the mines, but the miracles he performed made him so popular he set out to administrate a religious society in Chersonese. He preached with such power that he gained innumerable followers who assisted him in the establishment of seventy-five churches.

Clement's influence over the people terrified Aufidianus. Accordingly, he condemned Clement to be drowned in the sea three miles from shore by means of an anchor around his neck. Clement's followers from Chersonese prayed for the recovery of their leader, and to their astonishment their prayers were answered. The sea retired a distance of three miles (an exceptionally low tide) and left a firm, dry passage. When the Chersonese citizens followed the passage, they found a chapel, apparently built by angels, and within was the body of Pope Clement with an anchor secured to it. The sea continued its retreat for seven days, then returned to normal strength. This phenomenon continued to occur at the same time each year, revealing the chapel, with the incorrupt body of the saint within.

Simeon Metaphrastes, who lived seven hundred years afterwards, also makes mention of this annual event. He assures us that the miracle is authentic. During the same period, Cyril and Methodius, apostles of the Slav counties, recovered the body of Pope Clement, together with the anchor. These relics were later entombed in the church of San Clement in Rome, where Pope Saint Clement is regarded Patron of lighthouses and lightships.

Saint Clement is celebrated on November 23rd. The accounts of his life are recorded in Church History, by Nicephorus Callistus.

Open Door

Tenskwatawa, the great Shawnee Indian prophet was born one of triplet brothers in early 1775. His father died before he was born and after being weaned from his mother, he never saw her again. He was named Lalawethika and was raised by other Shawnees, including Black Fish, a war chief. At an early age he brought great shame to his people through his indulgences in alcohol and promiscuous activities.

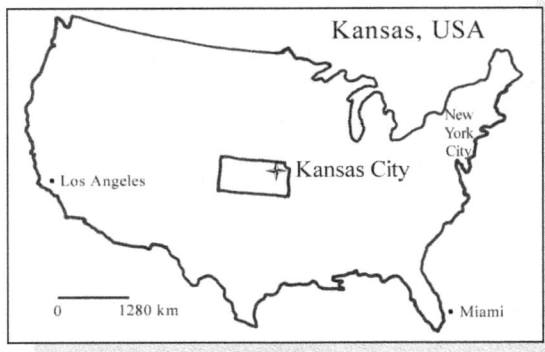

At the age of thirty he became deathly ill and was believed to be dead, but before his funeral ceremony was concluded, he revived and told his people that he had been carried to the spirit world by two young men who had been sent by the Master of Life. There he was shown the past and the future and was permitted to look at paradise, where the spirits of good Shawnees would go. He was also shown a world of fiery tortures that awaited the souls of evildoers. He vowed to amend his evil ways and give up drinking. He changed his name to Tenskwatawa (open door) to symbolize the open door he had entered to heaven.

In the months that followed numerous visions occurred whereby Tenskwatawa was instructed to develop a new teaching for his brother and sister Shawnee. He declared that his sole mission was to reclaim Indian people from bad habits and to have them live in peace with everyone. He denounced the consumption of alcohol, violent behavior, polygamous marriages and promiscuity. His teaching was essentially nativistic and encouraged a return to communal life. He utterly dominated the Indian movement attracting followers, first, to Greenville, Ohio and then to Prophetstown on the Wabash. However, the Battle of Tippecanoe, fought on November 7, 1811 was a devastating defeat for the prophet who assured his people it would be a victory for the Indian nation.

His movement ended with his exile to Canada and little more is recorded about his activities there. In 1832 he posed for artist George Catlin who painted him in his religious attire. He died in November, 1836, and was buried somewhere near what is now Kansas City, Kansas.

This account is given in The Encyclopedia of Native American Religions. Catlin's painting remains part of the Smithsonian Institution's National Museum of American Art.

Great Balls of Fire

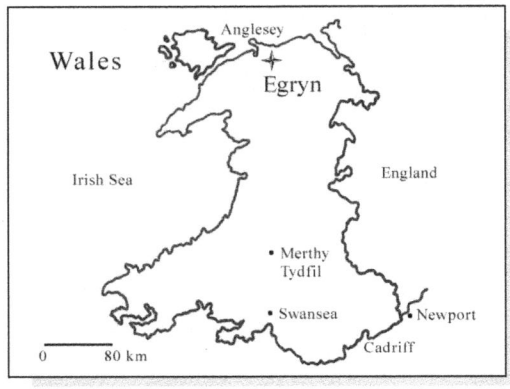

The most popular evangelist of the Great Welsh Revival was Mary Jones, a thirty-five year old housewife from Egryn in North Wales. Whenever she preached mysterious lights were seen in the sky, above or near her assembly. The lights, seen by thousands of witnesses, resembled bright stars or fireballs that "zigzagged" as they moved.

The following report was written by a journalist for the London Daily Mail who was sent to Egryn to cover the event.

". . . At 8:14 p.m. I was on the hillside, walking from Dyffryn to Egryn. In the distance, about one mile away, I could see the three lighted windows of the tiny Egryn chapel, where the service was going on. It was the only light in the miles of countryside. Suddenly at 8:20 p.m. I saw what appeared to be a ball or fire above the roof of the chapel. It came from nowhere and sprang into existence instantaneously. It had a steady, intense yellow brilliance and did not move.

Not sure whether or not I was deceiving myself, I called to a man a hundred (yards) down the road and asked him if he could see anything. He came running to me excitedly and said, 'Yes, yes, above the chapel, the great light.' He was a countryman and was trembling with emotion.

We watched the light together. It seemed to me to be at twice the height of the chapel, say fifty feet, and it stood out with electric vividness against the encircling hills behind. Suddenly it disappeared, having lasted about a minute and a half.

I leaned against the stone wall by the wayside and watched for further developments, the countryman leaving me and making his way alone. Again the chapel windows were the only light in the countryside. The minutes crept by and it was 8:35 p.m. before I saw anything else. Then two lights flashed out, one on each side of the chapel. They seemed about a hundred feet apart and considerably higher than the first one. In the night it was difficult to judge distance, but I made a rough guess that they were a hundred feet above the roof of the chapel. They shone out brilliantly and steadily for a space of thirty seconds. Then they both began to flicker like a defective arc-lamp. They were flickering like that while one could count to ten. . ."

Similar sightings were recorded throughout Wales during the years of the revival (1904-1905).

Thousands of Monks

Julian, like a zealous knight, was always ready to resist the unjust indignities thrust upon him by ignorant men of power and means. He was the leader of a religious community comprised of thousands of monks during the reign of Emperor Maximus II. 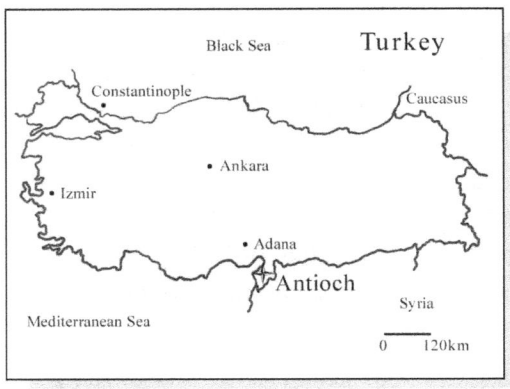 Maximus had no love for Christians and was determined to remove them from his empire. He dispatched Lieutenant Marcian to extirpate the entire Christian population of Antioch. Marcian's first act was to summon Julian before him, whereupon he commanded him to abandon his faith and offer incense to the idols of Rome.

Julian replied, "Neither I, nor any of my disciples will forsake the God whom we adore. Nor will we offer incense to sticks and stones, the work of men's hands." Blind with rage at Julian's reply, Marcian dispatched his soldiers with orders to set fire to all four corners of Julian's monastery. Not a single man survived.

Manager Guerin, Chamberlain to Pope Leo XIII, recorded that for years afterwards, celestial music proceeded from the ground at the sight of the holocaust. Many healings and miraculous cures were also reported by the citizens of Antioch. The dates of Julian's life are unknown.

Miraculous Medal

The following narrative on the great apparition of the Miraculous Medal is given in the words of its visionary, Saint Catherine Laoure.

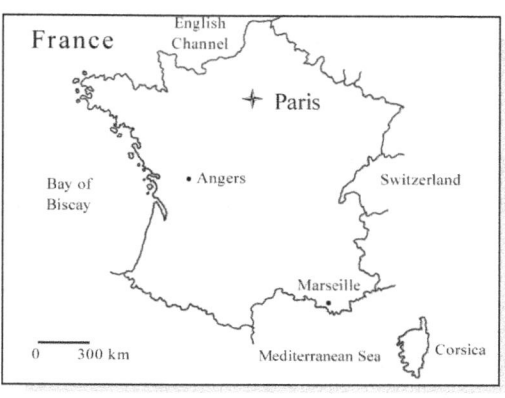

"On November 27, 1830 . . . at five thirty in the evening, in the deep silence after the point of the meditation had been read—that is, several minutes after the meditation—I heard a sound like the rustling of a silk dress from the tribune near the picture of Saint Joseph. Turning in that direction I saw the Blessed Virgin at the level of Saint Joseph's picture. The Virgin was standing. She was of medium height and clothed all in white. Her dress was of the whiteness of the dawn. . . . A white veil covered her head and fell on either side to her feet. Under the veil her hair, in coils, was bound with a fillet ornamented with lace. . . . Her face was sufficiently exposed, indeed exposed very well, and so beautiful that it seems to me impossible to express her ravishing beauty.

Her feet rested on a white globe. . . . There was also a serpent green in color with yellow spots.

Her hands were raised to the height of her stomach and held. . . a golden globe surmounted by a little golden cross. . . Her face was of such beauty that I could not describe it.

All at once I saw rings on her fingers, three rings to each finger . . . . Each ring was set with gems, some more beautiful than others; the larger gems emitted greater rays and the smaller gems, smaller rays; the rays bursting from all sides flooded the base, so that I could no longer see the feet of the Blessed Virgin.

At this moment. . . I heard a voice speaking these words: 'The ball that you see represents the whole world. . . . and each person in particular. . . .(The rays from the rings) are the symbols of graces I shed on those who ask for them. The gems from which rays do not fall are the graces for which souls forget to ask.'

At this moment, I was so overjoyed that I no longer knew where I was. . . Then the voice said: 'Have a medal struck after this model. All who wear it will receive great graces; they should wear it around the neck. Graces will abound for those who wear it with confidence.'"

So it was that the medal was struck. And as promised, miraculous favors occurred by the millions. The catalog of miracles ascribed to these medals seems literally endless. The number of Medals minted since 1832 is beyond counting; it is easily in the hundreds of millions. The Medals are worn by Catholics, Protestants, Jews and members of all faiths. Clearly its miraculous favors rise victoriously above religious distinctions.

Saint Catherine Laoure died peacefully on December 31, 1876. She was canonized by Pope Pius XII in 1947. Her incorrupt body lies beneath an altar built on the spot where Our Lady of the Miraculous Medal first appeared at the motherhouse chapel of Our Lady of the Sun on Rue du Bac, in Paris, France.

Recluse of Siope

Auxintius was the resident recluse of Siope, a community near Chalcedon. Rumors and tales of this hermit had long been running wild, and many in the neighborhood claimed he lived entirely without food. To resolve the matter, a small party from the community decided to put the recluse to the test. They collected baskets of vegetables, dates and other foods and placed them in his hermitage as a gift. They also lit a candle to ensure that they could watch him both day and night. A child was chosen to be the spy and was concealed at a spot where it was easy to see the hermit's activities.

Several days later they returned to discover the results of their experiment. They found that the food in the baskets they had brought was untouched and remained as fresh as if it had just been picked. Moreover, the candle which they had lit several days earlier had not consumed a single drop of wax. They asked their young spy what he had seen and the child informed them that he had watched the hermit eating daily. Every day a heavenly bird appeared in the sky, carrying with it a portion of food which the recluse received with great praise. Thus, the issue was resolved.

Saint Auxintius lived until A.D. 410. The original manuscripts of his life are found in the Bibliotheque de la rue Richelieu, in Paris.

Somewhere To Gather

On November 29, 1932, the Virgin Mary made her first of thirty-three historic appearances in Beauraing, a village of two thousand people in the French-speaking corner of Belgium. She appeared to five children, all but one entering their teens.

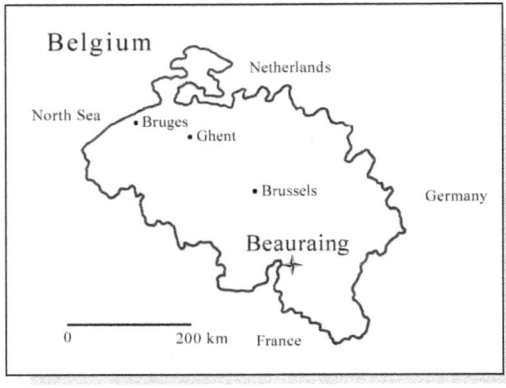

The Virgin looked young, about eighteen years old. Her smile was magnetic. Her eyes were radiant blue and beams of light spread from her head. She wore a long white heavily pleated gown that gave off a luminous blue light. During the apparition the children would speak to the Virgin, at which time their voices would involuntarily assume a high pitch, far different from their natural voices.

As expected, the children's reports were not believed. Friends teased them, officials threatened them and their parents dragged them to their family physicians. But on December 8, 1932, when the apparition was predicted to occur again, the children's parents, doctors and fifteen thousand curiosity seekers came to discern fact from fiction.

When the Virgin appeared, the children were transfixed. Their eyes were locked on the vision that they alone could see.

Doctors, meanwhile, busied themselves checking pulses, picking and pricking and shining flashlights into the children's eyes. All were oblivious of any distractions. One doctor held a flame under one of the children's hands, while another slapped and pinched all five of them. There was no reaction and no trace of burning whatsoever.

When the vision concluded, one of the children explained, "I could see nothing, neither fence, nor tree, nor crowd; only the Holy Virgin who smiled at us."

Another said laughingly, "Just think, Daddy, they tried to make me believe they had pricked and burned me."

The appearances continued daily until January 3, 1933, after which they stopped. The message conveyed through the children was simple and clear. The Virgin wanted people to gather at this spot and pray. How they chose to pray was their own decision, but she wanted them to gather at this spot in Beauraing.

The previous account is one of many hundreds of documented appearances of the Virgin Mary in this century. Because the frequency of such appearances seems to be increasing, it has become popular to refer to the twentieth century as The Marion Age.

No Peace In the Hermit's House

How hard it was for Hilarion to find peace. No matter where he hid or how hard he tried to disguise himself, he was always discovered and sought after to perform miracles. One day while he was still young and determined to live a hermit's life, a woman came to him.

He motioned to her making signs for her to go away (customarily hermits do not entertain ladies), but she addressed him with tears, "Blessed sage, pardon my boldness, but my sorrow is very great. Take pity on my grief. Remember that a woman was thy mother, and a woman is the mother of all blessed saints."

Hilarion could not withstand these words, and asked his petitioner what she wanted and why she wept.

"Fifteen years have I been married," she replied, "dearly wishing to be a mother, yet still I have no child."

Hilarion, moved to pity, blessed the woman and granted that her desire would be fulfilled, then again he motioned for her to go away.

After a year had passed, the woman returned with an infant son in her arms and said, "Behold the child of thy blessings!" Hilarion blessed the child and bid the mother tell no one what had happened. It was too late, however, for shortly following this incident, he became the most sought-after saint of his time. (See October 21)

Hilarion was born in Gaza in A.D. 291. Although he intended to be a hermit, he eventually took on disciples of both sexes. When his life became too hectic, he fled Palestine, first for remote caves in Egypt, then Sicily (where his disciple Hesychius found him), then Dalmatia, Cyprus and finally Paphos, where he died in A.D. 371.

The accounts of his life are recorded in Ecclesiastical History, by Nicephorus Callistus.

December

1 Many Pass Unnoticed
2 Saintly Pioneer
3 Momentarily Speechless
4 The Hand of Justice
5 A Difficult Roommate
6 Santa Claus
7 Delicious Levitations
8 Mystical Rose
9 Singing Eagle
10 Our Lady of Loreto
11 Reunited
12 Love of Country
13 Why Ask Me?
14 The Tailor's Son
15 The Service of a Slave
16 Liquefying Mystery
17 Something in the Sky
18 Freedom Fighter
19 Mule Power
20 The Weatherman
21 A Letter From Jesus
22 God Bless America
23 Unusual Baptism
24 A Family Tree
25 Christmas Day
26 Legend of Thyrsus
27 Son of Thunder
28 Thirsty Workmen
29 Our Lady of the Americas
30 Rare Distinction
31 Net Worth

Many Pass Unnoticed

Who had ever noticed Antony Bonfadini? Born into the good Bonfadini family of Ferrara in the year 1400, he went almost entirely unnoticed in his community until at age thirty-nine, he joined a monastery in his native town, where he distinguished himself as an excellent teacher. Nothing further was ever reported about Antony other than his death, of old age, in 1482.

He died and was buried at the village of Cotignola in the Romagna region of northern Italy. Years later, hundreds of incidents of unexplained cures and miraculous favors were reported at the burial site of this holy friar. Further, his body was disinterred and found to be miraculously incorrupt. In the course of years, miracles continued at Antony's tomb site and permission was given to transfer his body to a church in Cotignola where it is honored to the present day.

Antony Bonfadini is one among the saints who must have passed through this world unnoticed and unrecognized. Little doubt there are countless more who have never been known to us.

Beatified Antony Bonfadini lived from 1400-1482. His cultus was approved in 1901.

Saintly Pioneer

After one hundred and six years of processing and investigation, Marguerite D'Youville was officially declared by Pope John Paul to be the first Canadian-born Catholic saint.

Marguerite was born in Varennes, a small village not far from Montreal and her life has stirred much controversy. It seems she inherited slaves from her fur-trader husband who was also a notorious gambler and bootlegger. It is believed that she may have in some way participated in his dealings. However, her husband died when Marguerite was only thirty-two years old, after which she accepted religious vows and devoted herself to helping the sick and homeless.

In 1737 she founded the Sisters of Charity, commonly known as the Grey Nuns, and saved what is now the Montreal General Hospital from ruin. She treated both French and English soldiers despite the fact that the English were protestants and enemies to both her church and France.

The Vatican began collecting evidence toward her canonization in 1884 and has credited her with several miracles and healing powers. Miracles associated with her intercession occurred as recently as 1978. Over twenty-two hundred people went to Rome for the official ceremonies in December 1990, and ceremonies in her honor were also held throughout Canada.

Momentarily Speechless

An unusual event was recorded during the voyage of Francis Xavier from Ambon, capital city of the Maluku islands to Baranula, Indonesia. His ship was overtaken by a violent storm which threatened the 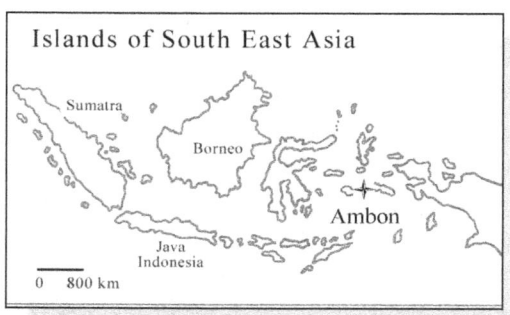 lives of every passenger. The vessel had taken on considerable water and wreckage seemed imminent. In an attempt to save the ship, Xavier removed the crucifix from his neck and held it in the sea. But at the same moment, the boat lurched and the crucifix flew from his hand and was lost in the water. The sea settled slightly, bringing partial relief to the captain and crew, but it was morning before the waters had settled completely.

The next day their ship arrived safely in Baranula and the moment Xavier stepped ashore, an enormous crab leaped out of the sea carrying his crucifix, "devoutly, and in an upright direction between its fins." The crab found its way straight to Xavier, delivered the crucifix to him, and returned to the sea. Xavier was speechless. He fell prostrate on the ground for thirty minutes where he remained in tears until his shipmates helped him back to his feet.

Saint Francis Xavier lived from 1506-1552. He was born at the castle of Xavier in Navarre, Spain. After his death, his body was returned to Goa, India, where he had spent a large part of his life. His shrine, in Goa, has long been the object of popular pilgrimage, as Francis' body remains miraculously incorrupt to the present day. This anecdote is documented in Cardinal de Monte's speech before Gregory XV, at the canonization of Francis Xavier, 1622.

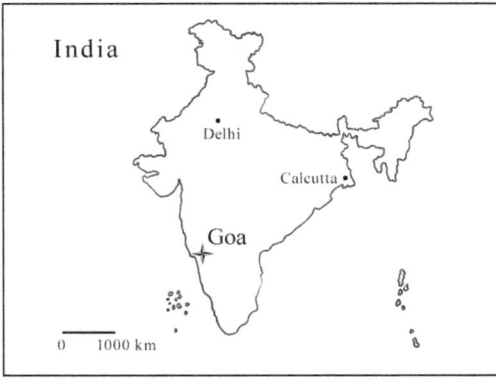

The Hand of Justice

John Damacene was a doer and achiever. He was a monk and prolific writer of Christian theology, but inside he was a warrior. The quiet, peaceful existence of the monastery was insufferable to him. His battles, therefore, were fought with pen in hand. His writings earned extreme displeasure of both the ruling Christian emperors and ruling Muslims under whose territory he resided. It followed that for political reasons, his right hand was cut off and fastened to a pole in a public market. The deed being done, John returned to his private chapel and prayed to the Virgin Mary thus:

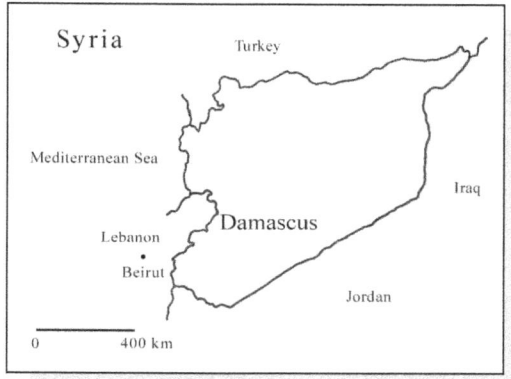

"O pure and holy Virgin, mother of God, thou knowest why the caliph has cut off my right hand and thou canst, if it pleases thee, restore it to me again. I pray thee grant me this grace, that I may employ it as before, in celebrating the praises of thy Son and thee."

During his sleep the Virgin appeared to him and said, "Thy prayer is heard and thy hand restored. Continue composing and writing my praise, according to thy word." When he awoke, he found his hand had been restored. The only indication that it had ever been lost was a thin red line around his wrist.

When the news reached the Sultan who had authorized the punishment, he realized that John had been unjustly victimized. Accordingly he restored him to his former honors and office and John continued his writing as before.

Saint John Damascene was born in Damascus, Syria in A.D. 657, where he remained until his death in 749. The most popular and influential of his writings is The Fount of Wisdom. In 1890 he was declared a Doctor of the Church, his celebration being ascribed to December 4th. This record is taken from the Acta Sanctorum, Bollandist, Volume II.

A Difficult Roommate

Sabas lived in a cave on the face of a cliff, at the bottom of which ran the brook Cedron, in the deserts of Israel. Among the stories told of this saint is how he came to establish a monastery there. He was searching for a peaceful home in which to live a solitary life when he lay down to sleep in a cave that happened to be the den of a lion. When the lion returned home he clawed hold of Sabas' clothes, while he was still asleep, and dragged him outside the cave. Unperturbed, Sabas returned to the cave and tamed the lion to a considerable degree of friendliness. However, the beast proved to be a rather difficult roommate, so Sabas told him if he could not live with him in peace, he had better go away. So the lion left.

On another occasion, a terrible drought devastated the area from Jericho to Jerusalem. Many people fled to other regions, but those who remained on their lands were unable to find enough water to quench their thirst. They implored Sabas to help them, and moved with compassion, he agreed. The moment he knelt to pray, rain began to fall, and in such an abundance that the cisterns were filled to overflowing.

A miraculous spring still flows in this spot and Saint Sabas' palm tree still bears stoneless dates.

Saint Sabas lived from A.D. 439-532. He is celebrated on December 5th. His chief monastery, called Mar Saba or the Great Laura, still exists in a gorge of the Cedron, ten miles southeast of Jerusalem towards the Dead Sea. After a period of ruin, it was restored by the Russian government and is now inhabited by monks whose lives are worthy of the example of its founder. Mar Saba is one of the oldest inhabited monasteries in the world, and one of the most remarkable.

The preceding stories are given in The Life of Saint Sabas, *by Cyril.*

Santa Claus

Santa Claus, or Saint Nicholas of Myra, was neither a fantasy for children at Christmas nor a Nordic magician. He was a natural born miracle worker who grew up at Patara, Lycia, a province of Asia Minor. "He was exceedingly well brought up by his parents and trod piously in their footsteps." At age five he began to study the sacred sciences, and "day by day, its teaching enlightened his mind and encouraged his thirst for truth." The life of this saint, Santa Claus, is filled with miracles both during and after his death, and curiously enough, his greatest popularity is found far from his homeland, in Canada, the United States and Russia.

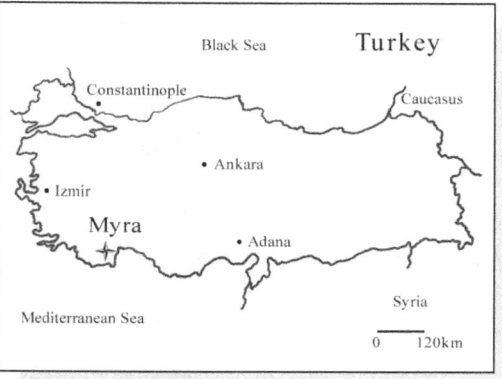

The following miracle is mentioned by almost all the biographers who have written on Saint Nicholas.

The young son of Cerrone and Euphrosina, two devout followers of Saint Nicholas, was kidnapped by the Agarenes and carried to Babylon. One day, on the feast of Saint Nicholas, the child was unusually sad. The king asked why his eyes were filled with tears and the child replied that Saint Nicholas could make wishes come true. The king said jeeringly, "If Nicholas is so mighty, bid him carry thee away and deliver thee." The child had the king's cup in his hand at the time and before he could set it down, he was carried off by the hair on his head from the king's palace, in Babylon, to the church of Saint Nicholas in Lycia. Here, his mother and father had come to celebrate the saint and mourn their lost son. When he appeared to them, borne though the air and set down at their feet, their joy was elevated far above common joy.

Saint Nicholas lived during the fourth century and died at Myra, where he was buried in his cathedral. There was a great competition for his relics as they were said to possess the miracle of fulfilling wishes. Eventually they were acquired by the faithful of Bari, Italy, where they remain. The celebration of Saint Nicholas was ascribed to December 6th. He is regarded as the Patron of children and seafarers.

Delicious Levitations

Saint Teresa of Avila is one of the few mystics who recorded her inner subjective experience of levitation. She explains how it felt to be lifted into the air:

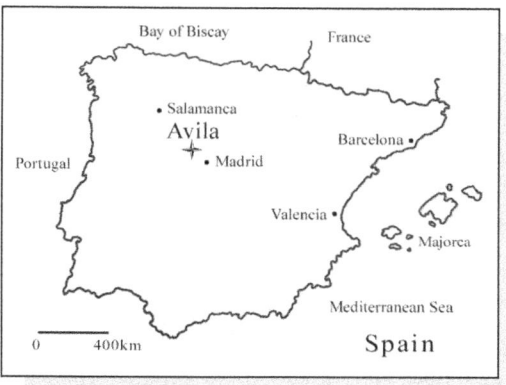

"I repeat it: you feel and see yourself carried away you know not whither. For though we feel how delicious it is, the weakness of our nature makes us afraid at first. . . so trying is it that I would very often resist and exert all my strength, particularly at those times when the rapture was coming on me in public. I did so, too, very often when I was alone, because I was afraid of delusions. Occasionally I was able, by great efforts, to make a slight resistance, but afterwards I was worn out, like a person who had been contending with a strong giant; at other times it was impossible to resist at all; my soul was carried away, and almost always my head with it—I had no power over it and now and then the whole body as well, so that it was lifted up from the ground. . . . I confess that it threw me into great fear, very great indeed at first; for in seeing one's body thus lifted up from the earth, though the spirit draws it upwards after itself (and that with great sweetness, if unresisted), the senses are not lost; at least I was so much myself as to be able to see that I was being lifted up. . . . After the rapture was over, I have to say that my body seemed frequently to be buoyant, as if all weight had departed from it, so much so that now and then I scarcely knew that my feet touched the ground."

Saint Teresa was born in Avila, Spain in 1515 and died in 1582. During one of her ecstasies she wrote:

"I saw an angel close by me, on my left side, in bodily form. He was not large but small of stature and most beautiful—his face burning as if he were one of the highest angels who seemed to be all of fire. I saw in his hand a long spear of gold, and at the iron's point there seemed to be a little fire. He appeared to me to be thrusting it at times into my heart and to pierce my very entrails; when he drew it out, he seemed to draw them out also, and to leave me all on fire with a great love of God. . ."

Saint Teresa's body remains miraculously incorrupt to the present day and may be seen at Alb de Tormes in Spain. Her heart was meticulously examined by researchers from the University of Salamanca and noted to have small perforations, similar to dart holes. They confirmed that the preservation of her body could not be credited to any natural or chemical means (See October 15).

Mystical Rose

Montichiari, a small village not far from the city of Brescia in northern Italy, is famous for the miracles associated with *The Spring of Grace*.

In 1947, Montichiari was home to less than fourteen thousand people, one of whom was a local hospital nurse, Pierina Gilli. During the spring of that year, while Pierina was praying in the chapel hospital, she was suddenly subsumed in a vision of the Madonna, who was dressed in a mauve colored gown and bathed in celestial light. The Madonna appeared hopelessly sad, with tears in her eyes, her heart being pierced three times with swords. This was the first of a series of seven great apparitions which appeared to Pierina during that year.

In the second apparition the Madonna appeared with three roses —red, yellow and white—replacing the swords of the earlier vision. She asked that a new religious order be formed and honored under the title, *Rosa Mystica* (Mystical Rose).

The Madonna or Mystical Rose appeared to Pierina on five other occasions during that year, the final time being on December 8th. She appeared standing on a white staircase decorated with roses and declared, "I am the Immaculate Conception. It is my wish that every year on December 8th, at noon, the hour of grace for the world be celebrated. Many divine and bodily graces will be received through this devotion." A secret was entrusted to Pierina and the apparitions discontinued.

Pierina retired to a small convent where she lived as inconspicuously as she could, working in the kitchen and waiting in silence for nineteen years. Finally, in the spring of 1966, a new series of apparitions occurred. This time the Madonna spoke of her Divine Son giving miraculous powers to a local spring which she named *The Spring of Grace* and asked that people do acts of charity for the sick who would come there to be healed. Following the conclusion of this new series of apparitions, Pierina was not heard from again. She retired to a convent, where she died peacefully twenty-five years later, on January 12, 1991. She is lovingly spoken of as one of the great mystics of our age.

Singing Eagle

It happened atop a one hundred thirty foot hillock in the wastelands north of Mexico City at dawn on Saturday, December 9, 1531. While on his way to join the Franciscan missionaries in mass, a poor fifty-seven year old Aztec Indian named Nahuatl (Singing Eagle) was halted in his tracks by what he thought was the burst of song birds. Although it was unheard of at that time of year, the songs were thrillingly clear. Standing atop the hill Tepeyac where a temple to the Mother-goddess of the Aztecs had formerly stood, he was utterly ravished by what appeared to be choirs of song birds intertwining melodies into one common harmony.

Suddenly the choir stopped, and there was an unnerving dead silence. Then he heard the voice of a lady calling to him from the ruinous rocks of the ancient temple. She called him by the name given to him by the Franciscans, "Juan! Juan Diego!"

Her voice sounded urgent, so he hurried to the top of the hill. When he reached the ruins, there she stood. It seemed to Juan that his sight had been magnified a thousandfold, for never before had he seen anything so clearly. It was a young Mexican girl, about fourteen years old, and wonderfully beautiful. Golden beams surrounded her person from head to foot, and everything around her gleamed like emeralds and gold. She spoke to him in his mother tongue and said, "Juan, smallest and dearest of my little children, where are you going?"

"I was hurrying to hear the mass," replied Juan.

"Dear little son," she said, "I love you. I want you to know who I am. I am the Ever-Virgin Mary, Mother of the true God who gives life and maintains it in existence. He created all things; He is in all places. He is lord of heaven and earth. I desire a temple at this place where I will show my compassion to your people who sincerely ask my help. Here I will see their tears; I will console them and they will be at ease. So run now to Tenochtitlan (Mexico City) and tell the bishop all you have seen and heard."

Then suddenly the Virgin vanished and Juan hurried to deliver the message as he was instructed. The bishop, however, found it somewhat difficult to accept that the Virgin Mary had appeared to a wholly uneducated Aztec, and further, that she desired a temple built at the sight of an uninhabited pagan ruin. Juan's heart sunk. He felt he had failed in his mission for the Heavenly Mother.

Returning to the hill, he hoped that she would be there, and she was. He explained all that had happened and added, "I am not worthy of your trusting me with a message so important. Please send someone else more suitable; for I am nobody. . . . Forgive my boldness in advising you."

The Virgin replied, "Listen, little son. There are many I could send. But you are the one I have chosen. Tomorrow morning go back to the bishop. Tell him it is the Virgin Mary who sends you, and repeat my great desire for a church in this place."

The following morning the bishop was surprised to see Juan again so soon. This time he was half convinced that Juan was sincere, but wondered if he was not suffering from deception or delusion. Accordingly he suggested that Juan ask the heavenly lady for a sign that would prove she was truly the Ever-Virgin Mary. So again Juan returned to the hill and told his tale to the Virgin. She was pleased to hear the news and responded, "Very well, my son. Tomorrow at daybreak, I will give you a sign. Go in peace and rest."

The next morning, Juan did not keep his appointment with the Virgin. For his uncle had fallen deathly ill, and there was no one to attend to his needs but himself. Before sunrise, the next morning, it was clear his uncle would not survive the day. He begged Juan to retrieve a priest to deliver the Last Sacraments. Juan hurried to do so, but on his way he carefully avoided the Virgin's hill lest she should delay him in his service to his uncle. But it didn't work. The moment he neared the hill he saw her descending in an angle that would intercept him just beyond the next curve. He was caught and very embarrassed. The Virgin spoke, "Least of my sons, what is the matter?"

"Forgive me!" said Juan. "My uncle is dying of cocolistle and desires me to fetch a priest. It was no heedless promise I made to meet you yesterday morning. But my uncle fell ill."

"My little son," she said, "Do not be afraid. Am I not your Mother? Are you not under my shadow and protection? Your uncle will not die. This very moment his health is restored. Ease your mind and go to the top of the hill. Cut the flowers that are growing there and bring them to me."

No flowers could be in bloom on that frozen hill, he thought, but he didn't hesitate to march to the top. Castilian roses—exotic, impossible—were covering the hilltop! He cut them quickly and wrapped them in his tilma (an Aztec cape worn in the front). Returning to the Virgin, he bowed low before her and held out the slightly opened wrap for her to see. She was not satisfied with the random arrangement and with her own hands rearranged them carefully. She then tied the lower corners of the tilma behind his neck so nothing could spill out. This being done, she said to Juan, "Little son, this is the sign I am sending to the bishop. Let no one see what you are carrying until you are in his presence. This time he will believe you."

Many were present in the bishop's office when Juan explained, for the third time, what had happened on the hill. When his story had concluded, he untied his tilma and watched as the roses tumbled onto the floor at his feet. He was proud to have, at last, delivered the sign for the Virgin. But to his amazement, within seconds, the bishop and his secretaries rose from their chairs and knelt in reverent submission at his feet. In the moment that followed, he too discovered that the Virgin had trusted him with an even more wonderful sign. Imprinted on his tilma was a perfect likeness of the Virgin Mother, just as Juan had seen her.

To the present day, this tilma, sanctioned *Our Lady of Guadeloupe*, remains on display in the most beautiful basilica in the western hemisphere, erected on the hilltop where the visions occurred. It has been scrutinized by every known method of modern science, yet the manner of paint or coloring, the techniques employed, and that it has utterly resisted all fading or fabric disintegration, elude any explanation.

The image stands fifty-six inches tall, but seems larger as one draws back from it. Surrounded by golden rays, it is clear in every detail, and brilliant in every color. Her star-studded outer mantle resembles that of an Aztec queen, just as Juan had envisioned her on the hilltop. Those who gaze on the tilma today see it exactly as it was first seen when the roses spilled from Juan's mantle over four hundred and fifty years ago.

Our Lady of Loreto

The Santa Casa is the reputed house of Mary and Joseph in Nazareth, where Jesus was raised. Surprising as it may seem, this house was seen floating through the air, carried by angels and relocated in Fiume, Dalmatia on May 10, 1291. The floating house was again seen by many witnesses on December 10, 1294, relocating itself to Recanati, Italy.

Even though there was no possible explanation for its sudden appearance, together with the undoubtedly authentic relics contained within, investigations confirmed what appeared to be unbelievable. In addition, a commission sent to Nazareth to investigate the matter, reported that the foundation was certainly there, but that the household had been removed. Also, the character of the stones and mortar matched precisely in material and dimension.

The history of this event is captured in a letter written by Paul della Selva, to King Charles II, of Naples:

"On Saturday, December 10, 1294, at midnight, a great light from heaven was observed on the banks of the Adriatic, and a celestial harmony was heard by many. Hundreds were roused from sleep and got up to gaze on the mysterious light and listen to the music. Suddenly there appeared a house in the air, blazing in light, and supported by the hands of angels. The angels set the house down in the midst of a wood, and the trees bent as if in reverence to it. Even to this day the trees are still bent. The spot was once occupied by a pre-Christian temple which was surrounded by a laurel grove, whence the name of the place, Loreto. At daybreak the rumor had spread in all directions, and all the inhabitants of Recanati went to see the mysterious house. Hundreds entered it and fell prostrate before the cedar image of Mary and Jesus. The crowd increased daily. In eight months the house left the forest and was set by angels on a hill, the property of Count Stephen and Count Simeon Raineldi. Offerings poured in, and a scandal arose that the offerings were misappropriated. In four months time, the house again shifted from the hill to a heap of stones near the highroad leading to Recanati, near the sea coast, and there it is still. The house has no foundation, and is exposed to the most violent winds and rain."

After 150 years, the miraculous house remained fully intact. Pope Paul II, in an official declaration dated October 15, 1464, says, "There can be no doubt of the miracles which proceed from the Santa Casa, for we ourselves have proved it in our own person."

This wonderful house is celebrated on December 10th, under the title Our Lady of Loreto.

Reunited

Francis Di Girolamo loved a challenge. He was a noted genius from childhood and despite the efforts of his family to deter him from the priesthood, his natural sanctity made it the obvious vocation. However, Francis was not satisfied with ordinary sins from ordinary sinners. He wanted to hunt down and destroy the very strongholds of sin. With an untiring and boundless zeal he melted stone hearts and reclaimed lost souls in prisons, hospitals and galleys throughout Naples. He set up over a hundred missions throughout the country and was very popular both for his strength of character and reputation for working miracles. Amid his numerous penitents was a remarkable French woman, Mary Alvira Cassier, who had murdered her father and afterward served in the Spanish army, disguised as a man. Under Francis' mastership, she witnessed many miracles and afterwards attained a high degree of holiness herself. The following account was recorded through her person.

It once happened that a poor woman lost her twelve-month-old infant. Not having money for a burial, she left it at the confessional of Father Francis. Francis later arrived in the church and knew by divine revelation what had happened. Accordingly he instructed Mary to go to his confessional and retrieve the infant who was lying there. Mary obeyed, but on lifting the covering, she exclaimed, "My father, the child is dead!"

"No, no, Mary," Francis replied. "Behold it sleepeth."

So saying he made the sign of the cross on the child's forehead and rubbed its lips with holy water. Accordingly the child began to breathe and opened its eyes.

"Go and call the mother," said Francis to Mary.

At first the mother refused to come, believing their tale was a trick. Even when she saw her living child in the same wraps, she would not believe it was her own. Soon, however, her maternal instincts and the unmistakable signs of recognition from the child reunited them in tears of joy.

Francis Di Girolamo was born in 1642 at Grottaglie, near Taranto, the eldest son in a family of eleven. He was a recognized saint in his own day, often being called The Holy Priest or The Apostle of Naples. He died at age seventy-four and was interred in the Jesuit church of Naples where he remains to the present day. He was canonized in 1839 (See May 11).

Love of Country

Finnian of Clonard was one of the most outstanding figures among the holy men of Ireland following the period of Saint Patrick. He was an inspiration of patriotic love and is credited with many miracles in defense of his country. He is celebrated for miraculously clearing the parasitic insects, worms and vermin from the island of Flathlom and the regions of Nantcarfan. And he is credited with saving Ireland from Saxon marauders by causing the raiders' camp to be swallowed by an earthquake.

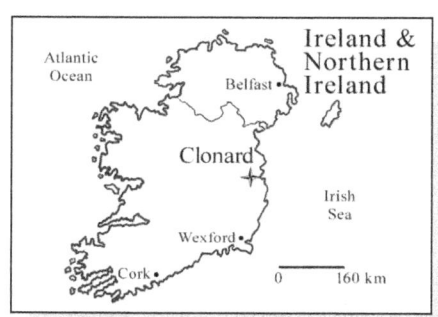

To his three thousand disciples, he was known as the *Teacher of The Saints of Ireland*. "Like the sun in the high heavens he sent forth rays of goodness and holy teaching to give light to the world." Finnian has been credited with developing a school whose graduates became saints. As a final act of love, he offered his life for his country during an epidemic of the yellow plague in the sixth century.

"As Paul died in Rome for the sake of the Christian people, lest they should all perish in Hell, so Finnian died at Clonard for the sake of the people of Gael, that they might not all perish of the Yellow pest."

Saint Finnian of Clonard lived until A.D. 549. He is celebrated throughout Ireland on December 12th. His relics were enshrined at Clonard but later met with destruction in the ninth century.

Why Ask Me?

Even as a child Lucy's will was astonishing, not so much for its intensity but for its quality. Eutitia, her mother, was aware that her child was exceptional, but she would never have guessed that her daughter was a saint.

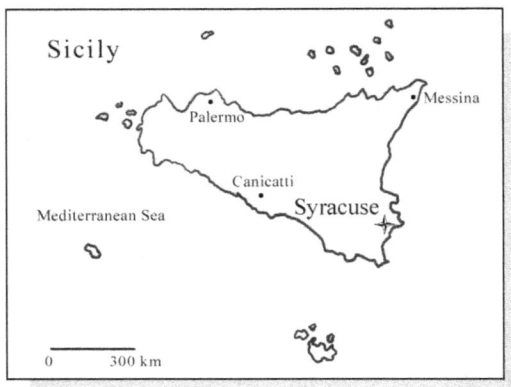

Lucy's mother suffered greatly with an incurable ailment which caused a considerable agony for the sensitive Sicily heart of her young daughter. She was induced by her daughter to join her in a visit to the shrine of Saint Agatha, in Cantania. When they reached the tomb, Lucy prayed that the saint would heal her mother. As the couple sat in silent prayer a vision of Agatha appeared before them with a host of celestial angels.

"Sister Lucy," she said, "why ask of me what you can give yourself? If the Creator of all things loves me, then surely you are loved no less. If He will harken to my prayers, so will He to yours. If I am honored as a saint here in Cantania, you shall be honored as a saint in Syracuse."

On hearing these words, Lucy rose from her knee and turning to her mother found she was perfectly restored to health.

Lucy was born in Syracuse, Sicily and lived until A.D. 304. Her celebration, on December 13th, is particularly popular in Sicily and Sweden where it has become a festival of light. The youngest daughter of the family dresses in white and wakes the remaining members with coffee, rolls and a special song.

In Venice, at a church near the railway station, a partially incorrupt body survives and is claimed to be hers. This account is recorded in Martyrology by Ado, Archbishop of Vienna.

The Tailor's Son

Vincent Factor was a Sicilian tailor who migrated to Valencia, Spain where he married a young woman named Ursula. In 1520 they bore their first son, Peter Nicholas, to whom miracles were common. His father wanted him to go into business, but Nicholas was a holy man at heart, and he longed for the company of others like himself. He made rapid progress in finding suitable friends when he joined the Friars Minor, a religious observance in his native town renowned for its sanctity.

This simple lifestyle elevated his spirit, and his raptures, visions and miracles were so frequent that St. Louis Bertrand described him as living more in heaven than on earth. He possessed a supernatural knowledge of the future and commonly announced forthcoming events as if they were recorded history. He was known and revered by all the royalty of Spain, from King Philip II downward. His personal circle of friends included St. Paschal Baylon, St. Louis Bertrand and John de Ribera, all of whom confirmed his superhuman abilities. We are told that he once received a message from the Virgin Mary through the mouth of her statue. During his ecstasies divine love so warmed his body, it required that he plunge himself into cold water which became heated almost to the boiling point.

It was under these circumstances that Nicholas lived a particularly joyful life. He was not a big talker, nor was he interested in impressing people with his talents. His single intention was to be one with his God and to this resolve he reserved all his energy and will.

Nicholas Factor died on December 23, 1583, at Valencia, Spain. He was beatified in 1786, his celebration being ascribed to December 14th. The accounts of his life may be found in all the Franciscan chroniclers.

The Service of a Slave

Nino was a captive slave who during her life converted the King and Queen of Iberia to her faith. Inspired by the miracles of Nino, the king commanded that a church be constructed in her honor, at Geogia. Three columns were to be placed in the facade.

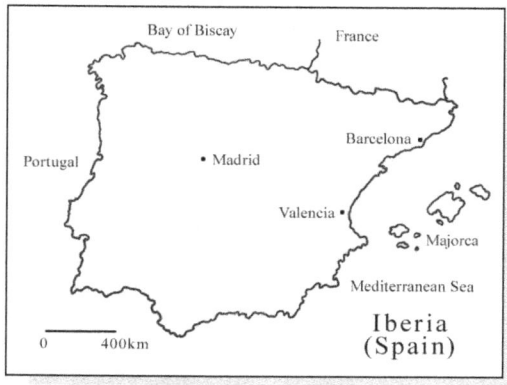

Two were erected, but the third, being larger, was so heavy neither man nor ox could move it. We are told that Nino approached the pillar and knelt beside it in meditative prayer. Shortly after, "the column rose into the air and, assuming a vertical position, was transported, entirely unsupported, to within a foot of the place where it was to be fixed." There it remained suspended for the entire evening. The following morning, one of the builders touched the pillar, as if to guide it, and it descended slowly, placing itself erect, in the required spot. We are told that there were ample witnesses and that all were overtaken with wonder. In time the Iberians came to understand what a treasure they possessed in Nino and were wholeheartedly confirmed in her teaching and guidance.

Much uncertainty surrounds the origin of Nino and how she came to be the captive of the Iberians, but we are told that even in captivity her days and nights were spent in long hours of meditation. Following a period in her life when she brought forth numerous wonders and miracles, she

retired to a cave on a mountain at Bodbe, Kakheti. There she died and her tomb is still in the cathedral that was built on that spot. Nino lived until A.D. 340. She is celebrated on December 15th. The accounts of her life were recorded in History, Book I, by Rufinus.

Liquefying Mystery

The miracle of the blood of Saint Januarius has eluded scientists for over two hundred years. Despite numerous investigations into the matter, no satisfactory explanation has been given as to why, several times a year, two vials of dried blood (that of the the martyr Januarius) continue to liquefy during ceremonies held in his honor. This ritual liquefication of blood has been carefully documented since 1659. Today the blood is preserved in a chapel within Naples Cathedral and kept under constant guard. The blood relics are exhibited publicly on December 16th, a date that commemorates a miracle that occurred at the time of the eruption of Mt. Vesuvius in 1631.

The blood, however, does not always liquefy according to the rule. For instance, it did not liquefy in May 1976, just prior to the worst earthquake in Italian history. Additional failures to liquefy that have also been chronicled coincide with various national disasters.

The liquefication of blood is but one of many miracles connected with this relic. Vast collections of supernatural instances are documented in thousands of books, articles and studies written in Italian.

Saint Januarius was a fourth-century martyr believed to be the Bishop of Benevento. He and several companions were thrown to the lions during a public execution at the city's amphitheater. The lions did not attack, so the entire company was beheaded on September 19th.

Something in the Sky

On December 17, 1826, after sunset, approximately three thousand people gathered for a jubilee ceremony at Migne, in the jurisdiction of Poitiers, France. All three thousand witnessed a magnificent luminous object shining "brighter than the sun" and "clearly not of this world" in the open sky above them. Records of this event indicate that the heavenly object resembled a cross, but by its description it hardly seems likely. The length of the celestial "cross" measured forty feet and its cross-member measured about four feet. The crowd was seized with excitement, and a general feeling of brotherhood and unity prevailed even long after the spectacle had vanished. Some wept, some raised exclamations of wonder, some lifted their hands to heaven, some studied and measured and scrutinized and others simply took note. The reason for this phenomenon has never been ascertained, as no one among the witnesses has ever offered a single reasonable insight.

Mgr. de Bouille published an account of this apparition and later received two brief from Pope Leo XII.

Freedom Fighter

No one ever forced their opinion on Sebastian of Narbonne. He judged what was right or wrong and let no one intimidate him. He was commander of the first Roman Cohort under Carinus, a position of considerable authority, and was utterly appalled by the abominable cruelties the emperor perpetrated against the Christians.

On one occasion he entered the court of Nicostratus, a Roman magistrate who had sentenced to death sixteen men for daring to express freedom of faith. Sebastian intervened on their behalf and delivered an exhortation with such power and passion as to utterly transform his audience. So much that Zoe, the wife of the magistrate, knelt before the soldier and looked steadfast into his face, but without uttering a word, for her tongue had been paralyzed for six years.

Moved by the genuine humility of this women, Sebastian raised his hand and said, "If I am a true servant of all that is holy, then your speech will be restored to you."

The words had hardly been uttered when Zoe exclaimed, "Oh holy soldier, you are blessed."

When Nicostratus heard his wife speak, he also fell at the soldier's feet. Accordingly, Nicostratus released the prisoners and under Sebastian's command hid them in his own house until their escape could be arranged.

In time, Sebastian was himself apprehended and delivered over to certain archers to be shot to death. His body was pierced with arrows and left for dead, but he was found still alive by Irene, a young widow, who concealed him and nursed him back to health. After his recovery, Sebastian deliberately stationed himself at a staircase where he knew the emperor

was to pass and denounced his cruelties. For a moment the emperor was speechless with surprise, but when he recovered, he ordered that Sebastian's life be conclusively terminated. And it was.

Sebastian was born in Narbonne, Gaul, and lived until A.D. 288. In the East he is celebrated on December 18th, as Patron of soldiers, physicians and freedom from disease. He was buried in ad catacumbas, where now stands the Basilica of St. Sebastian. This account is recorded in Lives of Saints by Baring-Gould.

Mule Power

"He was untutored in theology, in philosophy and in worldly knowledge, but in spiritual life and good works he was most learned. His holiness was made known by very many miracles both during his life and after his death."

William of Fenoli was an extremist of sorts, not one to be confined to conventions and certainly not one to require the assistance of anyone other than his God. Many of the accounts of his miracles have been preserved, the most colorful of which is given as a matter of public knowledge.

It happened that while William was returning from his field work, robbers surprised and attacked him. He was leading a mule at the time and having no weapon to defend himself, he grabbed hold of the mule's leg and pulled it from its socket. Wielding the leg like a saber, he thrashed his attackers so profusely as to put them all to flight. This being done, William restored the leg to its proper place and he and the mule went on their way uninterrupted.

William of Fenoli belonged to the charter house Casularum in Lombardy, Italy. He lived until 1205 and is celebrated on December 19th. His cultus was confirmed by Pope Pius IX in 1860. A greater part of the records of his life concern themselves with the miracles which occurred under his intercession centuries after his death. Historic art represents William with the leg of a mule in his hand.

The Weatherman

Ursus would have made a great farmer, not because he loved to work long hard hours with little pay, but because of his ability to influence the weather.

Ursus was an Irish boy, and not unlike Saint Patrick, he "prayed a hundred times every day and a hundred times every night." When he left Ireland, he journeyed to the Italian Alps, where he hoped to find a more spiritual life, and he did. He was soon recognized for his sanctity and miracles, and unable to avoid the responsibly of greatness, he was appointed Archdeacon of Aosta. The tale which follows is one of many which occurred during his life in Italy.

The Buthier River which passes Aosta had swollen with seasonal flooding and having overflowed its banks, threatened to inundate a large portion of the city. Ursus was officiating in the Church of Saint Peter. Many of the distressed, who had lost their homes, took refuge there, with Ursus caring for their needs. But the waters rose to the church leaving the occupants captive. Ursus, seeing the danger, prayed that the Almighty, who had restrained the waters in the flood of Noah's time and commanded the Red Sea to retire before Moses, would intercede and protect him and his people in this peril. As he prayed, the rains ceased, the clouds overhead broke up and the waters retired to their proper channel. After a short time, under the warm rays of the sun, all traces of the flood evaporated.

The commemoration of this miracle was celebrated every day in the church of Saint Ursus for eleven hundred years following his death.

Ursus lived during the sixth century. He is celebrated on December 20th. This story is given in The Life of Saint Ursus, Archdeacon of Aosta.

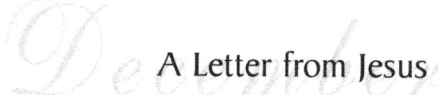

A Letter from Jesus

The Epistles of Jesus Christ and Abgarus, King of Edessa

Chapter 1: Abgarus, King of Edessa, to Jesus the good Saviour, who appears at Jerusalem, greeting. I have been informed concerning you and your cures, which are performed without the use of medicines and herbs. For it has been reported that you cause the blind to see, the lame to walk, do both cleanse lepers and cast out unclean spirits and devils, and restore them to health that have long been diseased, and raisest up the dead. All of which, when I heard, I was persuaded of one of these two, viz: either that you are God himself descended from the heavens, who does these things, or the Son of God. On this account therefore I earnestly desire you to take the trouble of a journey hither, and cure a disease which I am under. For I hear the Jews ridicule you and intend you mischief. My city is indeed small, but neat, and large enough for us both.

Chapter 2 (Jesus' reply): Abgarus, you are happy, forasmuch as you have believed on me, whom ye have not seen. For it is written concerning me, that those that have seen me should not believe in me, that they who have not seen may believe and live. As to that part of your letter, which relates to my giving you a visit, I must inform you, that I must fulfill all the ends of my mission in this country, and after that be received up again to him who sent me. But after my ascension, I will send one of my disciples, who will cure your disease and give life to you and all that are with you.

The foregoing narrative is taken from the manuscripts edited from the Bible by its compilers, the Council of Nice. In the early days of the church, the book from which this excerpt is taken was read aloud publicly, along with the other works of the New Testament.

God Bless America

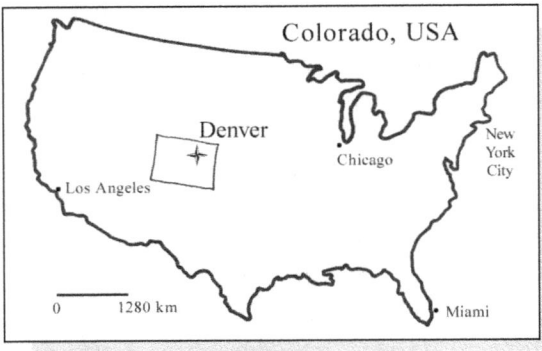

Maria Frances Cabrini, called Mother, usually got what she wanted. If it came easily, fine, but if it didn't, then she would build a bridge across her obstacle until it could no longer resist the force of her will. She possessed a powerful combination of intellect, principle and purpose and is best described as a woman of quiet force, whose scruples made her a dedicated, goal-directed person. She was the youngest daughter in a family of thirteen children and even as a child, growing up in the streets of San Angelo, Italy, she was well aware of the spiritual benefit of unbending discipline.

It would be impossible to mention a complete list of her accomplishments, as she traveled many times around the world founding the order of the Missionary Sisters of the Sacred Heart. In numerous countries she established more than fifty institutions, making them responsible for free schools, high schools, hospitals and other charitable institutions.

She had a natural knack for miracles as well, but seldom, if ever, revealed any sign of her inner life, often disguising her secret with a rugged hard-working display. There are several recorded instances that illustrate how Mother's prayers were rewarded with miraculous favors, but she made light of these instances and kept them to herself.

A minor story tells of one of Mother's pupils who suffered from varicose veins for many years. Her doctor had advised her to wear elastic stockings, but somehow she obtained a pair of Mother's cotton stockings and was cured the moment she put them on. "I hope you are not so foolish as to say my stockings cured you," said Mother Cabrini. "I am wearing them all the time and they do me no good. It was your faith that did it. Say nothing about it." She died peacefully in her room on December 22, 1917, at the Columbus hospital in Chicago, an institution she had founded in 1902. Despite the fact that she had disregarded any talk of "miracles" in her life, after her death more that 150,000 reports of miraculous favors were addressed to the pope by people from every walk of life in all parts of the world. Mother Cabrini was the first citizen of the United States to be formally canonized and have her sanctity recognized. She will always be dear to Italians and Americans. She is "a woman of fine understanding and great holiness. . . she is a saint," said Pope Leo XIII, long before her dedication.

Mother Cabrini was born in Italy in 1850 and immigrated to the United States in 1889. She became a naturalized citizen many years later and spent much of her time between Chicago, New York, New Orleans and Seattle where many of her institutions are established. Her body is enshrined in the chapel of the Cabrini Memorial School in Fort Washington, New York. Currently numerous miracles are occurring at her shrine near Denver, Colorado.

Unusual Baptism

During the baptism of Clovis I, King of the Franks, the church and the surrounding grounds were so densely crowded, mobility seemed impossible. As the ceremony proceeded, the king approached the font (fountain), and only then was it discovered that the holy oil had been forgotten. It would have been a great embarrassment to detain the king while one of the priests pushed his way through the crowd to retrieve the oil. Fortunately, a solution was found by way of a miracle.

At a moment when the crowd seemed to sense the dilemma, a dove suddenly entered the church through an open window. In its beak it carried a vial of holy oil which it placed in the opened hands of Saint Remi, the officiating prelate. When the vial was opened a magnificent perfume permeated the church causing great excitement in the crowd. When the gathering settled, the king was duly anointed. Immediately afterwards an order was given for a celebration to commemorate the unusual baptism of Clovis I during the month of December, A.D. 496.

This account is recorded in Life of Saint Remi by Hincmar, Archbishop of Rheims.

A Family Tree

Gregory the Great narrates his family life in his book Dialogues. In particular he mentions the life of his father's sisters, Tharsilla (the elder), and Emiliana, who lived with them as religious ascetics while Gregory was growing up. Tharsilla and Emiliana were bound more by their love for each other than by family blood, and the stories recorded by Gregory illustrate the divinity of their character.

Emiliana, nearing her fourth birthday, was playing alone in her room when suddenly a child appeared and began amusing himself near her bed. The child was of similar age and divinely beautiful. Thinking he was an angel, Emiliana said, "My dear child, have you nothing better to do than to waste your time in sport?"

The child answered, "What would you have me do instead?"

"Speak to me of the great God," said Emiliana.

The child replied, "In speaking of God, one can only speak in praise, and it is not well to praise one's self." So saying, the child vanished from her sight.

One year on Christmas eve Tharsilla was visited by a vision of her great-grandfather, Pope Saint Felix II. He revealed the temporary nature of life on earth and the immortal nature of life in Heaven and said, "Come, I will receive you into this habitation of light."

Immediately afterwards, she fell sick and prepared to breathe her soul into the hands of the Almighty. Her family gathered around intending to nurse her back to health, but she cried out, "Away! Away! My saviour is coming!"

Following these words she died peacefully. A few days later, Tharsilla appeared to Emiliana and invited her to come and live with her in the "habitation of light." Thus invited, Emiliana passed out of her body and joined her sister in the regions of Heaven.

Tharsilla and Emiliana of Florence lived until A.D. 550. They are celebrated together on December 24th. The accounts of their lives were recorded by their nephew, Pope Saint Gregory the Great.

Christmas Day

According to the ancient prophets, when all the proper conditions were met, God Almighty would incarnate as human flesh in the womb of a virgin, accomplishing one of His greatest mysteries, the birth of a Divine Son.

It happened that a decree from Emperor Augustus ordained all citizens to register in a census according to their family heritage. The descendants of the family of King David were ordered to register in Bethlehem, a town six miles south of Jerusalem. In obedience to the emperor's command, Mary and Joseph (a descendant of King David), undertook this journey even though Mary was pregnant and neared the time of birth.

After a slow journey, through sixty-four miles of mountainous country, they arrived safely in Bethlehem, but Mary's time had come and the birth was imminent. Despite her condition, no one in Bethlehem was willing to put them up. So they lodged in a large cave (found in the side of a ridge where Bethlehem is built) which was used as a stable and was still occupied by an ox and an ass. There Mary brought forth her son. She wrapped him in bands of cloth and laid him in a feeding trough which was all she could find for a bed.

On the same night, certain shepherds were watching over their sheep when suddenly an angel appeared to them. They were surrounded by celestial light and were greatly afraid, but the angel comforted them and said, "Fear not! For behold I bring you tidings of great joy, that shall be for all people. For this day is born to you a Saviour, who is Christ the Lord. And this is a sign for you: you will find an infant bound in cloth bands and lying in a manger."

Suddenly an army of angels appeared, and surrounding the shepherds they declared: "Glory in the heights above to God, and upon earth, peace among men of goodwill."

When the vision disappeared the shepherds hastened to Bethlehem where they found Mary and Joseph, and an infant lying in a manger.

"And seeing, they understood the words that had been spoken to them concerning this child. And all that heard wondered at those things that were told to them by the shepherds."

Two thousand years later, the life, teachings and miracles of Jesus of Nazareth still shape the political, religious and humanitarian evolution of this planet. No single personality has shaped our history to such a degree. Our calender, our philosophies, our wars and our religious administrations are all a measure of the impact of his life.

December 25th marks the celebration of His birth.

The cave beneath the Basilica of the Nativity at Bethlehem has an unbroken tradition of great antiquity. In its floor is set a silver star, around which is the inscription: Hic de vergine Maria Jesus Christus natus est; Here Jesus Christ was born of the Virgin Mary.

Legend of Thyrsus

In all the records of martyrs, none has exceeded in marvel that of Saint Thyrsus. In the reign of Emperor Decius, A.D 250, Thyrsus was condemned to death for supporting Christian causes. The proconsul of Apollonia was infuriated by his public declarations and sought to make a display of the revolutionary. But he did not succeed.

It was entirely in vain that the saint was scourged with whips charged with lead; in vain that he was hung by his thumbs to a tree; in vain that his arms were broken and his eye-lashes plucked out. Thyrsus remained miraculously unscathed and seemed to gain new force with every torment.

The proconsul, however, would not be defied. He charged that molten lead be poured into the throat of the rebel, but again the victim was unharmed.

Mad with thwarted rage, the proconsul ordered the saint cut to pieces, but at the moment the dispatchers tried to do so the assembly ground shook so violently with an earthquake, all hope of execution was abandoned.

The following morning, the proconsul commanded the "traitor" to abandon his support for Christians causes in exchange for his freedom. Thyrsus refused and was condemned to be thrown from a cliff. He was wrapped with chains which crumbled to dust as soon as they touched him, and then he was taken to a perilous cliff where he was thrown to his death. But nothing could extinguish this holy martyr, for "in the arms of angels" he descended to the ground as if he were a feather in the breeze.

He appeared utterly indomitable. Neither caresses, seduction, threats or tortures of any description could curb his resolve.

Finally, those judges who condemned Thyrsus were inexplicably struck dead and their bodies cast into an open ditch. Thyrsus, moved with compassion, prayed that they might be properly buried, and the earth of its own accord enveloped their bodies.

It seems that only death remained to be surmounted. So resolved, the holy martyr willingly surrendered his life and was joined by fifteen Roman priests of Apollonia who were moved to defend his cause and imitate his bravery.

Without a doubt, in all the lives of martyrs, none has exceeded in marvel that of Saint Thyrsus.

This transcription is taken from Les Petits Bollandistes, Volume II, published in 1880. All of which has been sanctioned by popes, archbishops and bishops.

Son of Thunder

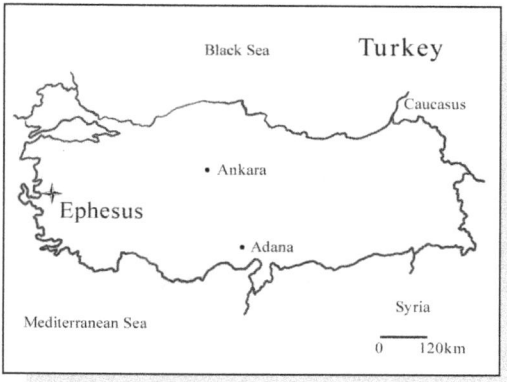

John was not only a good fisherman, but he was the "disciple whom Jesus loved." He first encountered Jesus with his brother James as they were repairing their nets on the sea of Galilee. Christ affectionately nicknamed them Boanerges, "sons of thunder," probably due to their loud and explosive dispositions. John held a very privileged status among the apostles, not because of his talents as a miracle worker, but rather because he was the youngest and the only one who did not die a martyr. Of those who stood at the foot of the cross with Mary, he received Christ's charge to care for Her as though she were his own.

This he did faithfully until the day of her passing, after which he was banished to the island of Patmos. It was there, in the silence of his banishment, that he received and recorded the deeply mystical inner visions known from the bible as *Revelations*.

"I, John, your brother and a sharer with you in the tribulation and kingdom and endurance in the company with Jesus, came to be in the isle that is called Patmos for speaking about God and bearing witness to Jesus. By inspiration I came to be in the Lord's day and I heard behind me a strong voice like that of a trumpet, saying: 'What you see write in a scroll and send it to the seven congregations. . . .'

And I turned to see the voice that was speaking with me, and, having turned, I saw seven golden lamp stands, and in the midst of the lamp stands someone like a son of man, clothed with a garment that reached down to the feet, and girded at the breast with a golden girdle. Moreover, his head and his hair were white as snow, and his eyes were a fiery flame, and his feet were like fine copper when glowing in a furnace, and his voice was as the sound of many waters. And he had in his right hand seven stars, and out of his mouth a sharp, long two-edged sword was protruding, and his continence was as the sun when it shines in its power. And when I saw him I fell as dead at his feet.

And he laid his right hand upon me and said: 'Do not be fearful. I am the First and the Last, and the living one, and I became dead, but look! I am living forever and ever, and I have the keys of death and of Hades. Therefore write down the things you saw, and the things that are and the things that will take place after these.'"

Saint Jerome writes that when due to age and weakness John was no longer able to walk, he asked to be carried to the assembly where he would repeat only these words: "My little children, love one another." When asked why he always repeated the same words, he replied, "Because it is the word of the Lord, and if you keep it, you do enough."

John lived until approximately A.D. 100. He was born in Galilee and died peacefully in Ephesus, Turkey, where the Virgin Mary is believed to have died John is celebrated on December 27th.

Thirsty Workmen

Third among the great miracles of Francis of Paola is the manifestation of water from a rock in Calabria, Italy. By merely striking a rock with his rod, he furnished much-needed water to thirsty workmen who had dedicated themselves to the completion of his monastery.

What renders this miracle more striking is the natural basin into which the water falls. Despite numerous examinations, no one has been able to determine its source. It is certain, however, that it continues to flow, in summer or winter. When the reservoir is emptied from washing or any other cause, it is full again in five hours.

In the same document, we are told that Francis once threw a dead trout into the basin, whereupon the fish recovered its life.

To date, the number of miracles and cures associated with the fountain reaches beyond statistical significance. Anyone traveling to Paola may visit the fountain and wash or drink from its waters. Every year when a celebration is held in honor of Francis and this miracle, enormous crowds gather to wash and drink his blessings.

This account is recorded in the Bull and other documents from the canonization of Francis of Paola.

Our Lady of the Americas

"Good morning daughter," spoke the Virgin Mary to Estela Ruiz of Phoenix, Arizona.

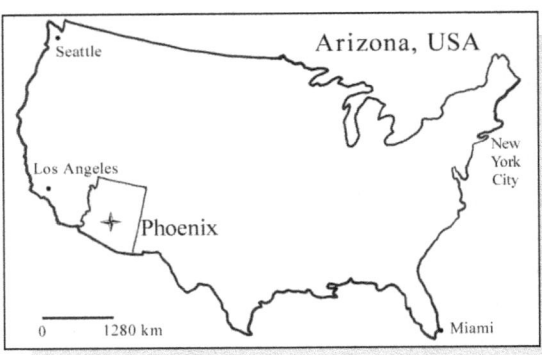

Her husband, a devout Catholic, was away at Medjugorje, Yugoslavia on a pilgrimage, while she remained at home, concentrating on career activities. When she heard this greeting from the Virgin for the first time, she could hardly believe her ears. She had always been a skeptic and had refused to accompany her husband on the pilgrimage.

"Why is she coming to me? I have never had any devotion to her," she asked.

Nevertheless, the apparitions which started during the fall of 1988, continue to the present day, every Saturday morning and evening at the Ruiz house hold.

The Virgin has asked that she be recognized as *Our Lady of the Americas*. "I have come to ask you to be my messenger, and I want to know if you will do it. I am going to help you and your children make many changes. There will be a period of time where I prepare the family and send many messages to the family."

Today as many as a thousand people show up every Saturday evening to receive the messages from the Virgin, whose primary emphasis is peace, prayer, penance and fasting. Numerous healings and other supernatural occurrences have been reported, such as the appearance of beams of light descending on the small shrine built in the Ruiz's back yard, or a ravishing fragrance of roses from an unknown source.

On December 29, 1990, this message was given by Our Lady of the Americas:

"Pray my little ones, for the coming events that this new year brings upon your earth. Pray so that the hearts of men will soften, especially those that are holding the fate of the world in their hands. War comes about because of the desire of men to have power and because of greed and hate. . . . Only your prayers and the prayers of many can and will make a difference. Pray that love and understanding of men for each other will prevail over the hatred and greed that exists. Be with me in prayer as I am with you. I love you and thank you for your love and prayers."

Further information regarding Our Lady of the Americas or the Ruiz family is available through Reyes Maria Ruiz, Phoenix, Arizona.

Rare Distinction

Colette was herself a miracle. She was often seen lifted from the ground and floating in the air, her face aglow with mysterious light. Miraculous favors were constant in her life. Once, while kneeling on the ground in the midst of her sisterhood, she saw the

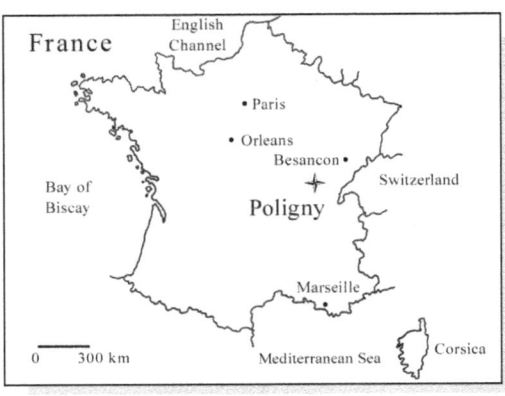

twelve disciples of Christ. She was subsumed in a breathless meditation at the time and watched as they lifted from the ground into the air. Spontaneously she rose with them and continued to elevate until she disappeared entirely from the sight of her companions. To the relief of her fellow sisters, she returned. This soon became expected during her prayer time, and occasionally, she would burst out in divine oratory with effulgent heavenly flames springing from her mouth.

"I am dying to see that wonderful Colette who raises people from the dead," wrote the Duchess of Bourbon about the child.

But a life filled with miracles is not always easy. In her early years she often met with violent opposition, being treated as a freak and accused of sorcery. In time, however, her true sanctity shone through and this simple woman of humble means attained the rare distinction of being made a saint in her own time.

Saint Colette lived from 1381-1447. She was canonized in 1807 as recorded in Vie de Ste. Colette, by Douiffet. Her body and relics are preserved in her convent at Poligny, thirty-five miles from Besancon, France.

Net Worth

Melania was unbelievably wealthy. Her estates were scattered throughout the Roman Empire, yet still she saw herself as poor. As it was clearly impossible to calculate her net worth, since it multiplied daily, the volume of her possessions became more of an obstruction than a luxury.

Eventually she was compelled to lay aside her great wealth for the sake of spiritual development. She realized that her family's wealth was gained through the working hands of her hungry neighbors whose efforts earned her more than it did themselves. "The rich man who gives to the poor does not bestow an alms," says Saint Ambrose, "but pays a debt."

To pay back her debt to society, she began the sale of her properties for the benefit of the needy. Her relatives, believing she was mad, prepared to profit from her liberal sale of properties and rights. But Melania protected her efforts by appealing to the emperor to take the equitable sale of estates under his protection. The proceeds were as numerous as the properties themselves: homeless shelters, hospitals, prisoner relief centers, bankrupts, pilgrims, churches, monasteries; thousands were endowed throughout the empire.

After two years she earned herself the title **Blessed Little One** and *Joy of Heaven*, and had given freedom to over eight thousand slaves. She later migrated to Tagaste in Numidia, Africa, to escape the invasion of the Goths. There she established two monasteries for men and women who had been slaves under her title. She endowed the new monasteries and lived among the women, taking care not to let them emulate her standard of austerity for she fasted every other day.

In A.D. 417, Melania, accompanied by her mother and husband, left Africa for Jerusalem where she settled into a life of solitude and meditation.

She established a convent that was noted for its mildness at a time when religious pursuits were measured through corporal austerity. For twenty-two years her reputation for sanctity and miracles offered a new direction for sincere seekers of truth. Early on a Sunday morning, December 31, A.D. 439, she spoke these last words and died. "The Lord knows that I am unworthy. I would not dare compare myself with any good woman, even those living in this world. Yet I think the enemy himself will not, at the Last Judgment, accuse me of ever having gone to sleep with bitterness in my heart. Now let me rest. As the Lord willed, so it is done." She was fifty-six years old.

Melania the Younger lived from A.D. 383-439. She is celebrated on December 31st. Fragments of her biographies are printed in the Analecta Bollandiana.

About the Author

Rodney Charles has spent fifteen years researching and writing about how the mind and body function to accommodate supernatural phenomena. He has delivered over a thousand lectures and taught courses in eight countries. His ability to bridge the gap between the religious and New Age community has given him a significant reputation. Born in Regina, Saskatchewan, he currently divides his time between Canada, the United States and India. He is available for lectures and may be contacted through 1stWorld Publishing. Email: **rodney@1stworldlibrary.org**.

See 1stWorld Books at:

www.1stWorldPublishing.com

See our classic collection at:

www.1stWorldLibrary.org

www.ingramcontent.com/pod-product-compliance
Lightning Source LLC
Chambersburg PA
CBHW022055150426
43195CB00008B/140